Editor: Ranald Lawrence

Graphic Design and Layout: Ivan del Renzio

Cover Image: Christian Ashton

Thanks to Chris Bowler, Peter Carolin, Gillean Denny and Jenny Willatt

© 2011 The Department of Architecture, University of Cambridge

All rights reserved. No part of this publication may be reproduced, stored in a retrieval system, or transmitted, in any form or by any means, electronic, mechanical, photocopying, recording or otherwise, without prior permission. Copyright retained by respective authors.

Scroope 20 has been produced by Part II students of the Department of Architecture, University of Cambridge. The running of Scroope Journal has now been handed over to a Committee, who can be contacted at:

The Editors
Scroope 21
Faculty of Architecture and History of Art
1-5 Scroope Terrace
Cambridge CB2 1PX

We regret to announce that there is no longer a subscription service available for Scroope. Copies can be ordered from the department, or www.scroopejournal.com.

Contents

RESEARCH

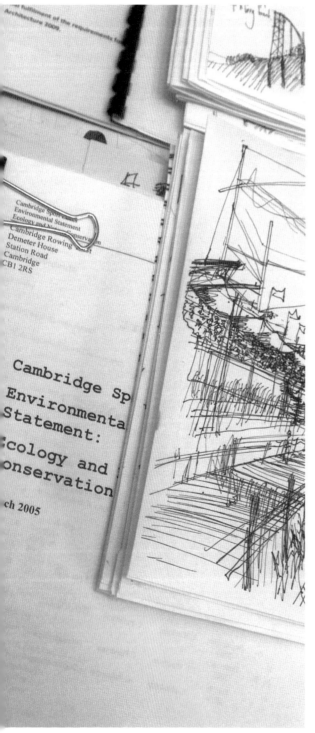

The structure of architectural education has changed little since the Oxford Conference of 1958. The Part II diploma in particular is often seen by students as 'more of the same', and by universities as a peculiar anomaly that maintains the principle of the five-year degree course in the face of an ever more capitalised market of postgraduate education. It was partly to address these concerns, and partly also to find new ways to compete for relevance in an industry that is becoming increasingly specialised, that the new Part II MPhil in Environmental Design was launched at Cambridge in 2008.

This new course presented a challenge as well as an opportunity: on the one hand, to design a new course that goes above and beyond all the criteria laid down by the ARB and RIBA for what a Part II course should be, in order to become relevant to contemporary practice as well as a wider research community; while at the same time, to offer the next generation of architects an opportunity to develop specific and in-demand techniques and skills that can again set them apart, after such a long training period, as professionals with the ability to lead in the building industry by example.

At the same time the studio – the testing and sharing ground of the ever elusive 'design process' – remains at the heart of the course. It was up to the first cohort

Editorial

to demonstrate how these often conflicting new aspirations could be reconciled in the realisation of design projects that were also thorough pieces of recorded research, which were applicable to contemporary practice. And so a thoroughly more careful and deliberate approach was taken, with every step and assumption questioned – often several times – in order that the result was as good a conjecture as could be. There is a fashionable tendency today to view architectural education – in particular studio work – as a place for 'blue-sky' thinking, where absurd propositions can be subjected to so many iterations and refinements so as to become a worthwhile end in themselves. The strength of the new Part II MPhil course at Cambridge is to attempt to consider and assess as many parameters in the design solution as are relevant and practical to a given situation, so that the proposed solution may be as engaged as possible.

The end result can often be unpredictable – it is truly 'parametric' (to reclaim an often misused word) in that the form can be an unexpected consequence that is the result of a balancing act between innumerable parameters, weighed up for their own particular worth. Through this process we learn to design critically as architects – to challenge our preconceptions about forms or priorities – as servants to the process,

rather than servants to the market.

This is an architecture which seeks to go beyond the facile 'wow-factor' stylings of an increasingly out of touch 'avante-garde', who seek change for the sake of the word alone.

This edition of Scroope celebrates the reinstatement of the Part II course at Cambridge, featuring several projects undertaken both by the new Part II students at Cambridge as well as in the undergraduate school, and explores the theme of what it means to be a practitioner of 'Environmental Design'. As students of architecture, we hope that our small contribution of this collection of essays may inform and widen the debate into what the future of our built environment might look like; how it might work; and how it might be lived in. From Alistair Donald's provocative call to expand the human footprint, to Kevin Fellingham's plea for a more holistic way of thinking about the environment and how we act within it, a wide range of views are encompassed that sometimes build upon and sometimes challenge a range of existing orthodoxies.

We hope you enjoy Scroope Twenty.

The Editors

Letters published below respond to and expand on the contents of the current issue of Scroope.

ENVIRONMENTAL DESIGN: RESEARCH AND PRACTICE

The present issue of *Scroope* includes a number of essays that, in one way or another, explore aspects of environmental design in architecture, but, and this is their virtue, they are broad and undogmatic, rather than deterministic and mechanistic in their subject matter and approach. What they emphasise is that environmental themes run through many aspects of research and practice in architecture.

Koen Steemers' overview paper looks back over the past thirty years of research and practice and forward to the next thirty, and offers a breadth of interpretation, with his references to the poetic writings of, amongst others, Rasmussen and Pallasmaa, as essential counterparts to the necessity to bring aspects of applied science to bear upon the design of buildings. Katia Papkovskaia's essay on Sverre Fehn's Norrköping Villa pursues the implicit phenomenology of Rasmussen and Pallasmaa back to its roots in the language of Heidegger, bringing fascinating insights to the interpretation of the experience of light in the villa. Further back in time, Henrik Schoenefeldt's studies of Paxton's Crystal Palace, strikingly demonstrate that the building was as significant as an environmental experiment as it was of the structural and constructional innovation that has previously earned it its place in the histories of architecture. The 'radiant' walls of Neave Brown's Alexandra Road housing project in the London Borough of Camden were a bold experiment when the project was designed in 1968. Lefkos Kyriacou's essay brings a perspective into the social consequences of technical innovation and to surprising and continuing popular support for a radical piece of environmental design.

Peter Clegg was one of the pioneers of environmental design practice in Britain and the achievements of Feilden Clegg Bradley Studios – in his practice's latest name – are widely acknowledged. Peter was a student in Cambridge some forty years ago and has generously acknowledged the influence that the teaching of Alex Pike – the author of the seminal Autarkic House project – and I had in shaping his and Richard Feilden's early interest in this field. But I want to offer a further memory from those days. I recall Peter's return from the year he spent at Yale as a Clare College Paul Mellon Scholar, where he had met Don Watson, then and still one of the most important figures in environmental architecture in the USA. Following that experience Peter was somehow able to articulate, better than we were able at the time, a sense of how environmental principles might inform the development of architecture; precisely the theme of his essay for *Scroope*.

All these years later Peter can draw on a deep well of experience in practice and, as his essay shows, bring this to bear as an effective critical tool. His comparison of the environmental bases of OMA's Seattle Public Library and FCBS's project for the City and University of Worcester library is particularly telling. In 2007 I had the privilege of writing the Introduction to FCBS's, The Environmental Handbook and suggested there that, in the best environmental architecture, the cross-section is almost invariably the key. The Worcester project seems to support this idea and thus joins a long sequence of buildings that serve as models for the future of environmental design. These include many of the works of Soane, Mackintosh's Glasgow School of Art, Louis Kahn's art museums and, to come full circle, the Oxford Law Library by Leslie Martin and Sandy Wilson, completed just before Feilden and Clegg arrived at *Scroope* Terrace.

Prof. Dean Hawkes
Cambridge

MAXIMUM CITIES

Well done Alastair Donald! His article Maximum Cities: Let's Expand the Human Footprint is refreshingly optimistic about humanity. After decades of gloom and doom in which humans have been portrayed as the culprits of everything – from destroying nature to destroying themselves – it is good to remind people of the contribution of mankind in creating resources and taming nature to the benefit of everyone.

I do agree that we need to act responsibly and plan our future in the best way that we can imagine, but the culture of self-imposed restraint – from reduction in population to reduction in mobility – flies in the face of the experience over the centuries. Population growth is contained by increased income, so we need economic growth to solve this problem. Human ingenuity and need generates discoveries that promise food sufficiency, defying the Malthusian forecast. Mobility and its globalisation effects improves the lives of everybody by providing access to better jobs, better housing, better and cheaper goods and, for producing countries such as China and India, a way out of poverty and illness.

The forecasts in 1970 by the Club of Rome, which utilised computer models (using exponential functions of demands), have been demonstrably proved wrong, as the world has not run out of resources. The big mistake of the Club of Rome was the complete misunderstanding of the role of prices. As resources become scarce prices rise, bringing alternatives in to the market, which were hitherto uneconomic. An example was the development of the North Sea oil and gas after the hitch in oil prices. Nowadays the deep sea explorations in the Brazilian Atlantic and Canadian tar sands are examples of new resources brought to the fore because of oil price increases. But alternative technologies for transport are arriving fast – from hybrid to all electric cars – promising a revolution without losing the benefit of personal mobility.

Human behaviour is a reflection of aspirations and responds to price signals. To force people to do what they do not want to do, and pay for it, is bound to end in failure. The vast majority of people want space and mobility: to force them to live in flats at high density and walk everywhere – because suburbs make you fat or use too much land – will not succeed; as this will reduce their quality of life and restrict their ability to increase income.

Prof. Marcial Echenique
Cambridge

REPLACING THE CARBON FOOTPRINT

Alistair Donald is arguing for dynamism, not sluggishness, for more growth, not less. He is taking on the prophets of austerity, like the New Economics Foundation (NEF) and George Monbiot.

The 'Human Footprint' he wants to expand is about Creativity and Energy, as expressed in 'Maximum Cities'. But for two hundred years the Human Footprint has been tightly linked to the Carbon Footprint. Britain pioneered the industrial revolution based on coal. Twentieth century industrial growth was based on fossil fuels. The explosive growth of China today is based on a coal-intensive economy. Today's cities may look cleaner than in the past, but without billions of tons of carbon emissions from their energy supplies they would quickly grind to a halt.

Donald endorses 'geo-engineering and the development of new forms of energy infrastructure (whether nuclear, hydro-electric, solar, wave, wind or coal CCS'. Good. But we must not underestimate the radical transformation of our energy infrastructure that is a necessary condition for the urgent shrinkage or elimination of our Carbon Footprint. In October, Adair Turner told a Commons Committee that the UK had to shrink its energy-related carbon emissions by 90% within the next forty years to meet the targets implied by Climate Change legislation.

We can applaud a Human Footprint that

replaces the Carbon Footprint. Cities full of human creativity, yes, but only if they are increasingly de-linked from their historic dependence on a fossil-fuelled economy.

Donald quotes Edmund Bacon as arguing for 'Outgoing Man, ebullient, involved', and for humanity 'to rediscover the confidence to fail. To leap into space aware of the possibilities of failure signifies confidence that whatever the problems, humanity can emerge on the other side and reflect on the lessons, before trying again.' But the science of Climate Change is less ebullient: it suggests that failure to curb carbon emissions could, rather quickly, create some nasty tipping points, and that – some of humanity at least – would not have the chance of 'trying again'.

This is the danger of dismissing the NEF and Monbiot as perverse enemies of creative dynamism. We do not yet know if we can decarbonise the world energy system. Even if we did, it is not yet top of the agenda of most political systems. So some austerity in consumption is another method of delaying the date when the Carbon Footprint becomes irreversibly too much.

We have to be energetic in shrinking the use of carbon-based energy. If 'Maximum Cities' do this, then let us expand them. But if they ride on the back our traditional carbon-based systems, then they will take us rather faster towards using up our carbon ration.

Christopher Beauman
European Bank for Reconstruction and Development

IDENTIFYING WITH NATURE

'Mankind is obsessed with changing the position of matter in space.'

Bertrand Russell

There have been many human civilisations, and each has burned itself out by exhausting its resource base. The present incarnation is the first to encircle the globe and to commandeer all resources. Sir Martin Rees documented the consequences of oil depletion in his book Our Final Century, setting the scene for burnout. He argues that ambitions that may have served humanity well during our growth phase are unlikely to be helpful during the long descent that lies ahead.

The UK Foresight Programme, initiated by Sir David King, examined four scenarios for future development. None of them, he said during a talk in Cambridge, were an attractive prospect (in the context of a growth agenda). While a small elite exercise their creativity, 'the mass of men' in the words of Thoreau, continue to 'lead lives of quiet desperation'.

Our diverse culture includes those who would dominate nature and those who identify with nature. 'The sense of identifying with a place', Kevin Fellingham writes, 'is not that a place belongs to us but that we belong to a place'. The implied relationship with nature is widely felt throughout society but its value is only now being evaluated in monetary equivalent. To dismiss nature is not only to get the accounts wrong but also to steal something precious from humanity.

'Human consciousness evolved in response to the natural environment' and while we come to terms with the dynamic between the left and the right hemisphere in our own heads, nature must feed our evolutionary spirit.

Dr. Peter Pope
Cambridge

To respond to a particular article, or to continue a discussion, please write to:

The Editors
Scroope: Cambridge Architecture Journal
The Department of Architecture
University of Cambridge
1-5 Scroope Terrace
Cambridge
CB2 1PX

Foreword

This should be architecture's finest hour. The leap in our understanding of the earth's systems has profound implications for the built environment and presents huge opportunities to architects and engineers; opportunities for inventing and synthesising new ways of making and re-making buildings and settlements energised by the emerging knowledge of the complex equilibrium that we are part of. Such solutions are unlikely to appear as architectural trophies, for which there is still, despite the global recession, such strong demand. And there lies the rub; for, leaving aside possible venality, architectural culture finds it easier to celebrate the object than to consider its consequences. Conversely our increasingly risk averse, homogenising ways of commissioning buildings – you may spot that I am avoiding the weird word 'procurement' – seem altogether incapable of judgement of the meaning and emotional potential of architectural form and language.

The contributors to this edition of Scroope have in common the welcome inability to wander into either of these camps, and so they will not separate architecture and sustainability. Kevin Fellingham notes that there is no necessary connection between the phenomenological and technical agendas but sees their mediation as one of a number of acts of practice as medium. Others show how wide is the range of intellectual and moral positions within this construct. From the delicacy of Piers Taylor's work graciously acknowledging Glenn Murcutt's teaching, or the spirituality of Sverre Fehn as described by Katia Papkovskaia, to the trenchant demolition job that Alistair Donald attempts on current environmentalism that in his view is too deferential to nature. In Henrik Schoenfeldt's piece on Paxton and Peter Clegg's on his practice's patient researches I see the virtues of pragmatism, architecture and engineering interwoven to great effect.

Of course sustainability is a problematic term – the 'slipperiest piece of soap in the shower', as someone once said. But its imprecision is itself what will continue to make it unavoidable – at least until another word comes along to better express mindfulness of the interconnected nature of all parts of the natural/human system. The difficulty of understanding, mapping and gaining traction on this system lies not only in the vast numbers of parts but in its mix of different types of substructures and subsystems and the complexities of their relationships. The breadth of intellectual, emotional and moral grasp that is presented here seems to offer the right instruments for the mission.

Sunand Prasad
May 2010

Environmental Research in Architecture

by Koen Steemers

Koen Steemers is Professor of Sustainable Design, and Head of the Department of Architecture at the University of Cambridge.

What is environmental research in architecture, why do we do it and what impact does it have? I hope you will forgive me if I start with a brief outline of a personal journey. When I first started studying architecture at Bath University 30 years ago, and 'cut my teeth' as an architectural assistant at *Energy Conscious Design* (now *ECD Architects*) in the mid eighties, there was an emerging interest in energy efficiency in architectural academia. A hard-core group of my teachers and practitioners – including Peter Clegg, Derek Croome and even Peter Smithson at Bath University, and David Turrent and Nick Baker at ECD Architects – confirmed for me that energy in architecture was a creative and valuable pursuit. This was reinforced when I came to Cambridge to study under teacher and practitioner Dean Hawkes and physicist Nick Baker. My motivation was and remains to understand architecture beyond the spatial and physical dimensions – to get under the skin of form, space and style. My route in to this was through the study of environmental design in architecture not only in terms of the technical performance to meet energy efficiency criteria, comfort standards or required illuminance levels, but also in terms of sensory stimulation, human perception and occupant behaviour with respect to the conditions we design.

Alongside technical criteria and targets, environmental design is increasingly presented in terms of sensory and experiential design. Key precursors to this are Rasmussen's *Experiencing Architecture* (1959) and Heschong's *Thermal Delight in Architecture* (1979) but more recently this momentum has been accelerated with books such as our own *Environmental Diversity in Architecture* (2004), Pallasmaa's *The Eyes of the Skin: Architecture and the Senses* (2005) and Hawkes' *The Environmental Imagination* (2008). Underpinning such work is a wealth of research activity and academic papers that are beginning to influence design. The last two issues of the *Harvard Design Review* demonstrate how sustainability, understood in terms of sensory pleasure and architectural expression, is permeating avant garde teaching and practice.

Our current academic interests are building on the technical and cultural aspects of environmental design, but with a focus on the urban scale. Major research projects that are ongoing in Cambridge relate to: outdoor comfort and wellbeing in urban spaces, the design of sustainable neighbourhoods and energy efficient cities. Such projects involve architects, engineers,

economists and social scientists, and strive to develop new insights and strategies for integrated sustainable planning.

These issues are increasingly reflected in Government priorities and new directions for practitioners, with a focus on planning for low carbon development in the context of climate change. Architecture, renewables, community, jobs, infrastructure, adaptation and mitigation are now often discussed in the same brief or policy document. Despite the fact that we are expected and need to be taking up these challenges – meeting technical targets whilst designing better spaces for people, with an emphasis on neighbourhoods and cities rather than one-off buildings – there are still significant gaps between our understanding and practice. To demonstrate this, let us look back at what on the surface appears as the relatively straightforward issue of energy use in buildings over the last 30 years.

THE LAST 30 YEARS

Buildings consume more energy now than 30 years ago. I am not referring here to the cutting-edge low energy buildings of innovative designers but to the overall building stock in a climate of change.

In 1980 the annual energy demand for housing in the UK, accounting for 30% of the UK's total energy use, stood at 40 Million tonnes of oil equivalent (Mtoe). Today the figure is nearly 50 Mtoe. The only positive spin on this, apart from the emergence of exemplar singular projects, is that the 'dash for gas' has stemmed the CO_2 emissions associated with this increasing energy demand. Despite this, the underlying question remains: why are we using more energy now? The answer is in part associated with population increase, although the statistics show that the energy demand per person has also been rising (from 0.7 toe/person to 0.8 toe/person). The second part of the answer is that the energy increase is attributable to the increasing number of households, rising from 20 Million to 25 Million over the period, due to demographic changes such as an aging population and increasing divorce rates, with the net result of smaller household sizes. When we allow for these two key demographic factors, the annual energy demand per household in the UK has remained largely unchanged over 30 years, remaining at about 2 toe per household.

One might ask the question: why is it interesting that the energy use per household has remained the same over the last 30 years? During this period we have seen an increasing awareness of energy issues, initially triggered by the Oil Crisis of 1974, and the introduction of energy-related building regulations to reduce heating loads, which account for circa 60% of domestic energy demand. As a result, the use of wall insulation has risen from 2% in 1974 to 37% in 2004, and the application of double glazing has increased from 8% to 83% over the same period.

So why has energy demand not reduced? The simple answer is: people. A number of occupant-related factors have counteracted the technological advances made. Occupants have had the new energy standards imposed upon them and tend to exploit the opportunities that these provide. The most obvious of these opportunities is increasing comfort: the average household temperature in 1980 was 14°C whereas today this average is 20°C. This increased comfort standard – where more rooms are warmed to a higher temperature, even in the existing and poorly insulated building stock – would have resulted in a doubling of the energy demand, if it had not been for the improved thermal characteristics of the building stock. Greater thermal comfort has gone hand-in-hand with increased space standards (i.e. smaller households have resulted in increased floor area per person) and increased use of appliances (as a result of greater disposable income). Energy efficiency has thus delivered improved standards of life rather than reduced energy use.

A similar trend can be observed in non-domestic buildings, where increased comfort expectations have made the use of energy-intensive air conditioning increasingly the norm (stimulated in part by the ubiquitous use of air conditioning in hotels, cars, restaurants, etc.). Air-conditioned offices have on average consumed more than twice the energy use per square metre of naturally ventilated offices. Along with this fact there is also increasing awareness that when we modelled non-domestic building designs to predict the energy use, there was an inability to anticipate occupant behaviour and their interface with control systems, resulting in a two-to-one discrepancy between measured and predicted performance.

To date, our energy efficiency policies have managed to stem an increase in the energy demand of buildings but have not yet managed to reduce overall energy use, primarily as a result of what can broadly be summarised as 'human agency'. Only where there are common aspirations and early dialogue between client, user and within the multidisciplinary design team is it likely to lead to low energy buildings and, crucially, low energy users.

THE NEXT 30 YEARS

The context for the next 30 years is challenging: the climate is changing, the population is increasing (globally from 6.8 billion to 8.6 billion, and in the UK from 62 million to 74 million) and becoming older. Living standards, particularly in China and India, will continue to increase rapidly, resulting in a continuation of the trends outlined above. In the UK and elsewhere a concern is that householders will turn to domestic air conditioning during the anticipated hot spells, counteracting any theoretical advantages of reduced heating demand due to global warming. The air conditioning industry is targeting the economic potential of the lower end of the market (i.e. domestic air conditioning units) and air conditioning units are now widely available at your local DIY store in the summer.

An enormous refurbishment action, demanding war time effort, is required to tackle the 'backlog' of poorly performing existing buildings if we are to achieve the ambitious UK emissions target of 80% be-

low 1990 levels by 2050, dealing with both reducing heat loss and avoiding overheating. We can learn from vernacular architecture in southern Europe to avoid overheating, for example by the use of thermal mass and shutters, and from northern Europe where high levels of insulation and the use of earth sheltering to reduce ventilation heat loss is the tradition. Perhaps more importantly, we need to design and inhabit buildings in an adaptable way, not just to respond to changing seasons but also changing lifestyles, expectations and work habits. The term 'long life, loose fit, low energy' still resonates, although it was first coined in 1972 – before the Oil Crisis of 1974 – by the then President of the RIBA, Alex Gordon.

The challenges and opportunities are now bigger than the design of individual buildings, despite (and in part because of) the UK Government's target of 'zero carbon' new homes from 2016 and new non-domestic buildings from 2019. Buildings and ground transport in total account for three quarters of the UK's energy demand. This means that the way we design cities, including transport infrastructure, combined with renewable energy sources, has to be integrated and holistic. For example, when our urban transport becomes electric, and more importantly clean and quiet at source, our urban buildings might become more open and less reliant on mechanical systems. The use of urban vegetation, on buildings and in urban spaces, further facilitates this. Such passive design opportunities provide greater freedom of choice for the occupants and can deliver greater comfort as a result (it is typically the lack of occupant control that exacerbates thermal discomfort, and conversely increased control that increases tolerance to a wider temperature range). Combined with decentralised renewable energy technologies incorporated into the design of our cities (or suburbs for that matter), the targets can become achievable and deliver a more liveable urban environment.

May 2010

Figure 1. Seattle Public Library. Image: Jeff Wilcox.

Sustainability – A New Architectural Paradigm

by Peter Clegg

Peter Clegg is a Senior Partner with Feilden Clegg Bradley Studios, having established the practice with Richard Feilden in 1978. Widely regarded as a key pioneer in the field of environmental design, he has almost 30 years of experience in low energy architecture and is actively involved in research, design and education. Peter was the primary author of 'Feilden Clegg Bradley: The Environmental Handbook' (2007), a substantial account of the practice's sustainable design experience over the last 30 years and a primer on the implementation of environmental best practice.

It is an unusually bright winter's day in Seattle. I am in the new OMA-designed public library moving around to avoid the sun so I can focus on a computer screen. I am not too worried about this – there are plenty of free spaces and options as to where to sit down. The main entry level is, as Koolhaas has said, a new kind of 'living room for the city', a place where people can come to meet, hang around, and relax as they would in their own living room – only this one is a glazed pyramidal space seven storeys high that opens up on different levels to a multitude of spaces for study and relaxation *(fig. 1)*. Like everything else that Koolhaas does, it challenges our expectations of the typology – provides us with a new paradigm – eloquently conceived,

Figure 2. Seattle Public Library - Exterior envelope. Image: Bill Eager.

described and crafted. Here is a new take on the idea of a Library: the communal brain-space at the heart of the city – a place for everyone, not just for those naturally drawn to books – a civic space that everyone seems to be genuinely proud of.

But what, I begin to wonder, does it tell us about the civic sensibility around sustainability, which happens to be very strong in the pacific Northwest, in this city that is home to Microsoft and Amazon and likes to wear its green credentials on its sleeve. What about the large areas of south-facing glazing, the potential summertime heat gain and wintertime heat loss? The pyramidal structure inverts itself towards the ground so that some areas of the glazed skin face

downwards – perhaps a lesson in how to maximise heat loss through the envelope (fig. 2). I eventually notice that the building does have something to say about itself – or rather the City of Seattle does on its behalf – in a small sign in front of the largest expanse of glass, the City tells you that this is a green building because in between the two layers of glazing there is Krypton gas and a layer of aluminium micro-louvres. I wonder about the cost benefit of Krypton over Argon (five times the cost for a marginal improvement in efficiency) and realise that this is a very expensive way to solve an environmental problem that need not have existed if the area of glazing had been defined from the outset by taking into consideration energy and environmental criteria. It's an environmental bandage over a defective skin. Around the back of the elevator shaft I find a plaque to say the building has achieved a LEED (the US environmental rating system for buildings) 'silver' rating – nothing you would want to display more prominently when you have 'gold' and 'platinum' buildings elsewhere across the city.

So why is it that it is so much easier for us to reinvent the typology and form of a building than it is to develop an architectural language which addresses the issue of sustainability? Why are those architects who are most adept at formal exploration almost exclusively disinterested in buildings that might provide a useful commentary on the environmental agenda?

If we look at the history of social and political change it is quite often tied into a radical shift in architectural paradigms. The architecture of early Renaissance Italian cities became the embodiment of civic and political power. The American Revolution became associated with the pure classicism of pavilions in a controlled landscape that was Jefferson's choice of architectural language at the Universities of Virginia and Arkansas at Monticello. The biggest paradigm shift of all emerged about a century ago and freed architecture from its stylistic associations with the past, as well as heralding social and technological change through the revolutionary new language of the modern movement. It took another 50 years for this to become mainstream in the UK, but, when it did, it became associated with the biggest changes we have ever

seen in the way we run our society, and an anglicised version of modernism became the architecture of the welfare state – homes for war heroes and a new education system. Architecture was there to play a part in and to reinforce societal change.

So given that we now at least have a global consensus around the significance of climate change (salvaged from the detritus of Copenhagen last December), how should we respond in a way that helps us to generate the popular will to solve the unprecedented problem? In the recent past environmental architecture has tried to develop a new language to encourage a paradigm shift. Our new Environmental Office for the BRE fifteen years ago was designed as a test bed for ideas about natural light and ventilation, thermal mass and night-time cooling. It embodied all of these in a very explicit language on its south-facing façade (fig. 3). It met the client's brief, gave them plenty of technology to monitor, and we all learned a lot of simple lessons. We learned that the ventilation chimneys contributed only marginally to what was in effect a cross-ventilated building, that the glass louvres that shaded the south elevation didn't really need to be moveable, and that one of the most fundamental issues (that we failed to achieve first time round) was to achieve airtightness. What we did do, however, was to capture the public imagination for a short while about how environmental architecture might look different, though at the same time we knew that it didn't necessarily need to look like that.

Dean Hawkes, in a very balanced review

Figure 3. BRE - energy explicit south facade. Feilden Clegg Architects, 1993.

Figure 4. BedZED, iconic ventilation monitors. Bill Dunster Architects, 2002. Image: Tom Chance.

of the building, pointed out that only when we could produce low energy buildings that wouldn't necessarily depend on this language would we have begun to solve the problem.[1] The same comments could also be addressed to Bill Dunster's Bedzed housing scheme (fig. 4) which in 2002 pushed the boundaries of the architectural language of housing. The wind-powered roof vents have become an icon of the building but an analysis of these in comparison with a very simple mechanical ventilation and heat recovery system demonstrates the latter could arguably provide better control and lower overall carbon emissions and could be buried in the fabric of the building.

Both of these projects were to a certain extent led by a desire to create a new language of climate-responsive architecture, but in neither case was the architectural language essential to the performance. Basic considerations of orientation, the pro-

portion of transparency, and the effectiveness of ventilation are all essential considerations, but there is no reason to imagine a paradigm shift in visual appearance. The Elizabeth Fry building by Colquhoun and Miller (fig. 5) at the University of East Anglia remains one of the best buildings in the UK in terms of energy consumption simply because of its 'TermoDeck' ventilation system and a very low specific heat loss; but its external appearance gives no clue as to its environmental credentials.

So what are the popular characteristics of these credentials? They are often misinterpreted or over-emphasised. For many the prototypical 'green' building would have a lot of south-facing glazing, be clad in timber, have a green roof and photovoltaic cells. All of these characteristics are part of green 'mythology'. Very large areas of south-facing glazing contribute little to improving energy efficiency in the UK. For

Figure 5. Elizabeth Fry Building, UEA. Colquhoun and Miller, 2001.

Figure 6. The National Trust HQ - the roof snouts. FCBS, 2005.

a well-insulated building, the heat load is reduced to the three months of mid-winter when direct solar gain is minimal, and south-facing glazing is more likely to cause an overheating problem in summer unless it is carefully protected by external shading. Using timber in our buildings is a great way of sequestering carbon but using it on the outside it is more likely to rot and revert to CO_2. Green roofs are useful for rainwater attenuation thereby reducing the flood load on a storm water drainage system, but, beyond that, the claims about increasing insulation values, reducing the urban heat island effect, and increasing CO_2 absorption by photosynthesis are all dramatically overstated. And photovoltaics? They are obviously useful, though still difficult to defend in capital cost terms, and when they do become cost effective we are more likely to be farming energy in large quantities rather than clipping them onto our buildings.

If photovoltaics are part of the story a building tells it is sometimes a pity they are not generally visible. At the National Trust headquarters we developed a roof design where we maximized the solar 'harvesting' area of the roof both from diffuse natural light (the cheapest way to make use of solar energy in the UK) and photovoltaics (the most expensive way!) which are also used to shade the south-facing glazing. The purpose built roof 'snouts', which control the exhaust air as part of the natural ventilation system, also shade the roof glazing from low incident solar radiation in summer. Everything is doing more than its share of the work to contribute to the environmental control of the building.

But then this is nothing new. The buildings adjacent, which date from the mid-nineteenth century, also have smart roofs. But the delights and intricacies of the architecture are only seen by God and the maintenance engineers (figs. 6, 7).

Another lazy but pragmatic approach to the incorporation of solar energy systems is to hide them all behind a parapet roof – and then you don't have to worry about what they look like – so long as no one apart from God can look down upon them. But

Figure 7: The National Trust HQ - energy systems of the roof. FCBS, 2005.

then they really aren't part of the architectural solution – only a disguised piece of plant.

So the conventional green trappings are no guarantee of low carbon performance – on the contrary, they can cause confusion. Looking at our Stirling Prize-winning scheme for Accordia on the outskirts of Cambridge, it would be possible to think of it as a very 'green' scheme. Its appearance is both enhanced and softened by a strong underlying landscape concept, which not only provides high quality public spaces but redefines the garden and incorporates it into the house. Public landscape is represented by the preserved woodland, the riverine environment and the newly created village green, and children's play areas. Private open spaces are incorporated as courtyards, terraces and roof gardens, a series of inside and outside rooms on all levels. The communal landscape of the scheme serves to weld the community together around shared 'front gardens' and has turned out to be one of the most successful aspects of the project (fig. 8). But from a carbon perspective there is nothing special about it. The scheme more than meets building regulations but cannot be said to break new ground other than in the way in which open space is used to create positive, pedestrian-friendly spaces. But building a sense of community is almost more of a challenge than reducing carbon emissions, and indeed the former may well be thought of as a prerequisite for the latter.

When we were asked by Bioregional Developments to design a high-density mixed-use scheme in Brighton in accordance with their 'One Planet Living' principles we realised that the idea of Community was at the heart of their thinking about sustainable development. The higher the density of development the more precious the external spaces become, but outside space, for recreation and even for food production, was one of Bioregional Developments' core principles, and they were concerned that the reduction in carbon footprint should not simply be confined to household energy consumption. Their work analysing the energy footprints of vari-

Figure 8. Accordia Communal green space. FCBS, 2008.

ous occupiers of the original Bedzed project showed that the carbon savings attributable to reduced household energy consumption were only able to dint their overall carbon footprints by between 2 and 5%. We have to address equally serious issues such as transportation, food and the reform of our waste-oriented culture. So, apart from providing statutory spaces for the disabled, One Brighton will provide car spaces solely for members of their own car club. It will provide sky gardens for growing food (fig. 9) and a composting system to produce the growing medium. The scheme is designed to encourage waste separation and recycling, and will provide an intranet connection to each occupier with details of their household energy budget, how to buy from local food co-ops, and how to book a car from the club. For many who have already bought apartments this is a chance to really come to terms with one's carbon footprint, not only from a perspective of household energy use (the heating comes from a centralised biomass plant, the electricity from a PV array topped up with green electricity from an offsite wind generator), but also from all those other and less tangible ways in which we live that lead us to a lifestyle that, in Bioregional's terminology, assumes

we have three planets rather than one. As architecture it is supremely functional and quite self-effacing, but as a planned community it will go well beyond the capacity of architecture to produce energy saving: we are talking about a paradigm shift in lifestyle. One Brighton shows that significant carbon savings do not necessarily mean a new architectural prototype, and that the background architecture of our cities does not need to change fundamentally in appearance to meet the carbon targets that we are committed to: 30% by 2020, 80% by 2050. The problem is bigger than architecture and the solution has to extend further into every aspect of our lifestyle.

But what about those buildings whose clients nevertheless demand environmental icons? What would Seattle Public Library have looked like if Rem was motivated primarily by low energy considerations? It would be great to find out, as he has a way of redefining everything in his own terms. From our own practice's perspective we are developing a project for the City and University of Worcester that we hope will also radically redefine the concept of a library. Firstly it is the only combined facility in the UK for both university and city, and it

Figure 9. One Brighton - sky gardens, FCBS for Bio-regional developments, 2009.

will contain the city archive and an outpost of the local authority. So we do have a new mixed typology. But we are also building on what we have learned about distributing natural light and getting natural ventilation to work for us in a high thermal mass, deep-plan, building. The concept derives from an urban topography that has echoes of the pottery kilns that once provided the wealth of the city, as well as the Malvern Hills that are a constant presence to the west, but also has references in the environmental roofscape of the National Trust building. However (whereas the idea at the National Trust headquarters was to have an intelligent climate-modifying matrix structure that placed the whole of the workforce 'under one roof'), at Worcester, the roofs form an irregular series of sloping and truncated pyramids that create a variety of different enclosures below, reflecting the variety of spaces within the library brief (fig. 10). It may not create a living room for the city but we believe it will fuse the city (and its historical archive) with the new University in a building that we hope will be unique in its function and form, and maybe even set new benchmarks for low energy design that are both explicit and inspirational. We may not even need a sign to tell everyone how clever the building is.

Figure 10. Worcester Library - the interior.

(ENDNOTES)

1   Hawkes, D., 'The Functional Tradition', RIBA Profile (April 1997), pp. 18-27.

Architecture and Cultural Climates; A History of Year 2 Studio 1

by Miraj Ahmed
& Gregory Ross

Miraj Ahmed is a painter and architect and has been teaching at the department since 2006. He is also a Unit Master at the AA (since 2000). He has previously worked with Pierre d'Avoine Architects, Stanton Williams and more recently with Andrzej Blonski Architects on a range of theatre projects.

Students of Architecture now have a lot on their plates. Gone are the days of certainty, a confidence in the past or, indeed, the future. Architects used to be trained in traditional forms of building; typologies that represented given cultural norms and materials. Faith in progress and growth came with civilization. We still live with the same ideology of material progress and growth but have begun to see the damage.

In these uncertain times the effects of industrialisation, consumerism and globalisation are naturally affecting the way we think about architecture.

One response is that of 'sustainable' architecture where quantifiable environmental performance becomes the primary driving force. This is problematic in the same way

Figure 1. 'Please walk on the grass', video still. Chris Green and Maya Davies 2006-07

that the fascination with parametric computer tools can create architectures of empty form, for form's sake. Good environmental performance, or form-finding tools alone, do not necessarily make good architecture. Architecture is more – it has always been about the environment and sustenance through building. It is also about human relations, culture, body, mind and soul.

The need to provide 'sustainable' strategies is implicit but not the real challenge of architecture and architectural training. The question is how to create buildings that address cultural contexts, a sense of community and sensual atmospheres. To create cities that allow for civic life, debate and participation. Attitudes to the environment relate to cultural patterns and political systems. To be truly 'sustainable' requires transitions in the way we conduct our daily lives and routines. A shift away from the damaging corporate consumerism that is sold on the basis of creating individual comfort is a socio-political problem. In order to find ways to deal with changing climates, we first need to change our 'cultural climate'.

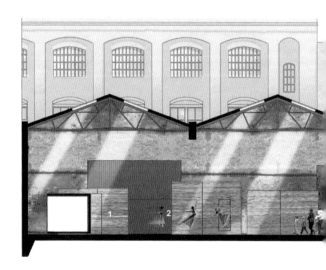

Figure 2. Theatre as civic space in Kings Cross. Mike Taylor 2006-07

Figure 3. 'Being a Gian' street performance. Joe Halligan, 2007-08

The second year at Cambridge Department of Architecture introduces students to an integrated way of thinking about architecture where technical and representational methods are brought together with social and theoretical ideas. Understanding of place, contextual connections and the creation of place are explored with variations through three studios with a common site.

In this context Studio I has, for the

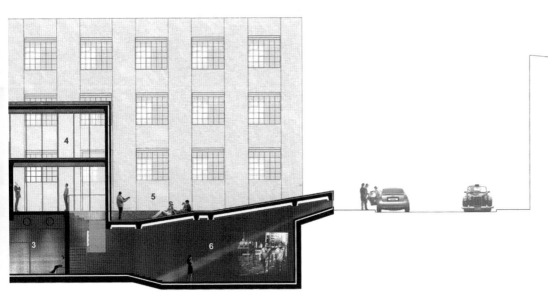

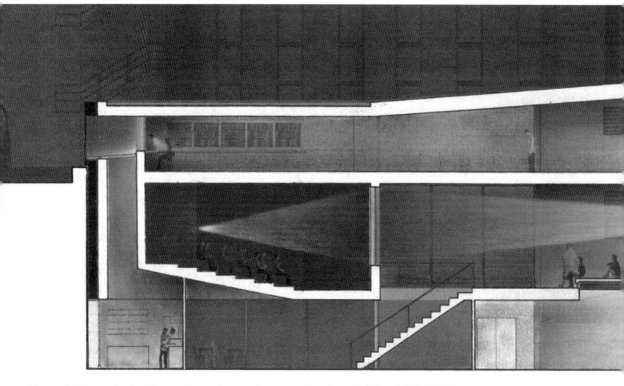

Figure 4. Film and television studios and screening space, Southwark. Adam Willis 2007-08

last four years, been focused on the connections between program, cultural and physical contexts and the poetics of space. Readings of George Bataille, Henri Lefebvre and Michel Foucault have been introduced to the pedagogy to create a link between cultural theory and the practice of space making, so that social readings of space compliment and reinforce the phenomenological and architectonic. Programs that foster cultural exchange – such as art pro-

duction and performance buildings – have been used as a vehicle to investigate space as a network of relationships.

PERFORMING SPACE

Between 2006 and 2008, Studio I (Miraj Ahmed and Teresa Hoskyns) explored 'lived' space through performance. Henri Lefebvre's 'Production of Space' provided a backdrop for discussion about the political dimension of space. Performance as politicised space can be traced back to Athens where the theatre was a vital aspect of the state where democracy could be performed. The critique of consumerist space and the challenge to create a more civic environment was investigated in sites around Kings Cross Station and later Borough Market.

'Architects should be much more aware politically while designing. If political plurality could be achieved architecturally, it could transform our cities and environments that we live in.'

Teresa Hoskyns[1]

Students created live street performances in order to map 'actor/audience' relationships and discover the spaces that are formed. The experience and analysis of the 'lived' space of performance led to the creation of Performing Art Centres that aimed to create spaces of production as public assembly and participation.

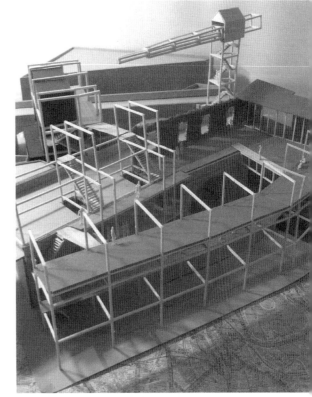

Figure 5. Perpetuating Performance, Immersive performance art colony. Paloma Gormley 2007-08

Figure 6 (above). Bottega set design , Live-in stage set for collaborative theatre and set design using 'found space'. Alex McLean 2008-09.

ORDER, DISORDER, FORM AND INFORME

During 2008/09 Studio 1 (Miraj Ahmed and Gregory Ross) continued to explore the political through an analysis of the order of city fabric. George Bataile's essays from Documents (1929) provided a theoretical backdrop. In his essays (Architecture; Slaughterhouse; Museum) Bataille was critical of architecture's capacity to repress society. Bataille was against the removal of the 'transgressive' from the everyday life of the city and the subsequent gentrification that represented authority. This provided an attitude towards the derelict site in Tottenham Hale, a disused bus/bomb shelter and surrounding Victorian workshops. Issues of re-use, and informal use of space, became key concerns in designing for art production and workshops. Strategies for the recycling of materials, the acceptance of decay and the poetics of 'base materiality' were applied to the design process.

Figure 7 & 8. 'The Art Yard', Bottega. Workshop created from re-use of existing buildings using re-cycled materials. Ellis Dodwell, 2008-09.

HETEROTOPIAS, MOVING BODIES AND MOVING IMAGES

The academic year 2009/10 was focused on Brick Lane – with its diverse culture and urban fabric. It has a history of being marginal and of hosting the 'other' with various occupations of immigrant communities as well as artists. The spatial condition of the 'other' was briefly explored in a lecture by Michel Foucault (Of Other Spaces, Heterotopias) in which he proposed an alternative reading of space. Fouacault's examples of Heterotopic space include spaces such as asylums, brothels, cemetaries, garden, cinemas and theatres. These suggest that society creates for itself certain types of space in which to perform aspects of culture that are outside of ordinary life. Within the cultural context of Brick Lane, the students have explored its conditions in order to propose a space for dance and film; a building for the production of dance films acts as a catalyst for collaborations between choreographers, filmmakers and the local community. An other space that reflects its location, but also a space of the imagination.

Figures 9 & 10. Urban farm art studios, Tottenham Hale. Artists cultivate allotments, rear animals as well as create and exhibit artworks. Amy Graham, 2008-09.

Figure 11. Heterotopia of Dance and Film. Louis Persent, 2009-10.
Figure 12 (overleaf).

Figure 12

(ENDNOTES)

1   Teresa Hoskyns, 'Designing the Agon, Questions on Architecture, Space, Democracy and the Political', Atmospheres of Democracy, Latour, B. and P. Weibel (eds.), MIT Press, Massachusetts (2005).

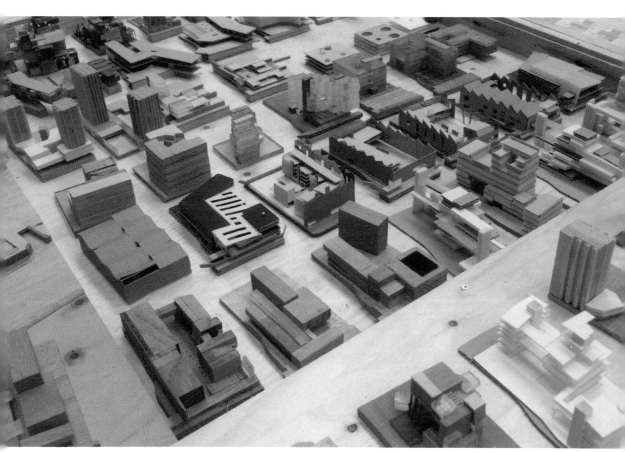

Third Year: Studio 1

by Jay Gort

Over the past six years, Studio 1's teaching projects have explored the capacity for buildings to contribute to the evolution of a city, and to form connections to a place and its people. We are able to ask a lot of modest scaled buildings through rooting them in a wider physical and cultural context whilst at the same time placing emphasis on the more immediate, experiential aspects of building. We aim to raise challenging issues or questions which architecture cannot answer alone, but which it can offer important clues towards solving. I intend to illustrate these ambitions through a description of our teaching methods and examples of past teaching projects.

Jay Gort has run Studio 1 jointly with: Nathan Jones (2009/10, 2008/09), Fiona Scott (2007/08, 2006/07) and Pete Manfield (2004/05, 2003/04).

Architectural design is not a linear process. We set projects that approach the design of a building through two scales

Figure 1. Print Sketch.

simultaneously – a room and an urban strategy – so that each will exert a different push and pull on the form of the building. The exercise requires leaps of faith, thinking through drawing and making, intuition and reflection. Work at the two scales will at first often appear quite unrelated, but through keeping both on the drawing board for the duration of the year an iterative process can lead to a strong idea for a building. We hope that the key properties of a strategy at 1:500 may define a detail at 1:5.

In this exercise the initial ideas of a specific room are supported by analysis of programme and typology, discussions relating to environmental issues and – more recently – the production of large precedent models. We are interested in how changes in scale, structure, material and the

light of a room create spaces with different atmospheres, which have a direct effect on our emotional perception and call on our memories. The location of the room in relation to the rest of the building and the wider context is also critical to our experience, and reading, of the space. The design always begins through imagining a particular human situation that, it is hoped, will occur in the room/building. Once an idea has been represented sufficient to describe its location and the atmosphere of the place, we can make judgements on appropriateness, relevance and are able to either reject or creatively expand upon this idea in order to build up a concept for what we want the building to be. We encourage the production of fast hand sketches, mono-printmaking (in the case of North Woolwich), or scrappy 1:50 models, which continue to be produced throughout the process but are joined by more refined photographs of models and drawings.

The formulation of the urban strategy, which usually begins at 1:1000 or 1:500, is underpinned by group site analysis. For a building to contribute to the evolution of a place, rather than simply gentrification, it is necessary to seek a strong understanding of its intended situation, which is not a quick or easy process.

We have set introductory projects to capture the relevant knowledge and empirical data, and to develop an empathetic understanding of the place. Documentary photographers, Henner and Lock, have joined the studio in recent years to run workshops. Alongside desk-based geographical and topographical mappings the portrait photograph has proven to be a useful vehicle for engaging with local people. It has enabled students to strike up conversations that have revealed a more complete, and at times surprising, reading of place.

Figure 2. AM

In choosing our sites, we have identified places which are experiencing urban change, whose physical and social fabric will provide a degree of creative friction with the architectural imagination, and where there is a relevant and current wider question or debate that we feel architecture can contribute towards – though not answer alone.

In 2008/09, our investigations took place in the context of a lively political debate on the regeneration of the town centre

Figure 3. ST

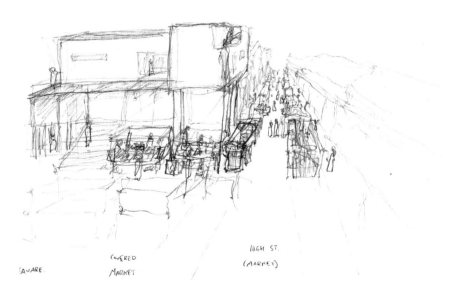

Figure 4. 1:500 models.

of Brixton, one of the most vibrant and diverse parts of Britain. Our site was an urban block housing a covered shopping arcade, a number of small dark service yards and a fringe of buildings varying from once grand terraces to chicken shop infill. Many of the existing buildings are down at heel, poorly maintained or unoccupied and this has led to questions over its future, intensified by the recent sale of the arcade

and associated buildings. This has raised a very pointed political debate as the low rent properties are home to shops and stalls of many ethnicities and the block is regarded by various communities as constituting the living heart of Brixton.

The core brief was a hotel or hostel. We asked students to interpret this in the way they felt resonated with Brixton. We were clear that the programme needed to be commercially viable, but also saw an opportunity for a civic building that would engage with the existing communities. The scale of the project was large enough to force the students to have an attitude towards the entire urban block (and which bits should remain) and to enable them to experiment with a range of different types and scales of rooms, spanning from the most everyday to the extravagant.

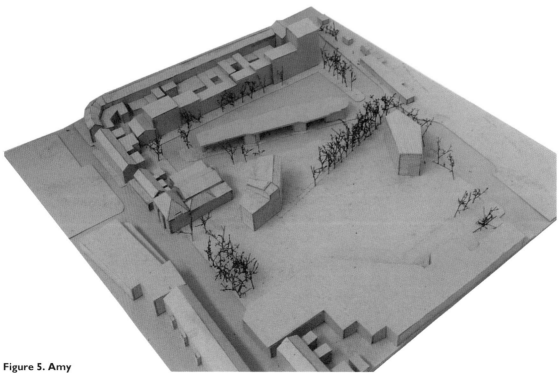
Figure 5. Amy

Students were expected to be radical in their propositions to meet the studio's intention that the building/urban proposal should anchor the block's role as a diverse urban centre in the long-term future. As Di Lampedusa stated in *The Leopard*, 'If we want things to stay as they are, things will have to change.'

At various points in the year, many of the students were hit by the realisation that although their proposals would certainly 'change' the urban landscape, they had to work very hard to ensure that this change was positive. Final propositions ranged from a series of light touch interventions through to comprehensive restructuring of the block.

Because we were sited on and within an existing piece of city fabric it is not surprising that all of the architectural moves have a

Figure 6. MN

Figure 7. AG

Figure 8 (above). EP. Figure 9 (below) LJ

direct bearing on an urban strategy. Other projects have had a less explicit engagement with a dense urban context but still required students to imagine the urban role of stand alone buildings. This is true of previous projects set in Abbey Wood, North Woolwich and Scarborough as well as this year's current student project in Walthamstow, more specifically the Town Hall grounds.

Waltham Forest Town Hall emerges without warning from the sea of terraced housing which typifies much of outer London. Completed in 1942, it was built in a heroic classical style, with an architectural ambition that recalls the great era of Victorian town hall building. Yet the building, set back from

Figure 10. LJ

the road within formal landscaped grounds, registers symbolically as a distant 'other' and fails to establish a more open and engaged relationship with the people whom it serves.

The main building project for the year proposes a new council building on the lawns of the existing town hall. The programme, which was clearly defined yet with room for interpretation/imagination, was to provide much needed office space in combination with collective space and facilities for borough-wide communities. The hierarchy of public spaces inside and outside the building has been our main focus. By making the building more inclusive, our hope was that it might, in a small way, ad-dress the 'them and us' perception of local government.

Like Brixton, though for different reasons, the territory is not a blank canvas and the act of building necessitates the destruction of an exiting setting which is cherished by some; in this case the front lawns of the Town Hall. This has again forced the students to commit to a strong attitude for their projects.

As in previous years, we asked students to keep the strategic investigations on the go at the same time as the more experiential. The location of the building in respect to others on the site, including the existing town hall, and outdoor spaces, has been a key consideration. To fully understand this conversation between their proposals and existing situations students have had to develop a sense of the life and material presence of the building. The projects that have responded to the brief are presenting rooms and sequences that are uplifting and grand in scale and ambition, and at the same time accessible, welcoming to individuals and accepting of the diversity, changes and conflicts of everyday life.

Figure 11. Urban Plan.

Reconciling Heritage with Environmental Performance in the Refurbishment and Adaptation of Iconic Post-war Buildings

by Christopher Bowler

Christopher Bowler completed the MPhil Option B in 2010 with a thesis focusing on readaptation of Modernist office blocks. During a course placement with Short and Associates his interest in conservation projects was put into practice whilst also contributing to work on an advanced low energy passively cooled building for a London university. Other collaborative projects have included an internationally award winning proposal for an algae powered domestic house. He hopes to continue his architectural studies with an interdisciplinary environmental design consultancy.

INTRODUCTION

To achieve national carbon emission targets, there is a need to address the environmental performance of the existing building stock. In cases where a building is deemed architecturally significant, and there is a desire to conserve at least some aspect of this significance, particular and interesting challenges and judgments exist in the consolidation of these potentially conflicting objectives. A focus on buildings from the recent past – taking an early 1960s office block as case study – presents unique technical and environmental characteristics that can accentuate the difficulty in this brokering process, not least because they can be severe enough to render the building inadequate in its intended operation.

This research investigates the following research questions;

What factors have lead to the perceived obsolescence of modernist office buildings and what are the barriers and opportunities for adaptation to new uses?

What reversible or irreversible design interventions are needed to accommodate these new uses satisfactorily?

How do adaptations of Modernist buildings compare to new-build developments in the quality of environment provided and levels of utility achieved?

THE PROMISE OF MODERNISM

During the 1950s and 60s the technologically orientated functionalism of late Modernism – derived from Le Corbusier's 'machine for living in' and Mies van der Rohe's glass towers – continued to exert a strong influence on the form of ongoing development across Europe. Ostensibly this cellular, formalistic, structurally efficient architecture was well suited to the task of quickly and boldly reconstructing urban environments devastated by two world wars and addressing the housing needs of the 'baby boomers' of the 1960s. However, by this time the Modernist idiom was already becoming outmoded, with much of the derivative late-Modernist architecture – that remains commonplace amongst our towns and cities today – struggling to address the cultural dimension of technology – ultimately, in many instances, failing in an attempt

to find a comprehensive response to the revitalisation of post-war societies.

TECHNICAL CHARACTERISTICS AND FAILINGS OF POST-WAR CONSTRUCTION

Parallel to this cultural dimension, the technical innovations and use of new materials and construction techniques that characterise buildings of this era had serious shortcomings in their intended performance and, along with rapid changes in user expectations, in many instances contributed to their premature obsolescence.

New and emerging construction methods led to a trial and error approach to establishing best construction practices and meant that performance and durability were often not sufficiently evaluated. Whereas previously a brick or stone masonry structure might have been the norm, increasingly steel or concrete framed buildings utilising cladding systems were employed.

During the sixties and seventies various versions of composite clad panels were evolved, generally with the aim of decreasing weight whilst increasing the level of thermal insulation. Primarily because a lighter weight, poorly insulated envelope had now been adopted, early Modernist buildings were commonly found to be overly sensitive to internal and external energy inputs. A poor understanding of the durability of many new materials – leading to high degrees of wind penetration among other problems – exacerbated this tendency towards poor modulation of climatic temperature extremes.

Improving understanding through the 1970s and 80s of the structural behaviour of new materials resulted in the dense column spacing of the early examples (typically 5 or 6 metre spans) quickly becoming outmoded as tenants moved away from old cellular partitioned layouts and came to expect large unobstructed open plan floor areas. Similarly, service provision requirements dramatically increased and the low floor to floor heights and smaller core sizes of older buildings were unable to accommodate modern day IT and air conditioning systems.

It is predominantly for these infrastructure factors that the market has traditionally rejected office buildings of this type and era, and led developers to conclude that potential rent levels achievable post-renovation do not better those possible through re-developing the site.

EXISTING GUIDANCE ON ASSESSING ARCHITECTURAL SIGNIFICANCE

Conversely, where the physical configuration does not represent an insurmountable barrier to reuse, the outward appearance will have a subsidiary effect on rental values. And so in the case of architecturally significant examples of the era, judgments must be made in resolving potentially three-way conflicting desires to satisfy market requirements, improve environmental performance and conserve the architectural fabric. Established conservation principles and

practices exist to assist in addressing the last of these objectives.

Orthodox conservation guidelines use quasi-objective methodologies to separate out the reasons for a particular building's significance, and distinguish original design intentions from actual building performance. Conservation Management Plans (CMPs) represent one such methodology through which architectural elements and organisational hierarchy of the building are catalogued – for example, wall finishes, particular elevations or the glazing detailing – in terms of their constituent contribution to the building's holistic significance. Whilst CMPs are recognised as specialised instruments to identifying significance, it is a contention of the author that the provision for identifying environmental intentions and performance is unduly lacking.

In making a critical linkage between the significance of each of the architectural elements analysed, an assessment of their respective environmental characteristics, and the degree to which they are integrated with the building structure, future conservation related decisions could be better informed. Curtain wall glazing details serve as a pertinent example when assessing Modernist towers; it is clear that the contribution to 'architectural character' and relative environmental performance could be relevant as conflicting interrelated factors.

THE CASE FOR MIXED-USE ADAPTATION

A third strand in the regeneration narrative concerns market pressures acting against adaptation in instances where the obstacles to maintain original use through renovation are too severe. Adaptation of office buildings to mixed-use programmes is especially unfavoured by developers. This is despite encouragement of appropriate mixed-use development in central government policy. Indeed mixed-use is frequently cited as an agent of sustainability; firstly in encouraging a reduction in transport use, and secondly as an aid to the creation of diverse, 'vibrant' communities – positively affecting social equality[1] and cultural and community level activity. Empirical evidence provides moderate support for these claims.

MARKET ATTITUDES AND CHALLENGES

The uptake of inner city mixed-use development in the UK, particularly 'hybrid' buildings containing a mixture of uses, has been slow. Caution and the minimising of risk are the priorities of the property developer and as an investment proposition mixed-use is perceived as high-risk. The traditional specialisation of developers and investors in one sector (i.e. residential, retail, commercial etc.) is cited by Prof. Colin Lizieri, Grosvenor Professor of Real Estate Finance at the University of Cambridge, as one such barrier to mix-use development. He confirms the tendency for 'firms and funds that are specialist (to) outperform those that are generalist', and that 'there is a tendency to (a) herd; (b) do what you understand; (c) be driven by short-term trends.'

SITE HISTORY

A host building suitable for re-adaptation was identified on a fringe location to the City of London *(fig. 1)*. St. Alphage House is a 20-storey slab tower, built in 1960-62, by architects Maurice Sanders Associates for the Corporation of London. In this particular instance an assessment of its significance must be made within the context of the ambitious regeneration vision of which it is part.

In 1959 a redevelopment plan by the Corporation of London and London County Council for a bold new business quarter was approved, amidst an area of London entirely blitzed by bombing in 1940. The plan consisted of a linear array of 5 parallel office towers regularly spaced along either side of a newly constructed four-lane highway; London Wall. The scheme was characterised by the uniformity of the architecture – The City stipulated the identical proportions and palette of materials for each block – to create a striking, and highly ordered urban vista. The real innovation of the scheme, however, was in the implementation of a segregated circulation system separating pedestrian from vehicle. Here, for the first and only time on any significant scale in Britain, this most quintessential of Corbusian Modernist ideas was realised, and indeed it

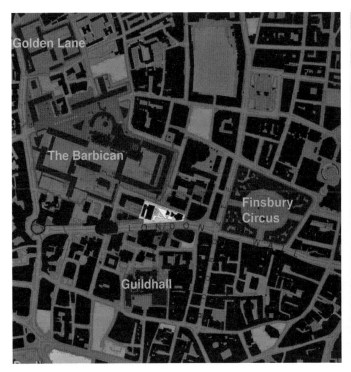

Figure 1. Proposed Site: View of St Alphage House along London Wall

was with great optimism that the scheme was presented; pedestrians were to enjoy a new, civilised car-free environment of pubs, restaurants, and generous civic spaces, all 5 metres above street level. The scheme was envisaged to be only the first phase of an expanded Highwalk network that ultimately was to cover the whole city.

In 1963 redevelopment of the remainder of the site to the north commenced and the residential Barbican Estate officially opened six years later. Architects Chamberlain, Powell & Bon utilised the same Highwalk grade separation as at London Wall, and together the two developments linked to form one pedestrian network.

Contemporary industry reaction to the scheme was overwhelmingly positive, e.g.;

'The need for vertical segregation has world wide recognition, in theory, yet in practice it is still impossible to point to a single instance where it has been carried out; that is on a scale sufficiently large to make it work. ...It is good news therefore that London is to be the first city to carry out a large scheme of this kind.'[2]

Considered in isolation from the Highwalk, in its construction and materials St. Alphage House is a typical, relatively early example of office towers constructed across the country during the post-war building boom of the mid 1950s and 60s.

Formally, it is an International Style slab block strongly influenced by the 'universal' towers pioneered by Mies van der Rohe and SOM.

The building features a rationally gridded concrete frame supporting a modular aluminium curtain wall. Reflecting the overall 'cut price' realisation compared to its American counterparts (typically specified with air conditioning systems), St. Alphage House was designed to be naturally ventilated and featured user-operable sash windows around its perimeter. These adversely contribute to the somewhat less elegant detailing of the curtain wall frame, the alternating mullion sizes contributing to a lack of visual unity to the grid. Altogether it struggles to achieve the lightness and 'membrane-like' quality of the most articulate iterations of Mies's Friedrichstrasse archetype.

As it exists today, St. Alphage House stands unoccupied and faces imminent demolition; all but one of its sister buildings having suffered this fate already. London Wall Highwalk is for the most part deserted, its kiosk businesses long since wound-up. Environmentally, the podium walkway fails to provide any differentiation in the intimacy and shelter of its spaces. It feels a very exposed, windswept place to be, and contrasts with the richness and complexity of the stepped and porticoed semi-public spaces provided in the neighbouring Barbican Estate (now Grade II listed). London Wall itself suffers from St. Alphage House's oblique, set-back relationship to the street, and indeed it remains very much the vehicular expressway it was intended to be with next to no human engagement by way of building entrances, visibly inhabited facades or pedestrian activity at ground level.

However, it is considered together as a component of the Barbican development that St. Alphage House derives its significance. The North and South Barbican developments together exemplify the development of Modernism as an architecture of grid-based planning and modular cladding systems through to a more complex, sculptural and expressive Brutalist language. The Highwalk forms an integral part of the most comprehensive post-war re-development in Europe. Whereas the London Wall Highwalk suffers for its lack of human scale, the criticism is levelled that the Barbican's design went too far in orientating the design to its residents' needs and that through its introverted relationship with the surrounding city it makes navigation across the site – via its Highwalk – and for visitors to the arts centre at its heart, difficult. Without completely isolating the Barbican, any adaptation of St. Alphage House would necessarily need to provide a Highwalk linkage of some form, and so an opportunity existed to re-imagine the failed London Wall Highwalk portion of the network.

ENVIRONMENTAL CHARACTERISTICS

The building axis is orientated north-south; inherently the most problematical orientation for control of solar gains is via the east and west facades. Evidence for poor modulation of external temperatures and high sensitivity to periods of high solar irradiance was extrapolated from a study of measurements taken from a nearby building of very similar size, site orientation, degree of over-shadowing, era and construction (Great Arthur House, Chamberlain, Powell & Bon, 1955).

An estimation of the energy loss:gain ratio was made in a steady state energy balance analysis. Estimations were made as to the thermal transmittance of each envelope material and a high rate of air infiltration assumed. The outcome of the analysis provided further evidence that the building, as anticipated for a building type with a high glazing ratio and a total lack of solar orientation to site or mitigation of gains by way of shading, suffers from very excessive solar gains.

In summary, St. Alphage House is representative of a ubiquitous building type that has hitherto been dismissed as obsolete by the real estate market. Its architectural significance is evident from urban scale analysis more than as considered as an individual building. Indeed it represents part of a uniquely extensive example of centrally planned post-war reconstruction and a Modernist utopian urban experiment. It suffers from environmental problems the resolution of which could be of significance across its building class, and is appropriate as a candidate for adaptation as an opportunity to question orthodox assumptions regarding its obsolescence, and to inform the debate on approaches to conserving architectural significance.

THE DESIGN APPROACH AND BRIEF

The design adopted a mixed-use programme as a means to re-invigorate and re-launch the site whilst providing the opportunity to test the feasibility of accommodating particular new programmes and mixes of programmes. Design challenges were created in catering for these groups of activities arising from patterns of compatibility and incompatibility between the various architectural, environmental and organisational configurations needed by each occupant group, and the physical constraints of the legacy building. Parallel to the re-adaptation of St. Alphage House, a design for a comparative new building, also with a mixed-use programme, was developed on an adjacent site.

The mix of programmes to be introduced was formulated from consideration of pragmatic real estate market pressures and of the successful existing juxtaposition of creative, residential, and business communities at the Golden Lane Estate and the Barbican. The concept for both St. Alphage House and the new-build was further influenced by concern for issues to do with ownership of public space and the market pressures that have the potential to compromise the interests of minority stakeholders in mixed-use developments.

Studies were made at EXHIBIT – a resident-run art gallery and sub-community of the Golden Lane Estate 500 metres north-west of the St. Alphage House site, and the Helen Hamlyn Centre (a design research department of the Royal College of Art with a design focus for research in inclusive design, patient design and workplace design). The two groups served as clients for the arts portion of the programme. The

Figure 2. Southern Elevation: the optimised shaded facade of the SkyDeck hub, and the SkyDeck linkage between the two buildings providing efficiencies in servicing and circulation, and providing a semi-outdoor / semi-public axis for creative industry activities.

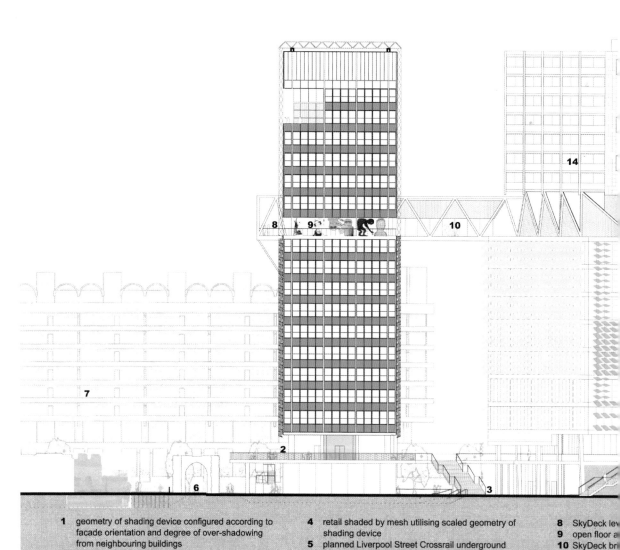

1   geometry of shading device configured according to facade orientation and degree of over-shadowing from neighbouring buildings
2   St. Alphage Highwalk cafe terrace
3   civic plaza leading to The Barbican

4   retail shaded by mesh utilising scaled geometry of shading device
5   planned Liverpool Street Crossrail underground interchange
6   ruins of St. Alphage Church
7   The Barbican

8   SkyDeck lev
9   open floor a
10 SkyDeck bri
11 SkyDeck do
    frame trans
    infilled with

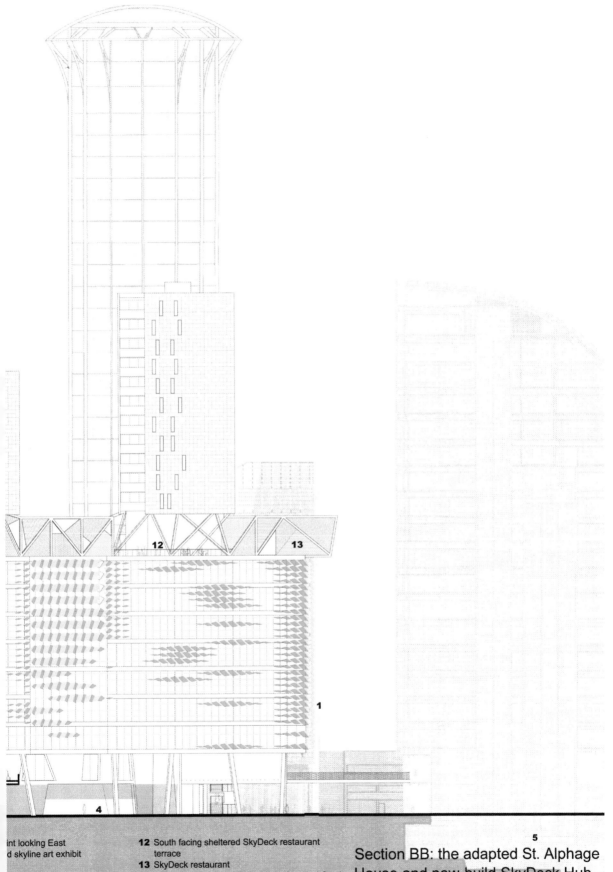

12 **12**

13 **13**

1

4

5

int looking East
d skyline art exhibit

st studios within space
toskelotal structure
el cladding and glazing

12 South facing sheltered SkyDeck restaurant
terrace
13 SkyDeck restaurant
14 residential: apartment balconies orientated South

Section BB: the adapted St. Alphage
House and new-build SkyDeck Hub
Scale 1:500 at A3

Figure 3. Section looking south: the SkyDeck and Atrium.

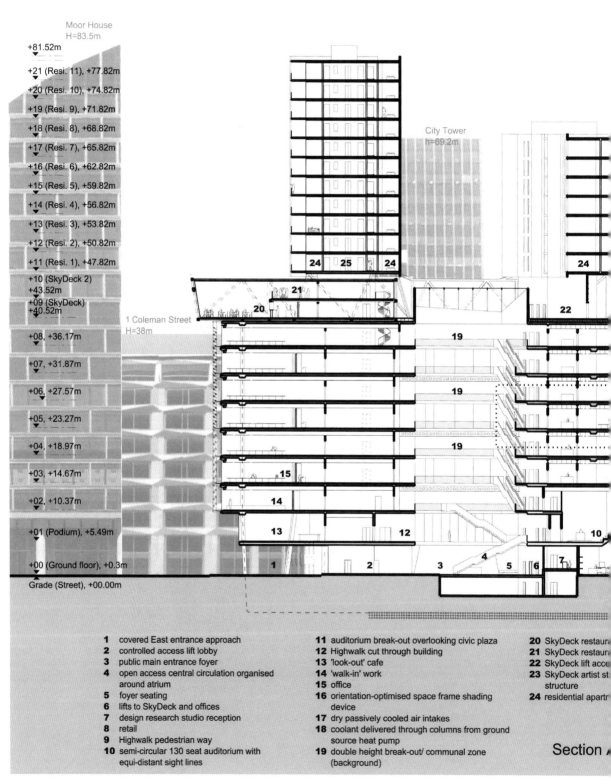

Moor House
H=83.5m
+81.52m
+21 (Resi. 11), +77.82m
+20 (Resi. 10), +74.82m
+19 (Resi. 9), +71.82m
+18 (Resi. 8), +68.82m
+17 (Resi. 7), +65.82m
+16 (Resi. 6), +62.82m
+15 (Resi. 5), +59.82m
+14 (Resi. 4), +56.82m
+13 (Resi. 3), +53.82m
+12 (Resi. 2), +50.82m
+11 (Resi. 1), +47.82m
+10 (SkyDeck 2) +43.52m
+09 (SkyDeck) +40.52m
1 Coleman Street H=38m
+08, +36.17m
+07, +31.87m
+06, +27.57m
+05, +23.27m
+04, +18.97m
+03, +14.67m
+02, +10.37m
+01 (Podium), +5.49m
+00 (Ground floor), +0.3m
Grade (Street), +00.00m

City Tower
h=69.2m

Section A

1 covered East entrance approach
2 controlled access lift lobby
3 public main entrance foyer
4 open access central circulation organised around atrium
5 foyer seating
6 lifts to SkyDeck and offices
7 design research studio reception
8 retail
9 Highwalk pedestrian way
10 semi-circular 130 seat auditorium with equi-distant sight lines
11 auditorium break-out overlooking civic plaza
12 Highwalk cut through building
13 'look-out' cafe
14 'walk-in' work
15 office
16 orientation-optimised space frame shading device
17 dry passively cooled air intakes
18 coolant delivered through columns from ground source heat pump
19 double height break-out/ communal zone (background)
20 SkyDeck restaura
21 SkyDeck restaura
22 SkyDeck lift acce
23 SkyDeck artist st structure
24 residential apartr

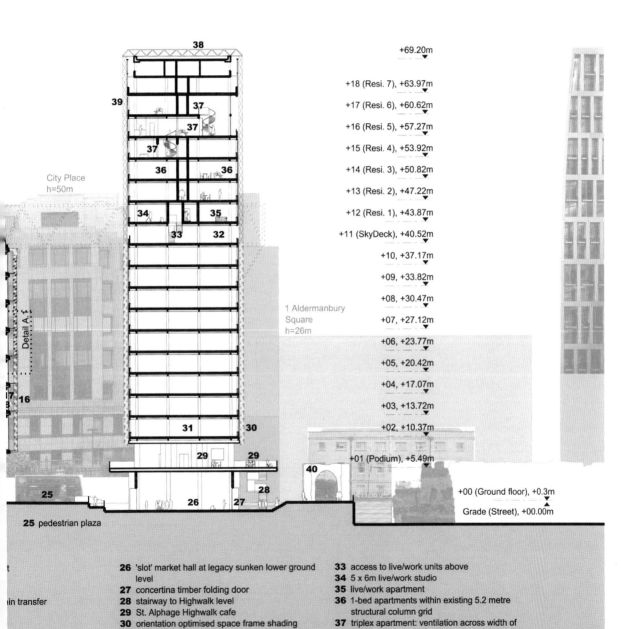

City Place
h=50m

Detail A: f

1 Aldermanbury
Square
h=26m

+69.20m
+18 (Resi. 7), +63.97m
+17 (Resi. 6), +60.62m
+16 (Resi. 5), +57.27m
+15 (Resi. 4), +53.92m
+14 (Resi. 3), +50.82m
+13 (Resi. 2), +47.22m
+12 (Resi. 1), +43.87m
+11 (SkyDeck), +40.52m
+10, +37.17m
+09, +33.82m
+08, +30.47m
+07, +27.12m
+06, +23.77m
+05, +20.42m
+04, +17.07m
+03, +13.72m
+02, +10.37m
+01 (Podium), +5.49m
+00 (Ground floor), +0.3m
Grade (Street), +00.00m

25 pedestrian plaza

1:500 at A3

t

iin transfer

26 'slot' market hall at legacy sunken lower ground
   level
27 concertina timber folding door
28 stairway to Highwalk level
29 St. Alphage Highwalk cafe
30 orientation optimised space frame shading
   device retro-fit to remedy excessive solar gains
31 start-up business
32 SkyDeck level: open floor art workshop/ exhibit
   space

33 access to live/work units above
34 5 x 6m live/work studio
35 live/work apartment
36 1-bed apartments within existing 5.2 metre
   structural column grid
37 triplex apartment: ventilation across width of
   building
38 roof truss on existing columns supports hung
   space frame shading device
39 support structure to shading device below
40 ruin of St. Alphage Church

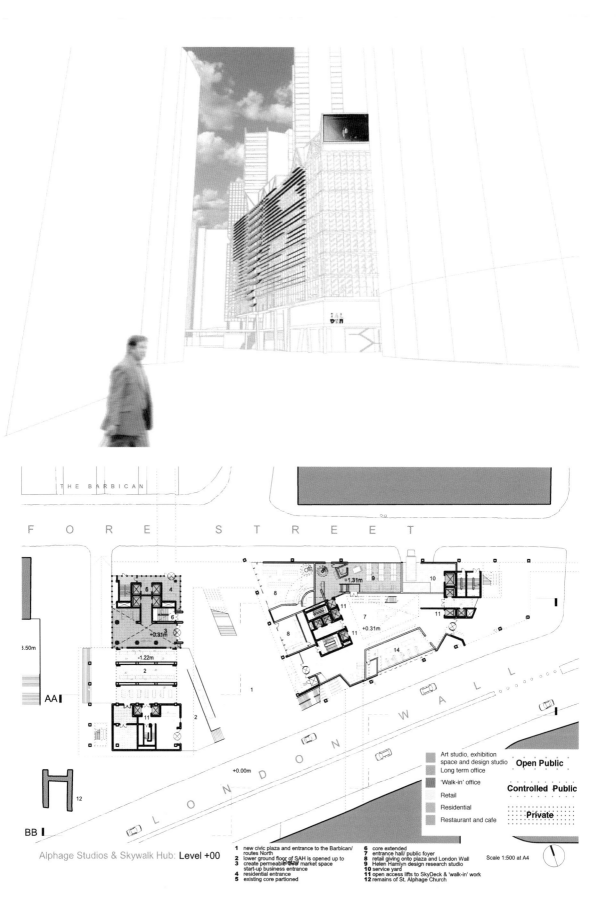

THE BARBICAN

F O R E   S T R E E T

AA

BB

L O N D O N   W A L L

+0.00m

3.50m

-1.22m
+0.31m

+1.31m
+0.31m

Alphage Studios & Skywalk Hub: Level +00

Art studio, exhibition
space and design studio
Long term office
'Walk-in' office
Retail
Residential
Restaurant and cafe

Open Public

Controlled Public

Private

1 new civic plaza and entrance to the Barbican/
  routes North
2 lower ground floor of SAH is opened up to
  create permeable/ quay market space
3 start-up business entrance
4 residential entrance
5 existing core partioned

6 core extended
7 entrance hall/ public foyer
8 retail giving onto plaza and London Wall
9 Helen Hamlyn design research studio
10 service yard
11 open access lifts to SkyDeck & 'walk-in' work
12 remains of St. Alphage Church

Scale 1:500 at A4

provision of commercial office space recognises the site's location within the Central Activities Zone and the associated market pressures commensurate with prime rental land values. It expands upon the layering of communities by providing for multiple occupancies for creative-industry businesses; sharing communal facilities and interstitial spaces where appropriate, whilst allowing for control of each of the constituent unit holders' private realms.

THE ADAPTATION OF ST. ALPHAGE HOUSE AND DESIGN OF A NEW BUILD COMPARISON

The new-build 'SkyDeck Hub' is organised spatially around a central atrium that splits the building in two, conceptually creating two communal shared zones – one outdoors between St. Alphage House and the Sky-Deck building – the other indoors in a series of double height atrium spaces that run between the two halves of the building, in which disparate users come together to utilise the shared resources of the building *(figs. 2-6)*.

Figure 4 (left). Perspective looking west along London Wall: showing 'look out' restaurant at SkyDeck level, Figure 5 (below left). Plan at Ground level,
Figure 6 (below). Plan at SkyDeck level, Figure 7. (overleaf).

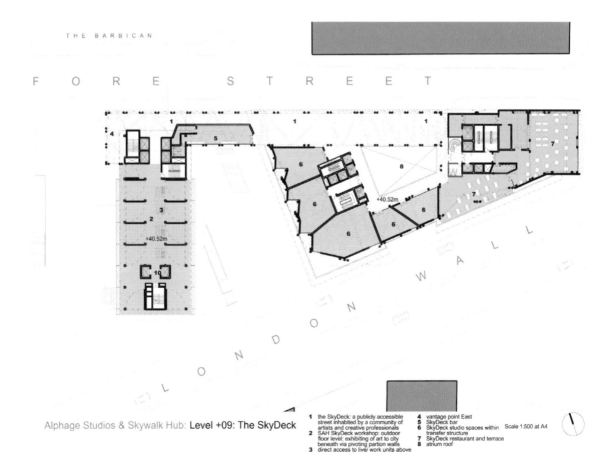

Alphage Studios & Skywalk Hub: Level +09: The SkyDeck

1 the SkyDeck: a publicly accessible street inhabited by a community of artists and creative professionals
2 SAH SkyDeck workshop: outdoor floor level: exhibiting of art to city beneath via pivoting partion walls
3 direct access to live/ work units above
4 vantage point East
5 SkyDeck bar
6 SkyDeck studio spaces within transfer structure
7 SkyDeck restaurant and terrace
8 atrium roof

Scale 1:500 at A4

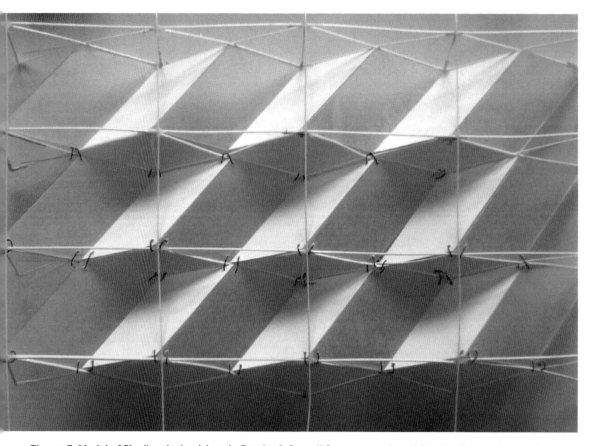

Figure 7. Model of Shading device (above), Graph of Overall Sun penetration of Shading Device (below right).

DESIGN OF SHADING DEVICE

As previously described, an exercise in evaluating net heat gains and losses across St. Alphage House identified a tendency towards severe over-heating. The unprotected expanses of glazing of the east and west facing facades contribute greatest to the excessive solar flux. The design of a retrofitted orientation-specific shading device addressed these problems whilst also reversibly transforming the appearance of the building and assisting in overcoming its perceived obsolete status as described above (fig. 7). This potential to aid the building's 're-invention' was a key benefit over the adoption of, for example, a conventional roller blind system.

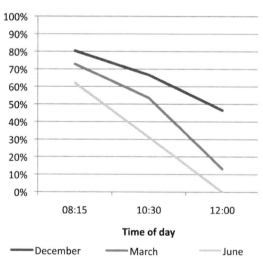

The shading device: by splitting the shading function between two panel orientations and opacities, the device was able to provide a greater amount of shading from low and Summer sun whilst allowing a greater percentage of mid-day Winter sun to penetrate when compared to a traditional 'Brise Solei' arrangement.

The design integrates the shading function within a lightweight rigid space frame. The geometry of the shading panels, as informed by analysis of solar geometry, and calibrated to allow maximum winter time/minimum summertime solar penetration, informs the node positions of the frame. Such a structure could be 'hung' from the roof of St. Alphage House and similar buildings; fixing to the façade only for lateral support and so minimising intrusion to the host building's existing envelope.

COMPARISON BETWEEN ST. ALPHAGE HOUSE ADAPTATION AND SKYDECK NEW BUILD

The proposed adaptation of St. Alphage House displays a variety of conservation approaches and combines reversible and irreversible interventions. The coexistence of the minimal intervention space frame shading device, with remodelling of the slab and curtain wall to form triplex apartments, is intended to begin to develop a 'shopping-list' of renovation design options for this building type. The insertion of residential occupancies in particular is much more satisfactorily resolved if the curtain wall can be modified to provide a more sophisticated relationship between interior and exterior (e.g. by provision of winter garden spaces).

A key conclusion is that the impact of additional stair and lift cores, as necessitated by building regulations to provide for the increased occupancies of mixed-use, is proportionally relatively greater on the small floor plan area of St. Alphage House compared to the larger areas of typical new-build developments. The linear nature of its layout means St. Alphage House does not afford the same opportunity to bring different users together into the 'heart' of the building.

However, the experiment of the SkyDeck shows that there is rich potential in the idea of the surrogate building; buildings working together and operating as one, sharing services and infrastructure. Future development of the scheme could explore the potential for a surrogate core; side-stepping the burden of inserting additional cores through the existing floor slab structure by supplementation with a service tower, potentially free-standing, serving multiple buildings at once.

The design of the SkyDeck Hub demonstrates that an holistic approach to interpreting architectural significance – in this instance the re-imagining of the 60s highwalk concept – in combination with provision for different occupancies, can enrich mono-cultural City architecture and public spaces, and that an architectural language can begin to emerge from the environmental qualities desired by the different building users.

(ENDNOTES)

1   Williams, K., *'Does Intensifying Cities Make them More Sustainable?'* in Williams, K. et al (ed.), Achieving Sustainable Urban Form, Spon Press, London (2000).

2   *Architects Journal* (June 1960), p. 858.

Future Hospitals

by Ivan del Renzio

Ivan del Renzio previously studied at the University of Kent. His MPhil design thesis was titled 'Reducing Energy Consumption in Acute Hospitals investigated through the design, simulation and evaluation of a 200 bed hospital in the UK'. During the MPhil in Environmental Design course he was seconded to Penoyre & Prasad working on an array of healthcare projects including the winning competition for Welwyn Garden City Local General Hospital. Currently Ivan is working for Foster + Partners as an Environmental Analyst in the Specialist Modelling Group.

INTRODUCTION

This research investigates the energy consumption of large acute hospital facilities in the UK. The NHS has recently set stringent carbon reduction targets which are unlikely to be met. Current hospital facilities are large consumers of energy largely due to their deep plan nature, utilising artificial lighting and mechanical ventilation to maintain internal environmental requirements. This research investigates how simple passive design measures (such as reducing plan depth of departments) could substantially reduce energy consumption; it is also suggested that the introduction of views to the natural environment may improve staff and patient well-being and increase productivity.

THE HOSPITAL AS A RECENT BUILDING TYPOLOGY

Over the past three decades, the hospital as a building type and in particular that of larger acute facilities has consisted of two typologies. The first typology is that of low rise, mat-plan, repetitive cruciform templates designed by the Architects Board of the Department for Health and Social Security, known as 'Nucleus' planning. The system allowed for a wide range of standardised departments and room types to be planned on a systematic template and planning grid. Nucleus planning allowed high flexibility in internal planning arrangements and to a certain degree 'passive' design with some notable examples.

The second typology has developed predominantly within the last decade.[1] Design and Build hospitals have been synonymous with PFI (Private Finance Initiative) design with a demanding brief, often amalgamating nearby hospitals onto a constrained site that is out of human scale, with deep plan buildings that are often separate from urban areas and the populations they serve, a notable example of this being the Norfolk and Norwich Hospital in Norfolk. The recent wave of PFI hospitals has seen the emergence of non-design or a non-typology in which health care planners arrange deep plan floor plates to exacting tolerances of floor area, with architects and designers left to design the entrance canopy, foyer, and possibly even the colour and pattern of linoleum if they are lucky.

THE 'MODERN' HOSPITAL AS A HISTORICAL BUILDING TYPOLOGY

From a historical context, when one talks of the 'modern hospital', as opposed to a Victorian hospital, the distinction can be drawn with the advent in technological advancements in science, engineering and social thinking.

Figure 1. Plan, St Mary's Low Energy Hospital, Isle of Wight.
Figure 2 (right). Recently completed Royal London PFI Hospital.

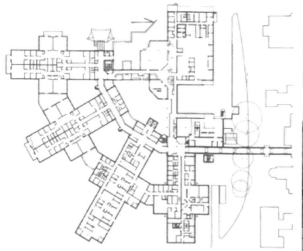

The hospital as a building typology has paradoxical origins with both the military and western Christian traditions. The hospital has always been a building associated with pragmatic requirements for mechanistic efficiency, but a counterpoint to this is the philosophical dimension of the provision of spiritual and medical care for the sick and ill.

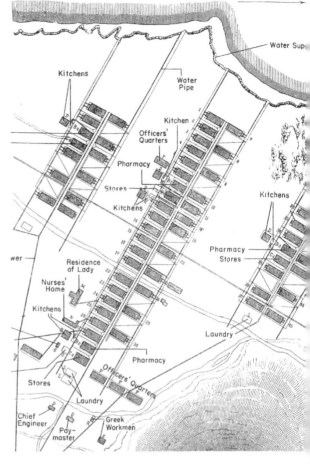

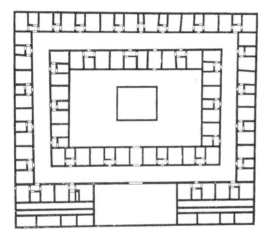

Figure 3 (above). Roman Barracks courtyard form (First Century AD) Windisch, Switzerland.
Figure 4 (above right). Plan of British Army Field Hospital, note long hospital street. Renkoioi, Turkey 1855.
Figure 5 (below). Section through a proposal of the new Hotel Dieu, Paris c.1750.

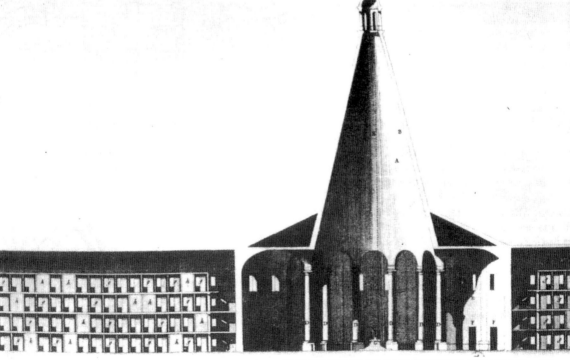

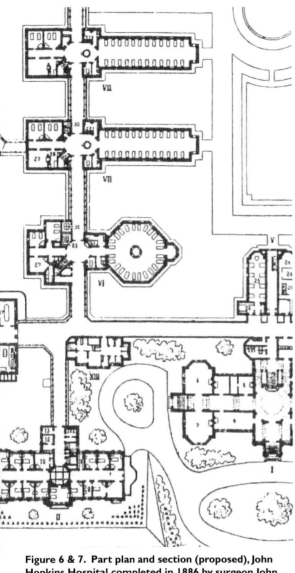

Figure 6 & 7. Part plan and section (proposed), John Hopkins Hospital completed in 1886 by surgeon John Billings.

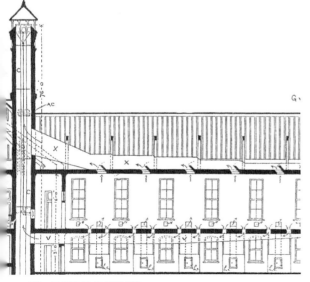

Early hospital forms such as the courtyard form in the Roman barracks at Wiendisch, modern day Switzerland, afforded efficient circulation and the provision of fresh air and light in the centre of the building. This led to the development of wards, with hospices originally inhabiting naves and monasteries, evolving into radial and cruciform plans allowing views for the sick and dying to the alter. This then evolved again with the development of pavilion hospitals, as championed by Florence Nightingale, with the 'separation and ventilation' principle negating the perceived 'miasma'.

The advancement and understanding of modern medicine, treatment, and diagnostics is constantly evolving at a rapid pace in ever increasing cycles of redundancy and obsolescence; from the discovery of germs through to the invention of penicillin and modern medicine through to an understanding of the human genome. However, as much as the activities and practitioners may change, the hospital building as a concept is still necessary, representing as it does civilisation, or even utopia.

A more modern example of this paradox is that of tuberculosis sanatoriums, built at the turn of the century to provide care to patients often by coastal towns or in countryside areas. Often sanatoriums were robust and well built, the thinking being that tuberculosis had been a prevalent problem for centuries, and would remain so into the future, and only fresh air and sun would cure the disease.

The use of deep plan buildings is not a recent phenomenon; the post-war period saw an abundance of cheap energy, and inexpensive artificial lighting and mechanical ventilation meant that large deep plan buildings such as Greenwich Hospital could be planned whilst maintaining environmental control.

Before this era of inconspicuous energy consumption, buildings, no matter how large, primarily relied on passive design, and narrow plan floor plates to allow for natural daylighting and simple natural ventilation as typified in the Nightingale wards still in use today.

One may argue that the hospital as a place of sanctuary and healing has not changed; while since the advent of penicillin treatment and equipment has evolved tremendously. This raises issues to do with redundancy and new types of infectious diseases.

THE MODERN HOSPITAL AS AN ENVIRONMENT

The modern hospital environment is often portrayed as that of the 'air-conditioned nightmare' in which the internal environ-

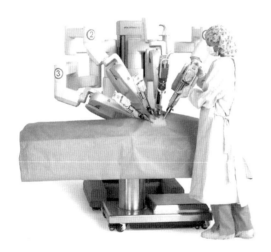 

Figure 8 (above). Equipment used in hospitals is constantly evolving, often equipment decreases in size but often new equipment can be invented such as the Da Vinci robot able to perform operations controlled remotely by surgeons.
Figure 9 (right). Internal windowless environment of a hospital.
Figure 10 (below). Plan deep plan US-style floorplate.

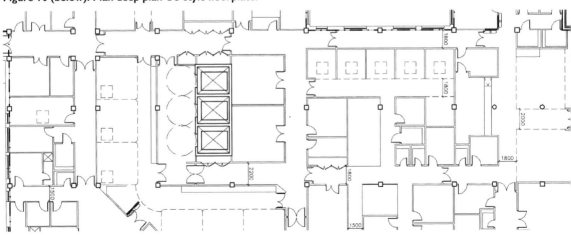

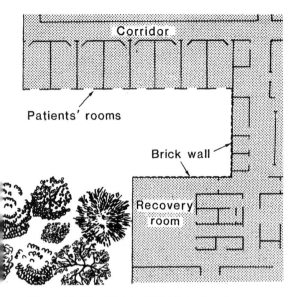

Figure 11. After Ulrich, 1974. View of patient recovery rooms.

ment is devoid of variation or clues as to the season or outside world. Constant lighting levels and temperatures have resulted in buildings that are not only badly designed but disorientating for both staff and patients' health and well-being. Anecdotally patients are often apprehensive to enter a hospital not only because of the perceived level of discomfort from treatment or examinations, but also because the environments that they will ultimately end up in for extended periods of time are so unforgiving and clinical ('white coat hypertension'). The stereotype of internal hospital environments is that of bland interiors, endless corridors, fluorescent lighting, stale air and no view out.

INTROVERT THE HOSPITAL ENVIRONMENT

The occurrence of 'staff burnout syndrome' is interesting in that it is a condition that predominantly affects staff who work in healthcare environments. Research has suggested that view outs may improve recovery times of patients who require prolonged hospital stay. Access to natural sunlight, and in particular the UV component, may have positive effects with improvements in staff morale, reductions in stress-related problems, and an increase in productivity and the quality of delivered care.

HOSPITAL ENERGY CONSUMPTION

Modern hospitals require large amounts of energy, with current 'best practice' benchmarks still in use from the early 1990's. Confusing metric data about energy consumption, such as 'GJ/100m3/year' are often used, making comparison with other non-domestic buildings difficult. When converted to a more standardised kWh/m2/year the comparison is staggering. One may argue that hospitals are high energy consumers because of the increased use of small loads from treatment equipment, but this simply is not the case. The largest proportion of energy consumption is from space heating in the winter and artificial lighting throughout the year.

The use of passive design currently employed in non-domestic buildings could substantially reduce energy consumption in hospital buildings, particularly with the introduction of shallow plans, increased floor to ceiling heights and Advanced Natural Ventilation techniques, which would not only reduce energy consumption but also have positive effects on staff and patients

Good Practice
Naturally Ventilated Office
135 kWh•m^2•year

Good Practice
Air-conditioned Office
220 kWh•m^2•year

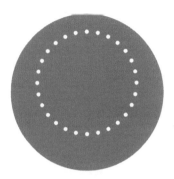

NHS EnCO$_2$de / BREEAM
target
282-443.5 kWh•m^2•year

Figure 12. Comparison of energy consumption between Office Good Practice ECG19 and current healthcare target.

Figure 13 (below). Extract of Environmental requirements for an array of space typologies normally found in acute hospitals.

health and well-being, as well as increasing efficiency.

ENVIRONMENTAL PERFORMANCE

Hospitals by their very nature are buildings with specific minimum environmental requirements for ventilation, thermal comfort, illuminance, lighting and acoustics; all of which are important factors in creating an efficient and safe environment for patients, staff and visitors. A review of current environmental performance requirements was undertaken drawing on work from Lomas.[2]

Environmental performance is currently set at a national level with guidance from the Department of Health (DoH) as well as national bodies such as the Chartered Institution of Building Services Engineers (CIBSE), although these bodies often refer to specific British or European Standards.

Space Name	Space Type	Environmental Requirement											
		Ventilation Rate (ach)				General Lighting (Lux)				Temperatre (°C)			
		RDS	HTM 03-01	CIBSE A/B2	NCM	RDS	CIBSE LLS	BS EN 12464	NCM	RDS	HTM	CIBSE A	NCM
Space Type 1	Waiting Area / Concourse / Atrium	-	-	2.4	3.8	200	200	200	200	21	-	19-21	
Space Type 2	Patient Bedroom	6	6	0.7	0.78	300-520	100	100	125	18-28	21-28	22-24	
Space Type 3	Consult / Exam / Treatment	-	-	1.9	1.9	300	300-500	300-500	300	21	-	22-24	
Space Type 4	Treatment Room	10	10	6	0.7	500-800	500	500	500	18-25	18-25	22-24	
Space Type 5	Imaging Room	5	15	-	7.9	400	500	300	300	21-23	-	22-24	>23
Space Type 6	Operating Theatre	Specific	25	39	15.8	500	1000	1000	300	20-22	18-25	17-19	
Space Type 7	General Circulation	-	-	0.9	1	150	200	200	100	16	-	19-21	
Space Type 8	Catering / Kitchen	-	-	-	1.9	-	300	500	500	-	-	15-18	
Space Type 9	WC / Shower / Utility	10	6	6	2.3	200	100-150	200		21	-	20-22	
Space Type 10	Store / unheated	-	-	-	-	-	100	100		-	-	N/A	

The DoH has also published several 'Health Technical Memoranda' which provide advice and guidance on design, installation and operation of hospitals at the building level, as well as overviews of requirements of certain specialised rooms or departments.

WARMING CLIMATE

According to the Stern Review of 2006, Climate change and global warming has largely been attributed to the relatively recent increase in Green House Gas Emissions. The impact of a warming climate will directly affect the consumption and performance of hospital buildings through increased cooling loads if current methods and designs of Hospitals are utilised. The warming climate particularly in the South of England poses a threat to elderly patients and will greatly increase the energy consumption in those hospital facilities which rely heavily on mechanical ventilation, cool-

ing and air-conditioning to maintain comfortable temperatures for patients and staff.

THE BRIEF

The design component of this research was based on a real life brief for Watford General Acute Hospital. The Schedule of Areas for a 600 bed hospital was scaled down to that of a 200 bed hospital; not only was this more manageable in terms of a small-scale design project, but it is also in line with recent plans by Lord Darzi for creating smaller specialist hospitals providing particular treatment areas within a hospital trust. Less urgent and technical procedures and examinations are to be carried out at a Primary Care level, in effect reducing the amount of patients who actually require the functions of a modern acute hospital.

Although the Schedule of Areas has been greatly reduced, the original brief is still

Figure 14: Comparison of hours over 25C, 28C and 32C between Current and Predicted Weather Data, 2020, 2050, 2080.

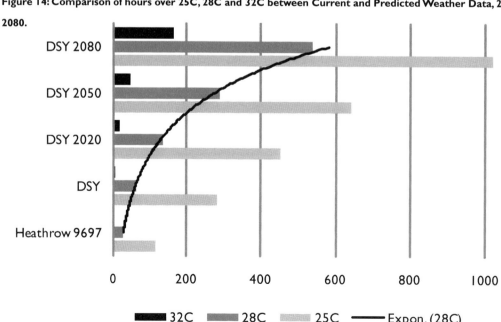

applicable; the four key criteria being: that the design is for a low energy hospital, that there should be separation of 'hotel' (ward) and 'factory' (clinical area) functions, that the wards are to be 100% single bedroom wards, and that the design should be flexible and adaptable.

It is interesting to note that the clinical areas are relatively small in comparison with the rest of the building. The Schedule of Areas has been divided into 11 separate typologies that have similar environmental performance requirements and functions.

SITE CONTEXT

The proposed new hospital is to be sited

south of the existing facilities which are proposed to be demoslished in the near future. The total site includes 65 acres of land belonging to several 'partners' including Watford FC, and adjacent allotement and industrial areas. The redevelopment will create a 'health campus' including leisure facilities, affordable housing for key NHS workers and a hotel and conferencing facility. The proposed 2008 'health campus' is to include B1 offices enabling a platform for start-up businesses related to the healthcare trust.

MASTERPLAN

The masterplan has been designed around the phasing of the current site divided into several 'Design Zones'.

Figure 15. Aerial view of site with site boundary.

Figure 16. Masterplan Zones.

Design Zone 1 is the proposed hospital site. In the future the hospital buildings are able to be expanded to the South.

Design Zone 2 is the current hospital site. The floor plates are to be reused and remodelled into a healthcare innovation site, with the current access road to be converted to pedestrian access only. The ground floor includes public amenities.

Design Zone 3 is adjacent to Watford FC stadium and will contain hotel and leisure facilities for both the stadium and the health campus. 'Car park towers' are to be created that allow a high density of parking without large scale multi-storey car parks

or large expanses of ground level parking. There is also a bus and taxi terminus.

Design Zones 4 and 5 comprise low rise mixed affordable and 'first time buyer' terraced housing which aligns itself to the urban morphology of the existing terraces. A pedestrianised street connects to artery roads via a 'drop off' area. Extensive greenery and planting is envisaged.

Design Zone 6 is returned to countryside with an ecological wildlife park created. Land bridges will cross the railway allowing a continuous wildlife corridor beyond to the south east and east of the site.

DESIGN AND MASSING

The massing of the hospital is based upon the separation between the clinical or 'factory' elements and the wards or 'hotel' element. The 'factory' element of the hospital is further differentiated into day functions such as the Outpatient and Day Surgery Departments, and 24 hour functions such as the Accident and Emergency and Maternity Departments. The two sub-elements are arranged with ease of operation and way finding in mind. The day functions are arranged around a central atrium space, allowing visitors who are more likely to casually find their own way to a procedure to easily identify the correct department (within these departments the waiting spaces face inwards into the atrium allowing users to easily identify their

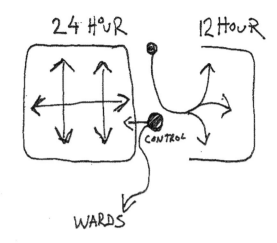

Figure 17 (above). Parti sketches massing and department strategy.

Figure 18 (below). Department layout and circulation.

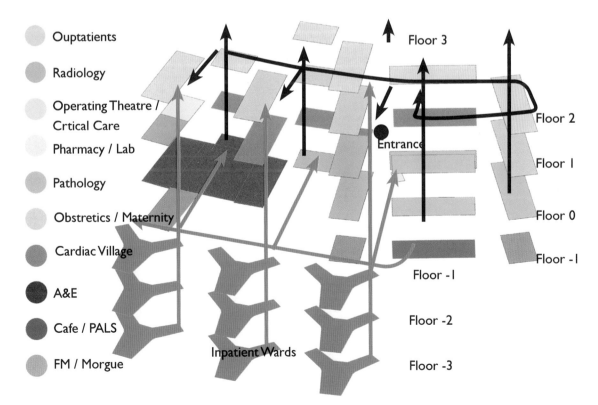

Ouptatients

Radiology

Operating Theatre / Crtical Care

Pharmacy / Lab

Pathology

Obstretics / Maternity

Cardiac Village

A&E

Cafe / PALS

FM / Morgue

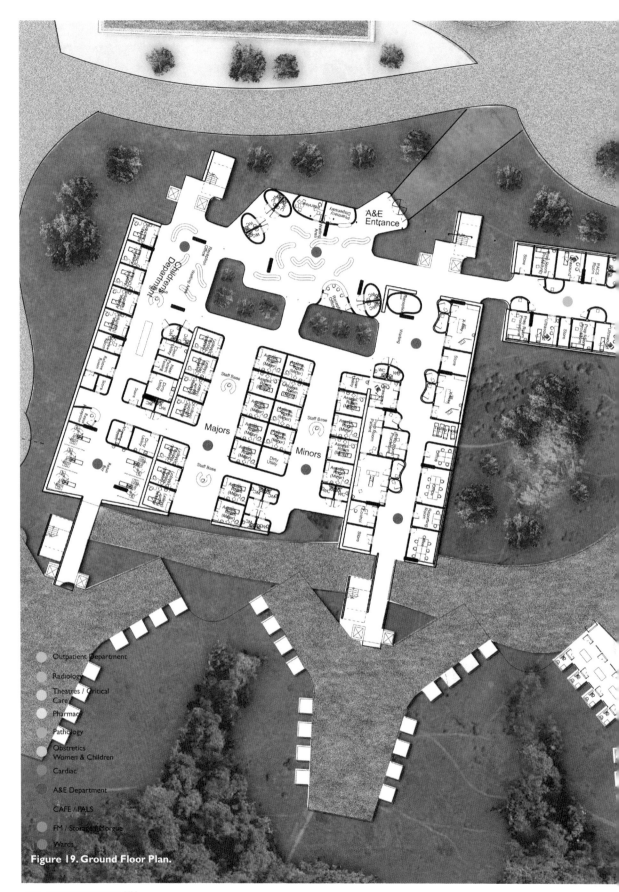

A&E Entrance

Children's Department

Majors

Minors

Staff Base

Staff Base

Staff Base

Outpatient Department
Radiology
Theatres / Critical Care
Pharmacy
Pathology
Obstetrics
Women & Children
Cardiac
A&E Department
CAFE / PALS
FM / Storage Morgue
Wards

Figure 19. Ground Floor Plan.

Main Entrance

Main Reception

Outpatient

Outpatient

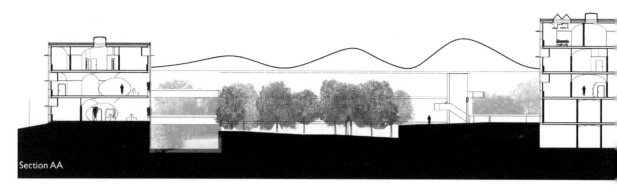

Section AA

Section BB

Section CC

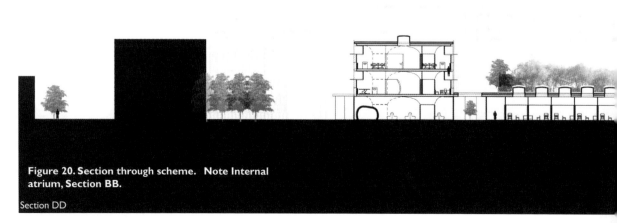

Figure 20. Section through scheme. Note Internal atrium, Section BB.

Section DD

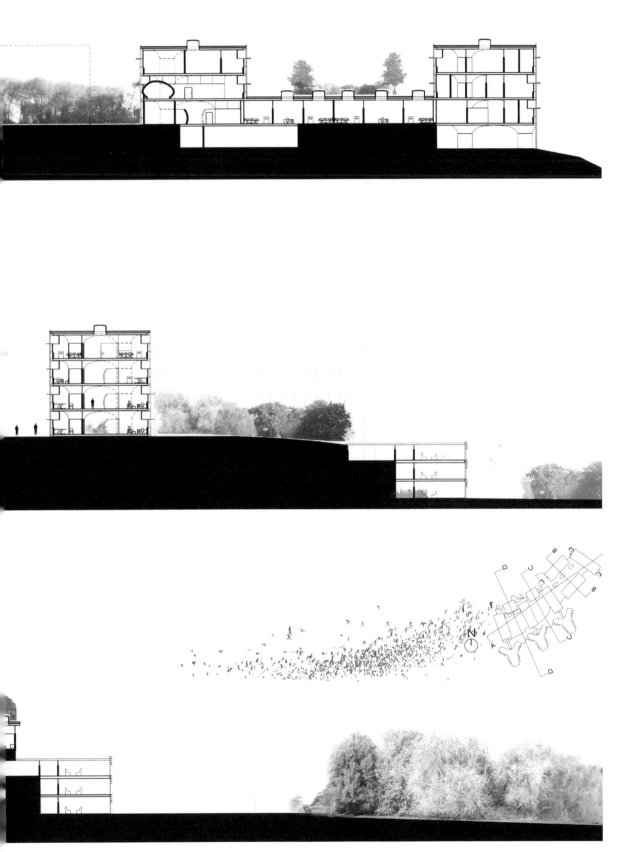

destination). The 24 hour 'factory' element is arranged with the majority of staff and patient circulation organised in a controlled fashion between wards and other departments. Waiting areas, staff offices and non-clinical utility rooms are threaded through the 'hospital street', off which the clinical facilities are located.

The primary pedestrian entrance is legibly articulated in the centre of the building. Other smaller entrances allow access into the atrium area in which visitors and patients are then able to re-orientate themselves to the correct destination. In both the day and 24 hour facilities of the 'factory' element departments are hierarchical, with 'public' services on the ground and first floors, more intensive or clinical departments located higher in the building, and operating theatres placed at the top; so that the vertical separation of the facility allows for increased control of patient movement and security. Similarly the wards can be accessed via the central atrium by visitors or directly from clinical 24 hour 'factory' areas via a second 'hospital street'. Security is achieved through a controlled level change; wards will also have staff bases with entrances to individual ward levels.

THE UNIVERSAL FLOOR PLATE

Each department is configured with an identical internal width of 15 metres. This allows for future adaption; the 15 metre span as used in the 'Nucleus' template defined a set of spatial rules, with common dimensional properties such as a 'universal grid' of 600 + 300mm for equipment and space planning. A standard room size of 16.2m^2 allows for the majority of functions across departments to be accomodated. The system allows almost any hospital department to be configured into the template. The floor to floor height is 4m, allowing for a floor to ceiling height of 3.7-3.8 metres, as well as the varying ceiling heights required by different types of accommodation; as a general rule a building can be sufficiently passively ventilated and lit from the perimeter up to two-times the floor to ceiling height.[3] The diaphram column is not only structural but is able to act as an adaptable downdraught ventilation shaft, servicing several floors.

Figure 21. Example floor plate with structural grid and column locations.

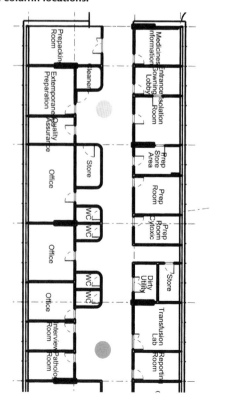

ENVIRONMENTAL STRATEGY

An array of low energy or passive measures have been utilised in the design. Heavyweight construction or exposed thermal mass, or materials with a specific heat capacity, are able to store heat in the structure or through thermal inertia, delaying the effects of outside temperature on the internal environment.[4] It is proposed that partitioned walls and ceilings offer as much exposed thermal mass as possible. Due to the cellular nature of the hospital, unlike open plan offices, utilising the high surface area of cellular rooms could make significant reductions in heating and cooling loads. Many of the space types have high acoustic performance requirements – current 'metsec' type construction relies on careful detailing to minimise the travel of noise. It is proposed that the partitions are constructed of 'unfired' clay earth blocks, which have substantially less embodied energy than traditional concrete blocks.

In preparatory studies and simulations, solar gains during summer periods caused unnecessary overheating in both 'hotel' and 'factory' areas of the hospital. The elevations of both areas were designed in such a way as to reduce unwanted solar gain during overheating periods (typically late April to August). The scale of the building does not allow the entire massing to be orientated north-south, so multiple orientations are utilised favouring views out. Extensive solar shading was utilised in both areas, with clinical 'factory' areas featuring a horizontal shading device as well as the 'Nuffield eyebrow', a solar reflector and shade devel-oped by the Nuffield Trust and University of Bath.[5] East and west elevations have been treated with vertical shading provided by climbing plants, while outboard en-suite bathroom pods, alternating between floors to afford both horizontal and vertical shading, provide solar protection to the ward or 'hotel' areas.

In order to reduce artificial lighting demand and take advantage of the health and well-being benefits of a full-spectrum of light and access to views to the outside, expansive glazing is provided to clinical 'factory' areas, and it is proposed that the 'Nuffield eyebrow' light shelf be utilised to provide reflected light to the rear of rooms. The corridor areas, often dimly lit, lengthy, and featureless, are enhanced with reflected clerestory lighting. The lighting strategy used is similar to the 'Permanent Supplementary Artificial Lighting of Interiors' (PSALI) concept.[6]

Natural ventilation is provided predominantly by operable windows in ward and inpatient areas, and it is hypothesised that the thermal mass of the room should provide sufficient thermal inertia to maintain internal temperatures within comfortable ranges. The introduction of internal stacks will allow for passive downdraught cooling and stack ventilation for areas of high internal heat gain such as imaging suites. Passive downdraught cooling captures air from prevailing winds in towers, where it is cooled with chillers, causing the air to fall freely through negative buoyancy down the stack. Passive downdraught, and passive downdraught evaporative cooling, have

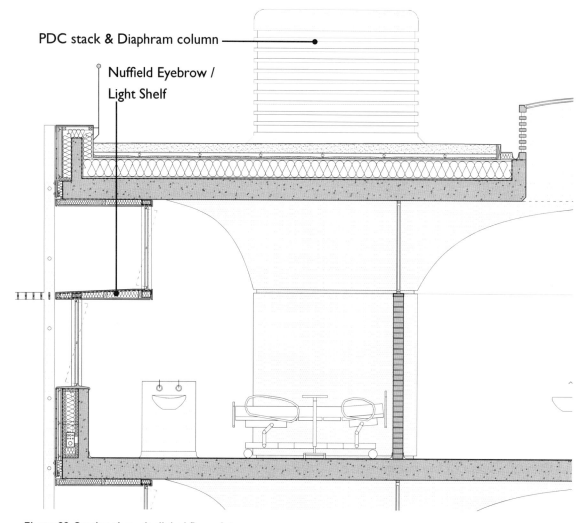

PDC stack & Diaphram column

Nuffield Eyebrow /
Light Shelf

Figure 22. Section through clinical floor plate.

been employed successfully in numerous non-domestic buildings.[7] Passive down-draught cooling will also be utilised in the atrium area, a covered space with a PTFE (polytetrafluoroethylene) tensile structure that is envisaged as a cool sanctuary in heat waves. The tensile PTFE structure allows the atrium to be easily dismantled when and if the building's use changes, reverting to an outside space or park. PTFE structures have several advantages such as a reduction in embodied energy due to the reduction in building materials needed to support a water-tight envelope, but there are several issues regarding its comparatively low thermal resistance, particularly in winter and summer.[8]

It is also envisaged that active measures will be utilised to reduce energy consumption, in particular Solar Domestic Hot Water (DHW) systems. Hospitals use substantial amounts of hot water, so it is proposed that solar panel water heater arrays be added to substantial areas of the external roof. Research suggests significant energy savings can be obtained from solar thermal energy in healthcare buildings.[9]

The resulting energy consumption of the departments was simulated for comparison with other representative departments simulated with benchmark constructions and systems.

Individual rooms and sections were also simulated, for example the imaging suite utilising the passive downdraught cooling and atrium area.

The resutling energy consumption dramatically reduced overall energy consumption through the four department typologies. The largest reductions occurred in artificial lighting and domestic hot water.

Figure 23. False colour daylighting simulation results. Room 1 (no light shelf or shade), Room 2 (no light shelf with shading), Room 3 (with light shelf and shade).

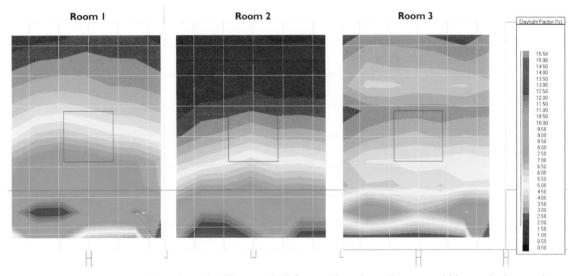

Figure 24. Air Velocity in PDC imaging suite. The use of PDC was able to keep the space within required operating temperatrures even with sensible heat gains of over 4000W.

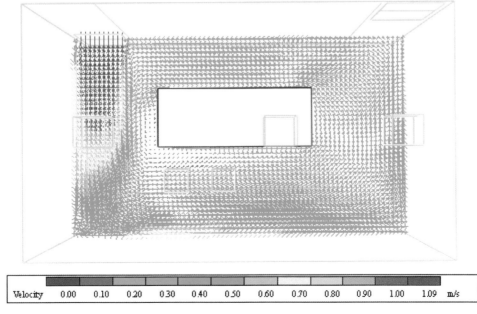

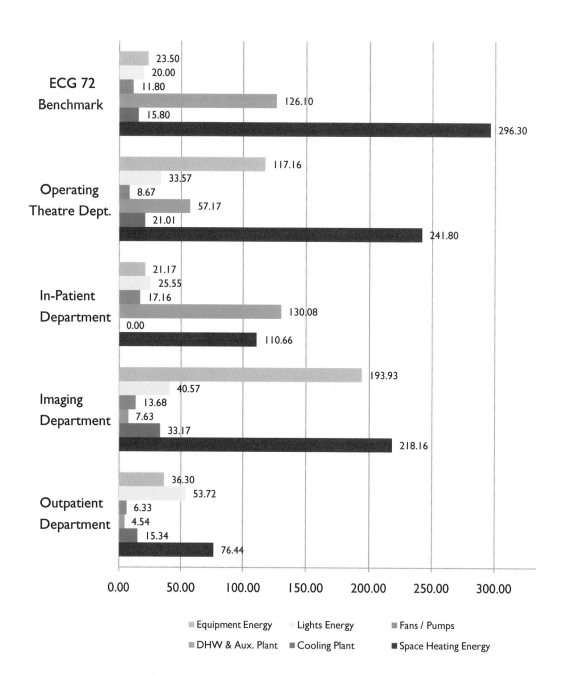

▦ Equipment Energy	▦ Lights Energy	▦ Fans / Pumps
▦ DHW & Aux. Plant	▦ Cooling Plant	■ Space Heating Energy

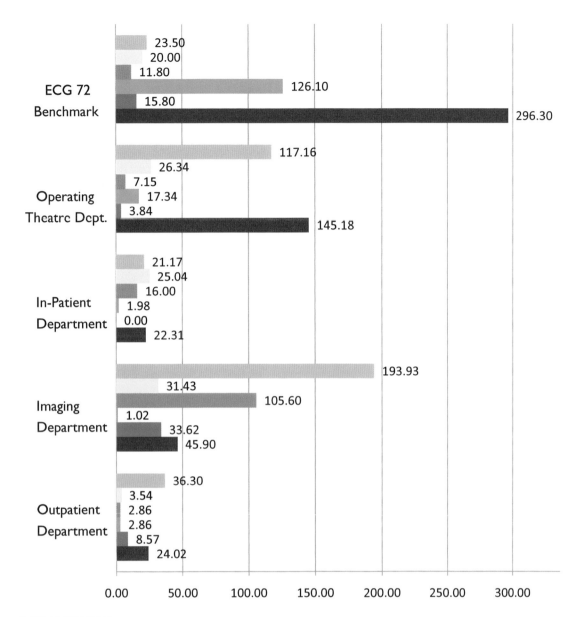

ECG 72 Benchmark
23.50
20.00
11.80
126.10
15.80
296.30

Operating Theatre Dept.
117.16
26.34
7.15
17.34
3.84
145.18

In-Patient Department
21.17
25.04
16.00
1.98
0.00
22.31

Imaging Department
193.93
31.43
105.60
1.02
33.62
45.90

Outpatient Department
36.30
3.54
2.86
2.86
8.57
24.02

0.00   50.00   100.00   150.00   200.00   250.00   300.00

(ENDNOTES)

1   The ambitious 'NHS plan of 2000' which oversaw the construction or extensive refurbishment of over 100 hospital facilities has recently been completed.

2   Lomas, K., Title, Institute of Energy and Sustainable Development, De Montford University, Leicester (2009).

3   Baker, N., and K. Steemers, Energy and Environment in Architecture, E&FN Spon, London (2000).

4   Givoni, Baruch, Climate Consid-erations in Building and Urban Design, Van Nostrand Reinhold, New York (1998).

5   Nuffield Provincial Hospitals Trust (1955).

6   Hopkinson & Longmore, Title (1959).

7   Bowman, et al., Title (1996); Short, Lomas, and Woods, Title (2004).

8   As opposed to cooling through the introduction of water droplets or Passive Downdraught Evaporative Cooling (PDEC),

9   Boonstra and Van Mil, Title (2003).

Therapy by Design: Can Specialised Environments Contribute to the Lives of People with Alzheimer's Disease?

by Jenny Willatt

INTRODUCTION

The aim of this research is to combine research methods with the architectural design process in order to put forward a current and relevant proposal for a supportive environment for people with Alzheimer's disease, their family and carers. A review of the literature identified the environmental design features considered most relevant to the topic. Visits and analysis of three 'exemplary' London-based dementia facilities revealed further design issues first-hand, whilst testing how successfully the issues identified in the literature review are integrated into real designs. User preferences were identified through first-hand conversations with relatives and nursing staff in the facilities visited and by consulting conversation threads in Alzheimer's forums, topical radio interviews and documentaries. This research was supplemented with findings from post-occupancy evaluations of psychi-

Jenny Willatt studied Architecture at Queen's University, Belfast, and has just completed an MPhil in Environmental Design at the University of Cambridge.

atric and dementia care units, conducted as part of the European Health Property Network (EuHPN) Design Impact Study.[1]

THE DEMENTIA EPIDEMIC

Dementia currently affects 750,000 people in the UK.[2] It is defined as 'the loss, usually progressive, of cognitive and intellectual functions, without impairment of perception or consciousness' and characterised by 'disorientation, impaired memory, judgment and intellect'.[3] The most common form, Alzheimer's Disease, was first described by German psychiatrist Alois Alzheimer in 1906 and affects around 417,000 people in Britain. It is 'the most common degenerative brain disorder' and is defined as a 'progressive mental deterioration manifested by loss of memory, ability to calculate, and visual-spatial orientation; confusion and disorientation'.[4]

There is no cure in sight and, despite the forecasted gravity of the situation, a mere 3% of the government's medical research budget is being spent on dementia research, compared with 25% being spent on cancer research.[5] Government forecasts estimate the number of dementia cases will rise by 70% to approximately 1.2 million by 2028, increasing further to 1.71 million by 2051 as life expectancy increases. Professor Martin Knapp, from the London School of Economics, predicts a rise of 88% by 2031, when close to 400,000 will be in long-stay institutions.[6] Despite this, nursing home places for elderly people with dementia have fallen by 9% over four years.[7]

THERAPY BY DESIGN: THE CASE FOR A NON-PHARMACOLOGICAL APPROACH

The challenging behaviour associated with Alzheimer's Disease often becomes unmanageable at home, or a danger to the individual, and it is at this point that most dementia sufferers move to a care facility. Due to the high demand this behaviour puts on staff, antipsychotic drugs are often administered unnecessarily for their sedative effect. However, research funded by the Alzheimer's Research Trust, has revealed that antipsychotic drugs cause a deterioration of verbal skills within six months whilst almost doubling risk of death over three years.

Recent research at the University of California has also revealed that stress hormones can rapidly lead to cognitive decline in Alzheimer's disease, with scientists suggesting that stress management and reducing the use of some medications could significantly stave off deterioration of patients.[8] The design of supportive environments could play a key role in stress reduction and thus improve quality of life. The Hearthstone Alzheimer's Family Foundation, founded in 1995, aims to focus on non-pharmacological approaches and supports research into 'the design of physical environment features to cue memories, support independence, improve way-finding, or produce positive emotions' and the 'use of nature, gardens, plants, and animals as therapeutic milieu'.[9] Anne Kapf also describes the benefits of a 'sensual environment promoting seeing, hearing, touching and smelling'.[10]

Recommended design features and criteria were accumulated and presented in one of the first products of this research; a booklet entitled Design for Dementia – A visual snapshot *(fig. 1)*.

USER PREFERENCES

Relatives of those with dementia know exactly what they like and dislike when selecting a home for their loved ones. The building seems to play as important a role as the care received in the selection of a facility. In response to many queries about how to choose a care home, a lady in one Alzheimer's forum described in detail the process she used for choosing a facility for her husband:

When I go to any care establishment, I look at the layout of the place. I have to bear in mind that Ken's particular form of

Connection with Community

Intergenerational exchange

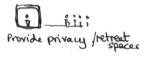
Provide privacy /retreat spaces

Visual connections (know only what they can see).

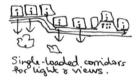
Single-loaded corridors for light & views.

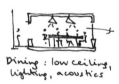
Dining : low ceiling, lighting, acoustics

Indoors & outdoors strongly connected.

Shading devices/structures.

Security

Design for casual meeting.

Adequate parking for visitors

Family privacy.

Encourage visitors.

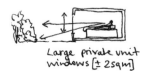
Large private unit windows [± 2sqm]

Raised planting beds

Figure 1.

dementia means that he needs to wander around constantly. If the home has only one room where residents are expected to sit around – then that is immediately crossed off my list.[11]

Snyder claims that meaningful activity is crucial for those with Alzheimer's, as 'there is often an imbalance between activities forfeited to the effects of Alzheimer's, and new activities established in their wake' which may in itself reduce quality of life.[12] The assumption that people in care homes are no longer capable of doing normal, everyday things can lead to a lack of meaningful activity and leave residents despondent and discouraged, with one person commenting:

I have some depression sometimes but I don't think it needs to be analysed. I attribute it to doing the same thing over and over and over. Day to day there isn't as much to look forward to.[13]

CASE STUDY BUILDINGS

The main observations from the case study visits included: social exclusion and lack of visitors; an institutional rather than homely feel; the success of a looped circulation route when it was present, and, when it was absent, restless pacing along dead-end corridors; a lack of personal space to accommodate visitors and personal belongings; and restricted access to outdoor spaces due to a lack of opportunity for efficient supervision. The location of residents in all three buildings was noted, showing that residents had a tendency to gather in centralised spaces. Analysis of the three case

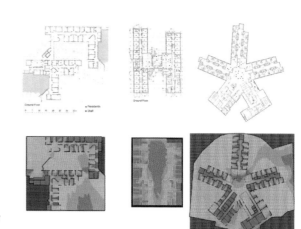

Figure 2.

study plans with Space syntax 'Depthmap' software showed that the spaces observed as being most populated in all three buildings were also the most integrated spaces *(shown in red, fig. 2)*. Syntactic analysis is 'the measurement of the relations between all parts of a system', with integration being defined as 'mathematical closeness', or as 'the proximity and visibility of each segment to all others in a system'.[14] Lack of such proximity seemed to correlate with residents being found more frequently in their own rooms.

One of the recent approaches to designing dementia facilities is to set them in an urban setting looking out on the world, as it is believed that this will provide residents with a connection to the community. However, most facilities need to restrict access to this 'outdoor world' for the residents' own safety. It is known that being able to see life and activity is uplifting and mentally stimulating for dementia patients, but research and guidance has also suggested that providing residents with views to places that they cannot access can actually increase feelings of confinement, confusion and anxiety.[15]

ARCHITECTURAL STRATEGY

The aim of the design component of this research was to explore the possibility of creating an easily legible and orientating refuge, which also invites people in. The location of the chosen site was to the west of Addenbrooke's Hospital (adjacent to the planned Clay Farm Residential Development of 2,300 homes) in Cambridge. In addition to the landscape the layout of the building also comprised a bowling green, tennis courts and a public building for hosting events, fairs, performances, school pantomimes, exhibitions and classes, with the aim of bringing the outside community in through the garden walls, and providing activity and life within the facility.

The architectural strategy of creating a beautiful walled environment set in landscaped gardens, establishing a community for both family members and the public, required a certain degree of control and clarity with regard to access to the facility, as well as a clear spatial hierarchy in the form of a privacy gradient, the lack of which is one of the distinguishing features of institutional buildings.[16] A 'back of house' theme was established to the north and east, and a 'public interface' to the south and west. This leaves a central core in which the rest of the accommodation can be enclosed (fig. 3). The deeper one ventures into the building, the more privacy there is, with the south and west edges of the building offering the greatest opportunities for interaction with the outside world. This is ideal for creating the security and privacy required by the residents of this facility, as well as differing degrees of mutual awareness for the avoidance of feelings of social exclusion.

Within this structure the building has been organised into a series of progressively private and secure spaces and courtyards.

Figure 3.

Figure 4.

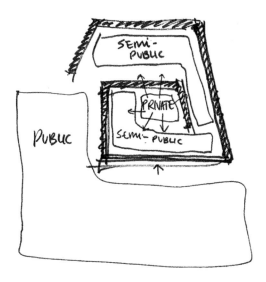

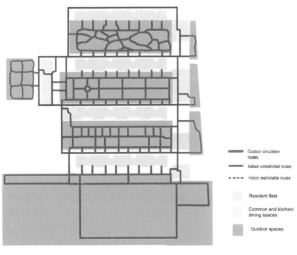

Diagram showing the looped circulation loops which link the private, common and outdoor spaces

The circulation between these spaces is arranged in looped routes to accommodate the wandering behaviour of residents; who find a sense of relief in continuous movement *(fig. 4)*. Distinct public, staff and resident areas provide zoning for both functionality and security *(fig. 5)*. Access control points block access between resident and staff zones, and allow mediation of access between the residential and public zones (should this be deemed necessary by staff).

order to facilitate efficiency. However, this is not something that should be imposed, as too much activity and interaction can be over-stimulating for some residents. Instead, the building should offer residents opportunities for adapting their position in relation to others. For example, they should have the opportunity to withdraw completely or to sit back and watch without actively participating.

A VARIETY OF COMMON SPACES WITH VARYING DEGREES OF PRIVACY

Evidence and guidance suggest that social interaction is important for maintaining physical and cognitive function, as well as personal well-being.[17] Some care models move all residents into one central room in

The smaller common rooms are much more secluded than the larger ones, as they only have a view out one side. This could be a problem for supervision but it will provide a quieter, more private common space. Its close proximity to the entrance kitchen should mean that staff are always close to the residents.

Figure 5 (below), Figure 6 (Right).

The larger common spaces (orange) are well integrated, which means that staff can keep an eye on residents inside and outside at the same time, and without intrusively supervising them.

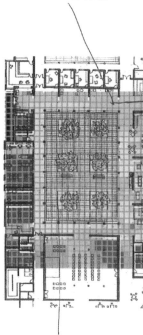

The degree of integration in the courtyard (red) means that this space will offer the highest degree of intervisibility and mutual awareness. This makes the space easy for staff to supervise which should mean that residents should be able to access it at all times. Previous analysis would also suggest that this characteristic will also promote social interaction and activity.

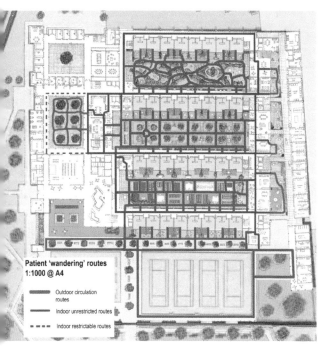

Patient 'wandering' routes
1:1000 @ A4

Outdoor circulation routes
Indoor unrestricted routes
Indoor restrictable routes

The amount of intervisib from the entrance co yard is one step less t that of the comr spaces, which ma sense for the semi-publi private transition.

A range of common and more private spaces is therefore provided throughout the building, in order to provide opportunities for varying degrees of social interaction and mutual awareness. Space syntax analysis of an individual courtyard can help to provide insight into how these spaces would be used *(fig. 6)*.

PERSONAL SPACE

One of the aims of this design was to provide residents with small flats, which would allow them to create their own homes within the scheme. At 43 square metres the size of the accommodation may be challenged, as most residents rooms in present facilities do not exceed 15-20 square metres. However, if the resident Is active it will give them space to live, arrange

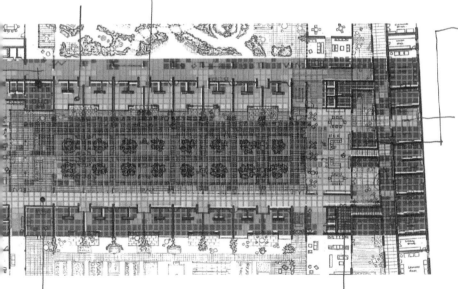

sident bedrooms are light e rather than dark blue. s means that they are are of the activity going on und them and connected n the outdoors, rather than ng isolated in their flats. ads can provide privacy en it is required, thus pro- ng adaptive opportunity.

A privacy gradient is provided from the flat, to the back of the terrace, to the front of the terrace and then to the courtyard. The further a resident retreats into their flat, the more private it will be, and vice versa.

Residents can find more secluded outdoor spots in the kitchen courtyards, should they wish to retreat or seek privacy. However, these courtyards are still vi- sually connected to the larger courtyards and resi- dents can choose the degree of intervisibility and mutual awareness they wish to experience.

View windows between the staff wing and common spaces allow the staff glimpses to the living wing from the service corridor and central kitchen. This allows the staff to feel con- nected to the activity in the rest of the facility.

Corridors have good inter- visibility for wayfinding but are more private than the courtyard and common rooms, which provides a pri- vacy gradient to the flats.

The service access points are not very visible from the resident accommodation, which is good as this will prevent residents being drawn towards locked doors, and allow staff to come and go unintrusively.

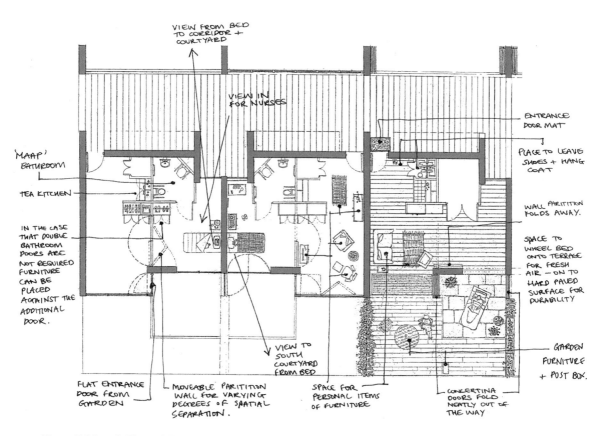

VIEW FROM BED TO CORRIDOR + COURTYARD

VIEW IN FOR NURSES

ENTRANCE DOOR MAT

PLACE TO LEAVE SHOES + HANG COAT

'MAAP' BATHROOM

TEA KITCHEN

IN THE CASE THAT DOUBLE BATHROOM DOORS ARE NOT REQUIRED FURNITURE CAN BE PLACED AGAINST THE ADDITIONAL DOOR.

WALL PARTITION FOLDS AWAY.

SPACE TO WHEEL BED ONTO TERRACE FOR FRESH AIR — ON TO HARD PAVED SURFACE FOR DURABILITY

VIEW TO SOUTH COURTYARD FROM BED

GARDEN FURNITURE + POST BOX.

FLAT ENTRANCE DOOR FROM GARDEN

MOVEABLE PARTITION WALL FOR VARYING DEGREES OF SPATIAL SEPARATION.

SPACE FOR PERSONAL ITEMS OF FURNITURE

CONCERTINA DOORS FOLD NEATLY OUT OF THE WAY

Figure 7 (above), Figure 8 (below).

personal belongings, take pride in their environment and even entertain visitors. The moveable partition at the centre of the room can allow shielding of the bed space during the daytime *(fig. 7)*. If the resident is bedridden it should help them feel less confined, as by folding it away the space is enlarged and the resident can become part of a living space. This means that visitors do not have to sit at the resident's bedside as if they were in a hospital. A homely and comfortable private space, enabling a spouse or family members to make themselves comfortable, could encourage longer and more frequent visits for the resident, thus improving their well-being.

A view window to the cloister corridor

in line with the patient's bed allows bedridden residents to observe activity both to the front and rear of their flat. This awareness should help them feel less isolated and allow light into the room from the north. A blind can be attached to the outside of this window to allow for privacy and so that

CHERRY STREET

nurses can observe residents without having to disturb them.

The flat appears residential from the outside, and can be accessed from a familiar 'street-scene' *(fig. 8)*. Objects from everyday life such as post boxes and street signs provide a sense of community and normality. Residents also have their own front garden and letter box for receiving mail. The openability of the facade means that residents' beds can be wheeled out onto the terrace on warmer days. This provides immobile residents with fresh air and daylight, whilst making them feel part of any activity going on in the courtyards. Flats on the upper floor have access to their own roof terrace, which also has a place for their bed.

MAXIMISING WAYFINDING AND STIMULATION OF REMAINING COGNITIVE ABILITIES

Those with Alzheimer's often experience 'difficulty organising sequences of events into a single process'[18] but studies have revealed that 'wayfinding and elementary problem solving remains unaffected when decisions are made in direct relation to explicit environmental stimuli'.[19] In particular, 'those with Alzheimer's retain the inbuilt responses to stimuli found in natural surroundings, such as sunshine, shade, flowers and trees'.[20] With cognitive deficits being a serious problem in those with Alzheimer's, the importance of identifying and maximising use of cognitive functions that are very much intact is paramount. Use of outdoor

spaces as useful external reference points for orientation is therefore particularly valuable. Different landscaping strategies will help residents to identify the location of their own 'living wing' within the overall layout of the building, with each courtyard also having a different name according to the landscaping theme.

Figure 9 (overleaf), Figure 10, 11 & 12 (below).

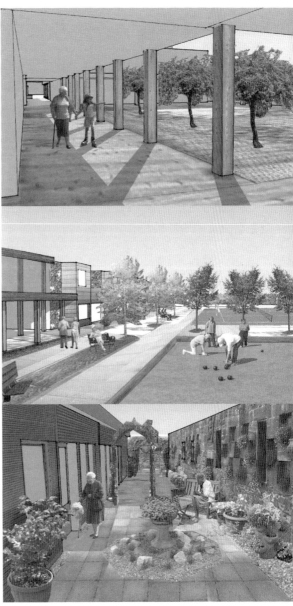

Planting chart showing choice of plants for year-round interest

January	February	March	April	May	June	July	August	September	October	November	December
Vibernum tinus	Vibernum tinus	Vibernum tinus	Lavender 'Imperial Gem'	Lavender 'Imperial Gem'	Lavender 'Imperial Gem'	Lavender 'Imperial Gem'	Lavender 'Imperial Gem'	Schizostylis coccinea	Schizostylis coccinea	Schizostylis coccinea	Vibernum tinus
Clematis	Clematis		Shrub Rose	Shrub Rose	Shrub Rose	Shrub Rose	Shrub Rose	Shrub Rose		Winter vegetables	Winter vegetables
Jasminum nudiflorum	Jasminum nudiflorum	Jasminum nudiflorum	Magnolia	Magnolia	Honeysuckle Japonica Halliana	Honeysuckle Japonica Halliana	Honeysuckle Japonica Halliana	Honeysuckle Japonica Halliana	Honeysuckle Japonica Halliana		
	Helleborus x hybridus	Helleborus x hybridus	Helleborus x hybridus	Wisteria	Wisteria			Prunus Malus Red Splendor	Prunus Malus Red Splendor		
Erica carnea 'Rosalie'	Erica carnea 'Rosalie'	Erica carnea 'Rosalie'	Erica carnea 'Rosalie'			Buddleja Davidii 'Black Knight'	Buddleja Davidii 'Black Knight'	Buddleja Davidii 'Black Knight'			
Lonicera x purpusil 'Winter Beauty'	Lonicera x purpusil 'Winter Beauty'	Lonicera x purpusil 'Winter Beauty'	Prunus Shirotae	Prunus Shirotae							Lonicera x purpusil 'Winter Beauty'

Figure 9.

SEASONAL ORIENTATION AND YEAR-ROUND INTEREST

Thought has also been given to the seasonal orientation of residents by ensuring that the planting strategy will provide sensory stimulation at different times of the year (fig. 9). For example, the Malus Spendour Crab Apple trees in the entrance courtyard (fig. 10) were chosen for their particularly vibrant autumn colours and fruit. These provide a visually stimulating feast of colour that also gives the fullest effects of the autumn season to help orient residents to the time of year. This fruit could also be collected by residents in order to make apple pie or crumble; an activity that may be reminiscent of times when they use to cook or eat in their family homes. The Prunus Shirotae Cherry trees put on an equally impressive performance in spring, with their pretty white blossoms fluttering in the breeze and decorating the ground around them.

The bowling green, tennis courts and associated public landscaping (fig. 11) aim to make reference to English sport and garden traditions, with their well-kept green 'lawns', beds of thornless roses and 'garden wall' perimeter (fig. 12). The activity of maintaining these lawns will help generate routine and provide interest. When not in use, the space will serve as a neat and expansive green garden for residents to look out on.

Walled courtyard gardens outside the kitchen and dining area provide intimate places for sitting or eating outside and will be more familiar to people who have been more used to compact 'city gardens' of terraced houses or flats. The variety provided in these four outdoor spaces means that they can provide the activity required by more able and energetic members of the community, as well as providing sensory stimulation and observable activity for those who are less likely to participate.

ENVIRONMENTAL STRATEGY

An environmental strategy to maximise both contact with and awareness of the outdoors was one of the main sources of inspiration for the use of a courtyard plan. Cox has described courtyards as 'organisational devices which provide sheltered communal space, privacy and security whilst maintaining contact with the changing seasons'.[21] The ability of the courtyard building to orient and relate people to the outdoors is particularly relevant to challenging behaviour known as 'sundowning', in which some residents experience the onset or exacerbation of delirium during late afternoon or early evening.[22] This behaviour is related to a disruption in circadian rhythms often associated with Alzheimer's Disease. As elderly residents in institutional environments often experience a lack of exposure to daylight and the outdoors, the building design could play a key role in regulating these rhythms by maximising indoor-outdoor connections.[23] The arrangement of accommodation around courtyards helps create shallow plans maximising views and contact with the outdoors from every point in the building.

EAST-WEST AXIS AND SOUTH-FACING ACCOMMODATION

As part of the environmental strategy, the courtyards are oriented with the major axis of the residential accommodation running east-west. With the major elevations oriented towards the north and south, passive solar heating in winter can be facilitated with south glazing, which can be more easily shaded in summer than east and west facing glazing.

Room orientation was identified as a problem in all case study buildings, with some resident rooms having more favourable orientations than others. Some may challenge this south-facing strategy, arguing that some older residents may not like the sun. However, studies on this topic have revealed that people would rather be offered the choice to block out the sun, for example, with shading devices, than be stuck with the static and grim orientation of a north-facing room.[24]

THERMAL COMFORT: ADAPTIVE OPPORTUNITY AND WINTER AND SUMMER MODES

In the case study facilities, the temperatures were extremely high (24.6-26.7°C) and seemed to render residents lifeless and drowsy. As institutionalised individuals often lack exposure to a range of tempera-

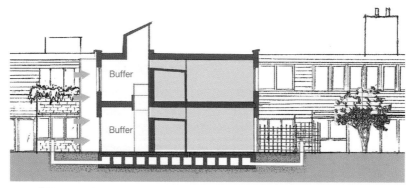

Cloister corridor as buffer space between resident flats and North facade

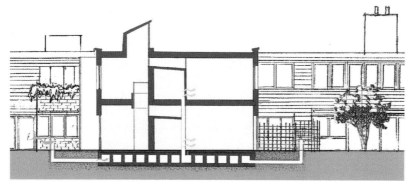

Concrete labyrinthe provides thermal mass, pre-cooling of ventilation air in winter and pre-warming in summer

Figure 13.

tures, their senses can become numbed and inert. The building is 'convertible' with both summer and winter modes, maximising stimulation of the senses via contact with the outdoors. The north facing cloister corridors, with insulating shutters applied at intervals along the facade, act as buffers to the north, shielding the north walls of the resident units from heat loss in winter. Opening up of the north and south facades will effectively provide two exposed walls in summer, which will increase the surface area available for cross ventilation and heat loss. Additionally, if the flat feels too warm,

it is also possible for the resident to sit outside their room in the cooler living and circulation space to the north. The building thus provides adaptive opportunity.

LIGHTING LEVELS AND QUALITY

High levels of natural light have been shown to be useful in regulating circadian rhythms of those with Alzheimer's, as well as providing heightened visibility for ageing vision. For this reason, the window heights in the bedroom are aimed at maximising light penetration to the centre of the room,

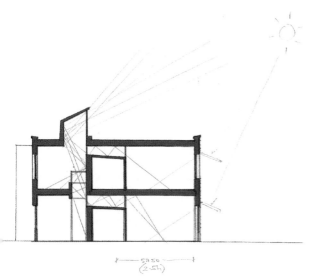

Daylighting of resident flats from both sides.
High summer sun is blocked by retractable awnings
Sunlight is admitted to the north cloister via a rooflight.

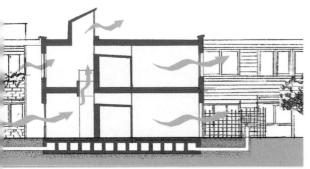

Cross ventilation via openable facades and a roof monitor

whilst clerestory glazing and a view window to the back of the room allow light penetration from the skylight and glazed cloister corridor *(fig. 13)*. This avoids dark spots to the rear of the bedroom plans, a problem that was encountered in the case study facilities.

CONCLUSION

This research has revealed the potential for architecture to improve quality of life in Alzheimer's settings. Design guidance suggests architectural features capable of compensating for cognitive impairments, reducing both challenging behaviour and use of anti-psychotic drugs. Despite this, case study visits and user consultation revealed fundamental flaws in current practice. Such problems included a disconnection from the surrounding community and a lack of visitors. Residents also appeared to be disorientated by the long corridors of undifferentiated accommodation. There was a distinct lack of both communal and private space, which meant that residents had very few personal possessions. The environment did not seem to allow for personal routine or individuality, which resulted in an institutional rather than homely atmosphere.

The design element of this research has aimed to provide an alternative 'image' for a building type currently surrounded by stigma. The creation of an attractive, spacious and homely environment amongst extensive landscaping aims to make visitors feel welcome. Access to large outdoor spaces and increased amounts of circulation help relieve stress by accommodating the wandering behaviour associated with Alzheimer's Disease. The ability to walk in continuous loops both inside and out will enable residents to release frustration, which can otherwise lead to aggressive behaviour. If residents are calmer, this could help reduce stigma surrounding the disease. It could also facilitate the work of staff and provide a less distressing experience for visitors and family members. This will ultimately benefit the patients, as the administration of anti-psychotic drugs will likely be reduced. As one of the ultimate objectives of any healthcare facility is to improve or prevent the decline of patients' medical conditions, benefits such as these help to highlight the potential of architecture to improve the quality of life and stave off cognitive decline in those resident in dementia care facilities.

(ENDNOTES)

1   Burt-O'Dea, *Design Impact Study - A European comparative study of design in relation to context: What is the relationship between design and context, and how does this impact on performance in healthcare environments?*, The European Health Property Network in collaboration with Plan & Project Partners, Durham (2005).

2   Alzheimer's Society UK, *My name is not dementia- Literature Review,* Alzheimer's Society UK (2010).

3   *Stedman's Concise Medical and Allied Health Dictionary*, Lippincott Williams & Wilkins, fourth edition (2001).

4   *Stedman's Concise Medical and Allied Health Dictionary*, Lippincott Williams & Wilkins, fourth edition (2001).

5   Alzheimer's Research Trust, www.alzheimers-research.org.uk (2009).

6   Donnelly, L., *'Dementia time-bomb 'will hit 1.2m'*, The Telegraph (18th April 2008).

7   Beckford, M., *'Care home places for Alzheimer's sufferers fall by 11,000 as cases rise'*, The Telegraph (5th December 2008).

8   La Ferla, *'Stress May Hasten Progression of Alzheimer's Disease'*, Journal of Neuroscience (30th August, 2006).

9   Hearthstone Alzheimer's Family Foundation, www.thehearth.org/foundation/ foundation.

10   Kapf, A, *'People who have lost their past still deserve a future'*, The Guardian (3rd December 2008).

11   *'Alzheimer's Talking Point; What to look out for when choosing a Care Home'*, Alzheimer's Society forum, forum.alzheimers. org.uk/showthread.php?t=14746.

12   Snyder, Lisa, *Speaking our minds: Personal reflections from individuals with Alzheimer's*, W.H. Freeman & Co. (2000).

13   Snyder, Lisa, *Speaking our minds: Personal reflections from individuals with Alzheimer's*, W.H. Freeman & Co. (2000).

14   Hillier, B., *'A new theory of the city'*, The Martin Centre Research Seminar Series, Department of Architecture, University of Cambridge (3rd June 2010).

15   Brawley, Elizabeth C., *Designing for Alzheimer's disease: strategies for creating better care environments*, Wiley & Sons (1997).

16   Thompson et. al, 1996, in Hanson, J., *Space in the Home: morphology and meaning in the home life of older people*, University College London (2003).

17   Alzheimer 's Society UK, *Home from Home: A report highlighting opportunities for improving standards of dementia care in care homes*, Alzheimer's Society UK (2007), Steeman, Els, B.D. De Casterle, J. Godderis, and M. Grypdonck, 'Living with early-stage dementia: a review of qualitative studies', Journal of Advanced Nursing (2006).

18   Zeisel, J., *I'm Still Here: A breakthrough approach to understanding someone with Alzheimer's*, Avery, New York (2009).

19   Passini et al., *'Wayfinding in dementia of the Alzheimer type: planning abilities'*, Journal of clinical and experimental neuropsychology, vol. 17, no. 6 (1995), pp.

820-832.

20   Zeisel, J., *I'm Still Here: A break-through approach to understanding someone with Alzheimer's*, Avery, New York (2009).

21   Cox, M., *Climatic influence of the Courtyard Form: A comparative study of climatic responses*, University of Cambridge (2006), p. 5.

22   *Stedman's Concise Medical and Allied Health Dictionary*, Lippincott Williams & Wilkins, fourth edition (2001).

23   Brawley, Elizabeth C., *Designing for Alzheimer's disease: strategies for creating better care environments*, Wiley & Sons (1997).

24   Choi, J., *Study of the relationship between indoor daylight environment and patient average length of stay (ALOS) in healthcare facilities*, Texas A&M University (2005).

Responding to the Cold: A New Institute of Architecture for the Glasgow School of Art

by Ranald Lawrence

Ranald Lawrence studied Architecture and has just completed an MPhil in Environmental Design at the University of Cambridge, where he is currently studying for a PhD on the environment of nineteenth century art schools and their development as a typology. He is editor of Scroope Twenty: The Cambridge Architecture Journal.

INTRODUCTION

Steven Holl Architects, working alongside the Glasgow office of JM Architects, won the widely publicised competition for the design of Phase 1 of the redevelopment of the campus of the Glasgow School of Art (opposite the Mackintosh Building) in September 2009. This design research explores the possibilities for a proposed Phase 2 development, with a potential third phase completing the campus renovation should funding be secured.[1]

While the main aim of the redevelopment is to consolidate the campus of the School of Art to bring the disparate community together on one site, the development of the proposed Phase 2 site also presents the opportunity to provide a new public face to

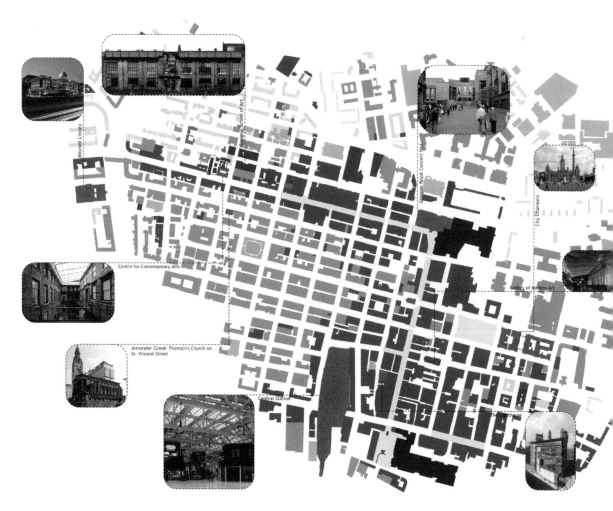

Figure 1 (above). Plan of Glasgow showing key civic buildings and Glasgow School of Art.
Figure 2 (right). Plan, Perspective and LT analysis, Bourdon Building.

the School, connected to the public realm of Glasgow (fig. 1). The key provision is for a new Architecture School and supporting functions, encompassing a library, lecture and teaching space, workshops, offices and social space. A further ambition is to provide a new home for architecture and design in Scotland to replace the Lighthouse, which used to be housed in Mackintosh's Glasgow Herald Building, but has now gone into administration.[2]

The present Mackintosh School of Architecture has a rigorous teaching pedagogy rooted in Glasgow's industrial past and its Victorian grid-iron layout, post-industrial decline and present-day regeneration. The city is distinctly European in its architecture and outlook, reflected in the far flung connections of the 'Mack' to other Architectural Schools in Europe (Porto, Venice, Oslo, Barcelona) and further afield (Beijing for example). Present day teaching is still very much rooted in the pragmatic and rational Modernist approach of renowned architect and former head of school Andy MacMillan.

The school considers this legacy as one of its main selling points, acting as a counterpoint to the increasingly frivolous and avante-garde agenda of other British schools. A key element of responding to the brief for the expansion of the school therefore is to consider how a 'hands-on' culture could be maintained at the school, with plenty of space for workshops, model-making and applied research alongside deskwork.

ASSESSING THE URBAN BLOCK

The proposed site was chosen due to its proximity to the School of Art, the potential of its location straddling the boundary between the city centre and the community of Garnethill, and due to the need for urban 'repair'. The Bourdon building (currently housing the Architecture Department and Library) bridges across Renfrew Street and divides the west end of the street from the rest of the city (fig. 2), while the 1970 extension to the Dental School is poorly constructed and insulated by today's standards (fig. 3). It is orientated east-west with all the associated solar gain problems, and reinforces the vertical divide across the block by creating an artificial ground plane that extends from Renfrew Street to 12 or 13 metres above Sauchiehall Street to the south, with no connecting public link.

While it is difficult to make directly quantifiable comparisons due to the different uses of each of the buildings in the

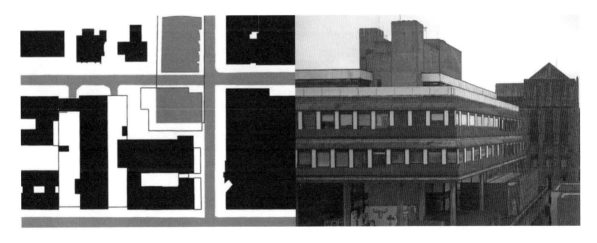

BOURDON BUILDING Type B Colleges 150 lux 20W/m²	Building Data				Specific Energy Consumption (MWh/m²)						Annual Primary Energy Consumption (MWh)			
	Location	Zone Area	Façade Glazing Ratio (%)	UHA deg	Lighting	UHF	Heating	UHF	Ventilation and Cooling	UHF	Lighting	Heating	Ventilation and Cooling	Total
PASSIVE ZONES	South	890	40	0	0.01	1	0.05	1	0.06	1	8.90	44.50	53.40	106.80
	East	1315	50	0	0.01	1	0.07	1	0.06	1	13.15	92.05	78.90	184.10
	West	1315	50	10	0.01	1.4	0.07	1	0.06	1	18.41	92.05	78.90	189.36
	North	504	30	35	0.02	1.4	0.07	1	0.06	1	14.11	35.28	30.24	79.63
	Roof	0	0	0	0	0	0	0	0	0	0.00	0.00	0.00	0.00
	Buffer	0	0	0	0	0	0	0	0	0	0.00	0.00	0.00	0.00
	Total	4024									54.57	263.88	241.44	559.89
NON-PASSIVE ZONES	Total	2803	0	0	0.05	1	0.05	1	0.06	1	140.15	140.15	168.18	448.48

Boiler Efficiency Factor		1.00	
TOTAL MHW	194.72	404.03	409.62	1008.37
TOTAL kWh/m²	28.52	59.18	60.00	147.70
Ratio of passive area to total area (%)			58.94

DENTAL SCHOOL 1970 Type C Offices 300 lux 30W/m²	Building Data				Specific Energy Consumption (MWh/m²)						Annual Primary Energy Consumption (MWh)			
	Location	Zone Area	Façade Glazing Ratio (%)	UHA deg	Lighting	UHF	Heating	UHF	Ventilation and Cooling	UHF	Lighting	Heating	Ventilation and Cooling	Total
PASSIVE ZONES	South	1874.4	50	25	0.03	1.5	0.02	1.75	0.11	0.93	84.35	65.60	191.75	341.70
	East	2436	50	0	0.03	1	0.03	1	0.11	1	73.08	73.08	267.96	414.12
	West	2184	50	0	0.03	1	0.03	1	0.11	1	65.52	65.52	240.24	371.28
	North	535.2	50	0	0.03	1	0.04	1	0.11	1	16.06	21.41	58.87	96.34
	Roof	0	0	0	0	0	0	0	0	0	0.00	0.00	0.00	0.00
	Buffer	0	0	0	0	0	0	0	0	0	0.00	0.00	0.00	0.00
	Total	7029.6									239.00	225.61	758.82	1223.44
NON-PASSIVE ZONES	Total	4526.4	0	0	0.13	1	0.01	1	0.11	1	588.43	45.26	497.90	1131.60

Boiler Efficiency Factor 1.00

	Lighting	Heating	Ventilation and Cooling	Total
TOTAL MHW	827.44	270.88	1256.73	2355.04
TOTAL kWh/m²	71.60	23.44	108.75	203.79
Ratio of passive area to total area (%)				60.83

Figure 3. Plan, Elevation and LT analysis, Dental School.

block, LT analysis[3] also revealed that the Bourdon building and the extension to the Dental School do not compare especially favourably with older buildings on the site in terms of their potential to perform well in terms of energy consumption, due to the large volumes of non-passive spaces on the inside.

A NEW INSTITUTE OF ARCHITEC-TURE

According to Hawkes and Baker,

'If the principles of atrium building design are extended to the re-development of areas in the centre of cities, through a combination of new buildings and the rehabilitation of existing city blocks, the possibility emerges of developing a network of glazed pedestrian routes which may be superimposed upon the existing street pattern, opening up the centre of the block which has traditionally been relegated to secondary functions.'[4]

The proposed Phase 2 design envisages the use of a generic roof to temper the environment of spaces in-between individual 'buildings', which are more actively environmentally controlled with different scales and atmospheric qualities appropriate to their function, to improve the energy performance of the whole. The generic roof in turn creates a succession of spaces with passive microclimatic tendencies that temper transitions between locations and activities, in order to improve comfort (fig. 4). In his essay, Intermediate Environments, Potvin characterises human adaptation as 'difficult', 'conscious' or 'subliminal', and argues that the most adept for promoting comfort is the 'subliminal' adaptation, such that the individual is gradually exposed in steps to a change in environment.[5] This theory is explicitly realised in the built form: individual 'buildings' within the development can be thought of successively as the beginning or end of a journey (from the library to the studios for example), while the generic roofed space that fills the voids between the 'buildings' may be passed through in a journey from one part of the building to another, or simply as part of a commute through the city block. In both cases, the generic roof acts to form either 'conscious' or 'subliminal' steps in one's movement through the building (dependent on how we define these steps and the conditions of the particular season). Broadly speaking, we might say that in winter the passage from the outside into the generic roofed space will be a 'conscious' transition in terms of temperature, but more subtle than the transition of entering an 'exclusive' building with a single imposed active environmental regime, and the transition from the roofed

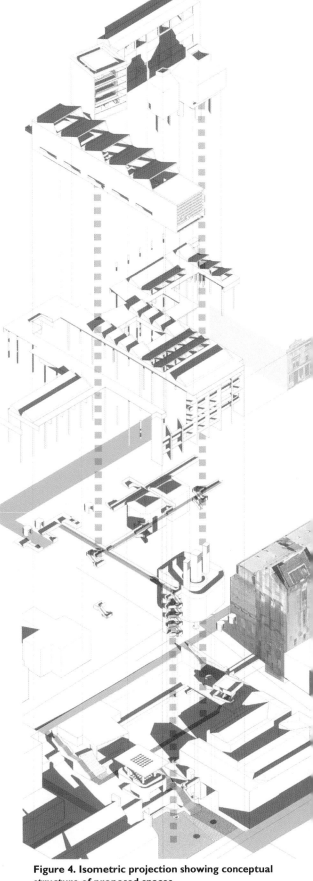

Figure 4. Isometric projection showing conceptual structure of proposed spaces.

Figure 5. Mid-level Plan.

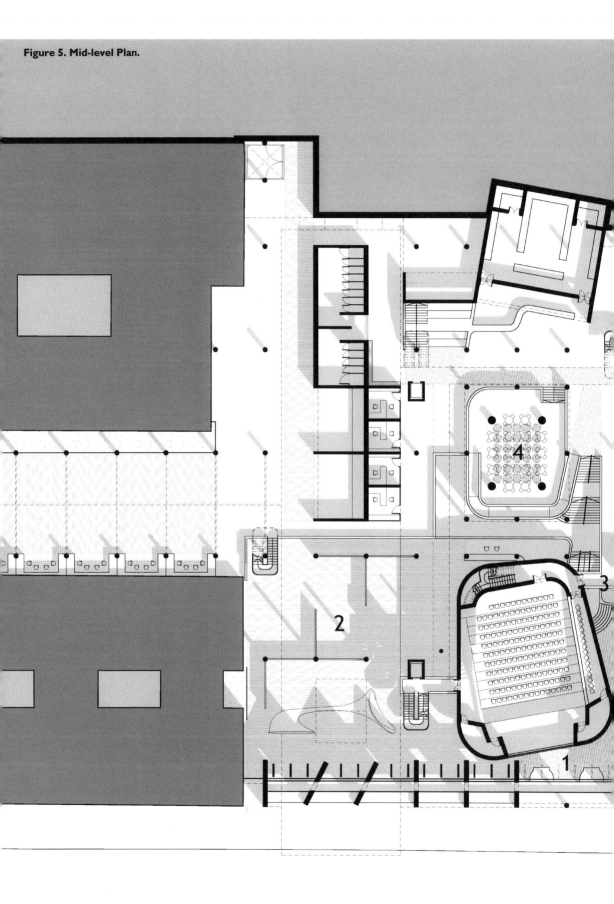

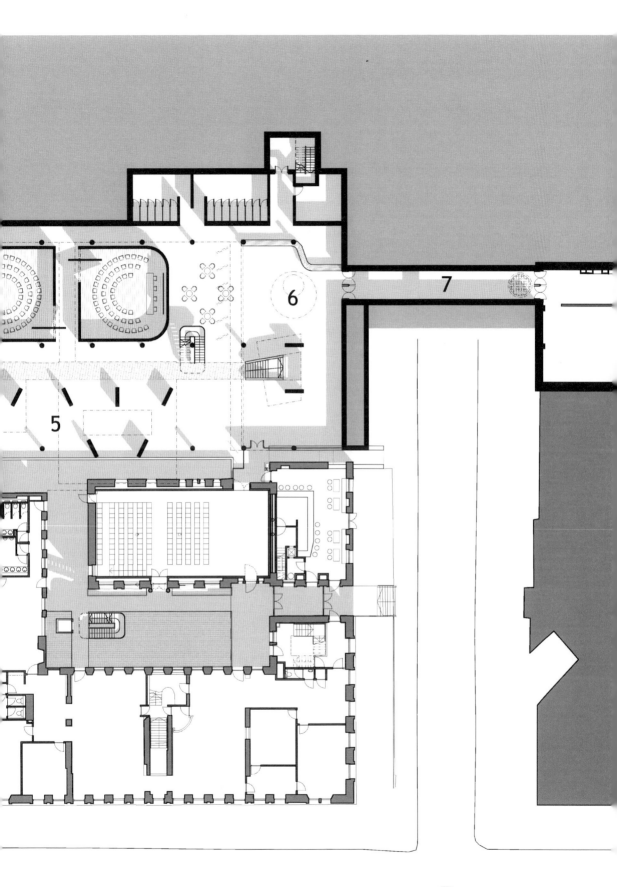

6

7

5

10m

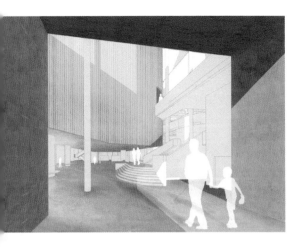 

Figure 6 (above left), Figure 7 (above right).

space to an individual 'building' will be more 'subliminal'; while in summer the transition from outside, to generic roofed space, to 'building' may be entirely subliminal.

In the proposed Phase 2 design, the public entrance to the building is on the north side of Sauchiehall Street, adjoining Alexander Thompson's Grecian Chambers, now the Centre for Contemporary Arts, to the east *(fig. 5, 1 on plan)*. The visitor enters between deep vertical concrete brise soleil and arrives underneath a rounded timber clad auditorium that fills the space above. This is illuminated by moving patterns of speckled light from the louvred south façade. To the left another massive structure, this time cast in in-situ concrete, soars 10 metres over a public gallery and punctures through the rhythm of the brise soleil to project over the street. This is the main studio block. To the right the original party wall of the Grecian Chambers is exposed and punctured through to connect the public atrium of the Centre for Contemporary Arts to the gallery of its new academic neighbour *(fig. 6)*. The rhythm of the brise soleil introduces the 5m longitudi-

nal grid that sets up the primary structure of the roof covering the 'generic' spaces. The roof establishes a horizontal datum for the space underneath: on the Sauchiehall Street façade it is about 18 metres, or five and a half storeys above ground level, while on the Renfrew Street façade to the north this is reduced to around 5 metres, a rise in ground level across the block of approximately 13 metres. This is negotiated in two 'steps'; the first of which, corresponding with the line of the rear of the Centre for Contemporary Arts, is negotiated by the main stair to the right of the information desk, giving access to the rear of the auditorium and the rest of the building beyond.

The gallery of the Institute *(fig 5, 2)* is designed as an extension to the street, a public forum to the centre of Glasgow that Mackintosh's original site could never allow. But the glass façade is not about creating 'inside-outside' space; it is a retreat from a hostile street environment of traffic, noise, and (especially in Scotland) wind and rain. The façade encloses an urban hall: in Scotland this is the equivalent of an Italian piazza *(fig. 7)*.

Figure 8 (above), Figure 9 (below).

Ascending the main stair the factory rooflights give a view of the sky to the north, drawing the visitor upwards into the heart of the building. The open space under the main roof enables visitors to orientate themselves, and find the auditorium accessed by a bridge behind (fig. 5, 3), the cafeteria raised on a plinth underneath an inverted glass aedicule (fig. 5, 4), and crit spaces and studios above (fig. 8). Turning to the right takes the visitor underneath two boxes held in the air by concrete legs reminiscent of the brise soleil on the south façade. This in-between space (fig. 5, 5) is quite dark, only lit by clerestory level windows to the south above the eaves of the Centre for Contemporary Arts, and any other remaining light filtering in from the periphery. Ahead, the famous Mackintosh west façade is glimpsed through more glazing (fig. 9), raised up at first floor level above an undercroft space below (fig. 5, 6). In this undercroft there is an entrance to an underground connection to the Mackintosh building itself (fig. 5, 7), as well as another

Figure 10. Upper level Plan

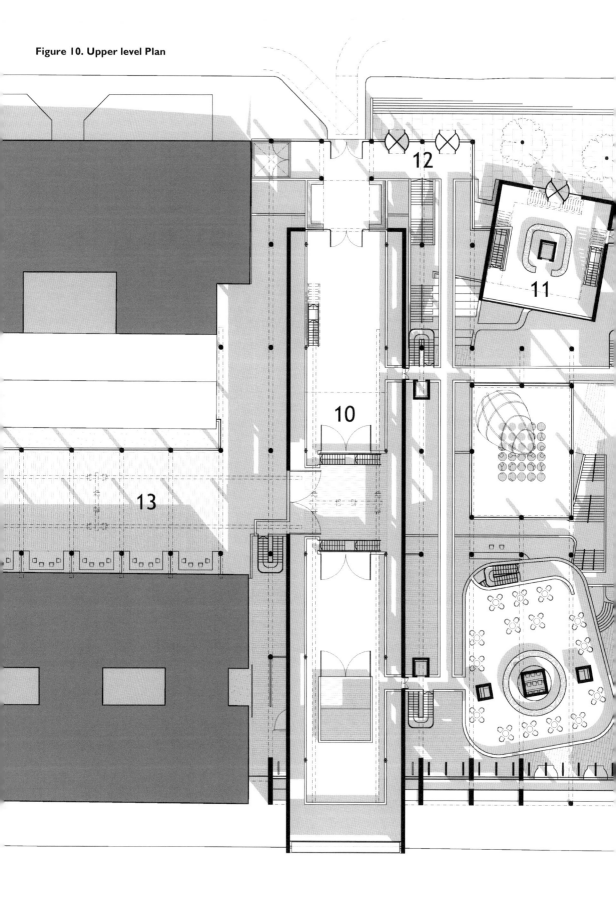

Figure 10. Upper level Plan

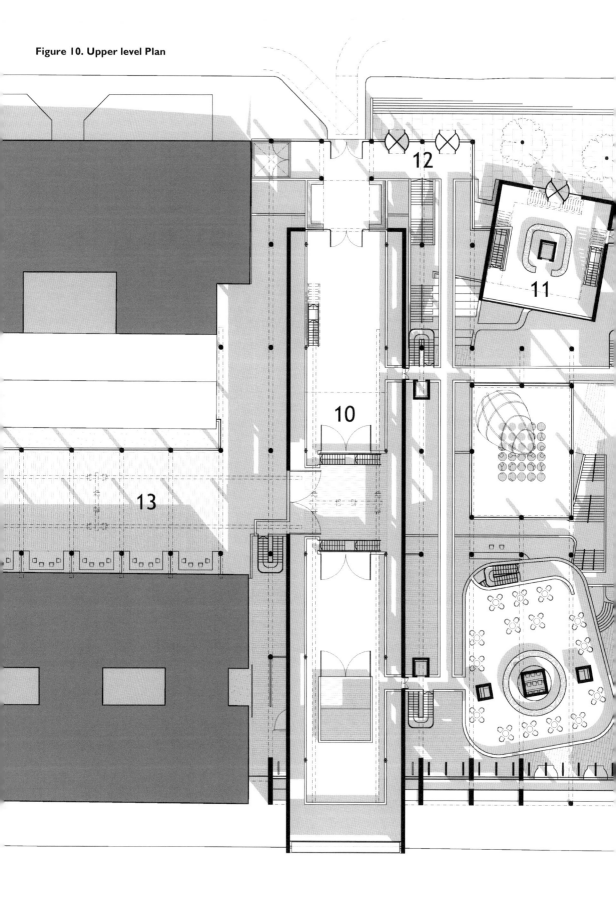

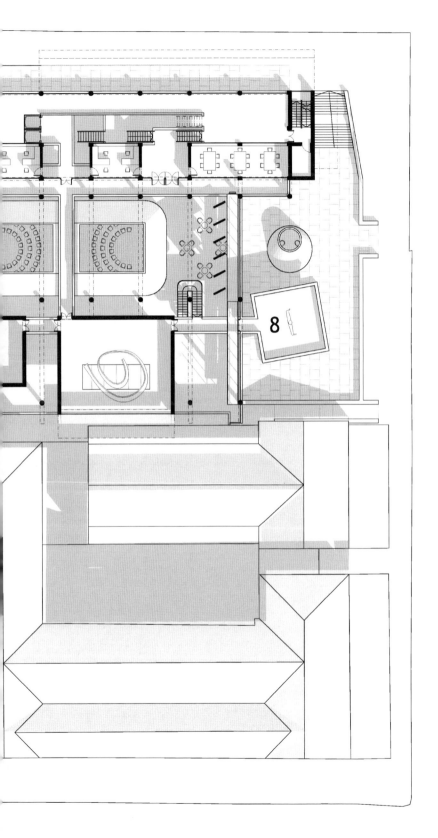

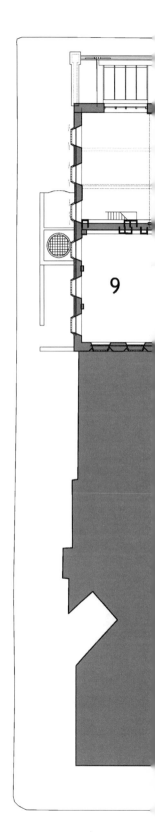

8

9

10m

Figure 11.

flight of stairs that lifts visitors into a glass pavilion that reveals itself to be a memory of the suspended boxes the visitor has already passed under, displaced and twisted off axis *(fig. 10, 8)*. At the top of the stairs, the exit to the street addresses the base of the library tower of the Mackintosh building directly *(fig. 5, 9)*.

The second major step that negotiates the change in level across the site corresponds with the southern edge of a new administration and research block that encloses the generic roof space on Renfrew Street. Another staircase *(fig.11)* rises up to Renfrew Street between the studio block *(fig. 10, 10)* and the library *(fig. 10, 11)*. At the top of the stair is the main student entrance to the building *(fig. 10, 12)*, giving direct access to the studios from the street (and the rest of the School of Art campus), without the need to negotiate the more public spaces below.

The studio block is lit by five large south facing factory-style rooflights angled at 25 degrees from the vertical *(fig. 12)*. This angle is enough to allow direct light into the

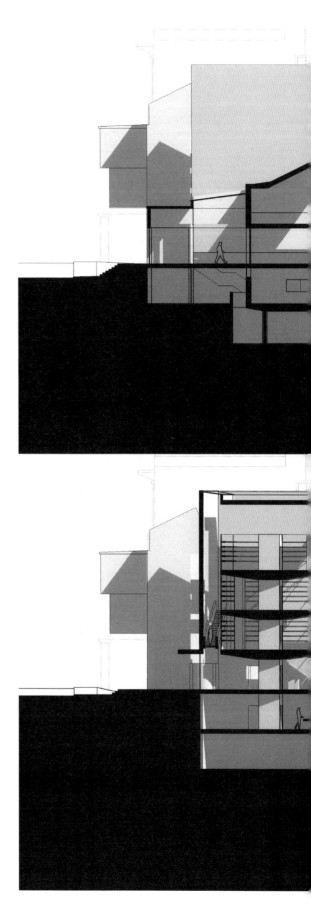

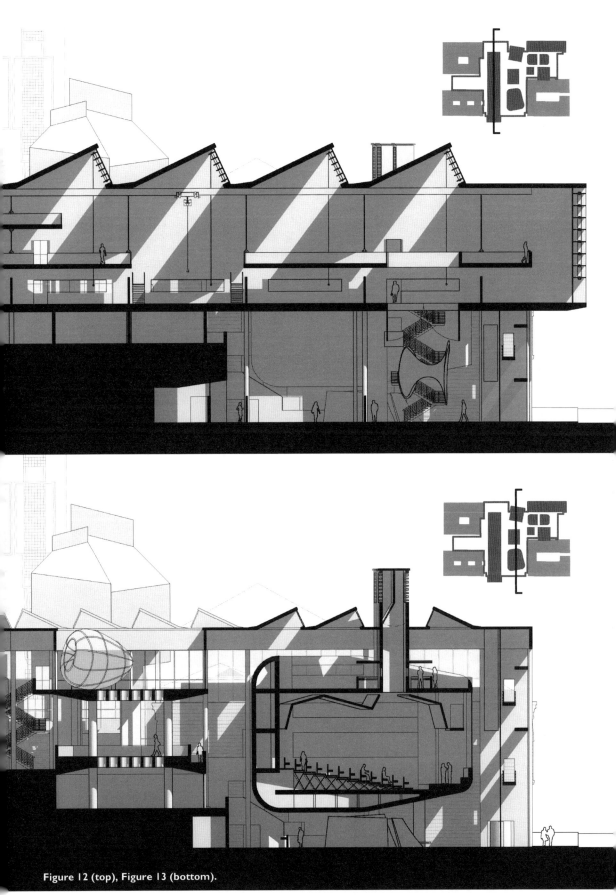

Figure 12 (top), Figure 13 (bottom).

studios at the winter equinox when the sun is only 10.5 degrees above the horizon at its southern azimuth, while also offering some protection from the highest sun angles of 57.5 degrees at the summer equinox. Further control of glare is provided by manipulation of small louvers on the inside of the glazing. The lowest level of the studios receives light that filters around the edges of the upper levels, which are suspended from the ceiling. It is intended as a darker, more secluded space for individual computer work, sketching, reading, or writing.

The upper levels are used for making large-scale models, and are served by an underslung crane that runs the length of the studios and travels in two axes. Fabricated components can be moved in and out of the workshops *(fig. 10, 13)* through barn-style doors on the west side, and finished models can be lowered through trap doors into the gallery space below the south end of the studios. Materials and components can also be delivered directly into the studio from a vehicle entrance on Renfrew Street.

The library is housed in a tower to the east of the entrance on Renfrew Street, inflected off the grid at an angle that emphasises its relationship to the Mackintosh building further up the street. It has a separate entrance at street level, with a model library a level below *(fig. 13)*. The main reading rooms are on a series of trays above, supported by a structural lift shaft,

Figure 14. View of Sculpture Courtyard looking towards Library

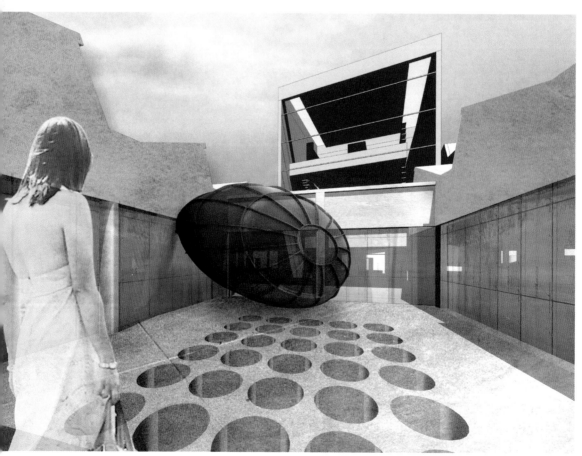

Figure 15 (above), Figure 16 (below).

reminiscent of Mackintosh's great American contemporary's tower at the Johnson Wax Building. The staircases are suspended in the void between these 'trays' and the envelope, which also serves to diffusely light the interior. The south façade is glazed to give views south over the city and the Clyde (fig. 14), and solar gain is controlled by a series of internal louvres.

The crit spaces are designed as sculptural boxes that reflect on the interior the mood of the ever-changing sky of Glasgow (fig. 15). They are held two storeys aloft to the east of the inverted aedicule at the top of the main entrance stair, and accessed by a network of aerial walkways also connected to the studios and the auditorium (fig. 16).

THERMAL ANALYSIS

The thermal performance of the building was assessed during the design process using a straightforward static model designed for planning passive houses by Simos Yannas.[6] First, the heat losses through the fabric of a given space, both to the outside and the rest of the building, are calculated, with assumed construction u-values. Heat losses due to ventilation are also calculated. Then heat gains due to occupancy, equipment and solar gains are calculated. The model is refined by considering the solar gains from six broad orientations: south, north, east/west, horizontal (reflecting horizontal ceiling rooflights), and a deviation from the horizontal of 70 degrees towards the south and north (reflecting the factory rooflights). Values for the irradiance of the sun in Edinburgh (which has similar irradiation values to Glasgow) at each orientation and in different seasons were taken from CIBSE *Guide J*.[7] Additionally, the model was expanded to calculate the ventilation flow rate in each space, which iteratively feeds back into the thermal calculations via the heat loss through ventilation, the thermal calculation then provides the temperature differential required to calculate ventilation flow rate. The thermal relationship between the spaces is also considered by iteratively connecting the models, so that the model for the generic space (encompassing the gallery on Sauchiehall Street, and the café and student union facilities in the centre of the building)

Figure 17.

GENERIC SPACE TEMPERATURES

	A m2	U W/m2 K	AU W/K
ROOF	2544.00	0.18	457.92
WINDOWS / DOORS/ ROOFLIGHTS	1944.00	1.40	2721.60
EXTERNAL WALLS (NET)	0.00	0.18	0.00
FLOOR	3977.00	0.18	715.86

							AU W/K	
SUBTOTAL BUILDING ENVELOPE							**3895.38**	W/K

	No. Occ	Q	Volume m3	Air changes/hour	m3/person hour	hrs/day		
FRESH AIR FOR VENTILATION	200	1.41	29830	0.17	25.30	6	**417.49**	W/K

TOTAL							**4312.87**	W/K

Heat Gains

	No. Occ	Watts	hrs/day				24-hr Mean	
OCCUPANTS	200	100	6.00				5000.00	W
APPLIANCES	12	100	24.00				1200.00	W

Solar Gains

	Glass Area m2	ISun kWh/d	Obstruction	Correction Factor	Transmitted	Absorbed	24-hr Mean	
SOUTH	715	1.3	45	0.50	0.70	0.90	12199.69	W
NORTH	384	0.2	40	0.56	0.70	0.90	1120.00	W
EAST/WEST	546	0.4	20	0.78	0.70	0.90	4459.00	W
HORIZONTAL	21	0.6	0	1.00	0.70	0.90	330.75	W
70 DEGREES SOUTH	104	0.5	0	1.00	0.70	0.90	1365.00	W
70 DEGREES NORTH	193	0.1	0	1.00	0.70	0.90	506.63	W

Other Gains

	Studios	Auditorium	Library	Classrooms	Offices	Crit Spaces	Total	
	2237.49	1848.09	1043.40	1118.75	559.37	559.37	7366.47	W

TOTAL GAINS							**35785.02**	W

AVERAGE TEMPERATURE RISE ABOVE OUTDOOR		35785.02	/	4312.87			**8.30**	K

Outdoor Temperature °C		1.0	3.5	6.0	
Predicted Mean Indoor Temperature °C		9.3	11.8	14.3	

Target Indoor Temperature (lower margin)	17.1	18.0	18.8	
Target Indoor Temperature (upper margin)	21.1	22.0	22.8	

	Inlet Area m2	Outlet Area m2	Stack Height m	Temperature Differential °C	Pressure Pa	Q	
VENTILATION FLOW RATE	1	1	11	8.3	5.78	**1.41**	m3/s

takes into account the thermal gains from the specific spaces within it (a product of the degree of enclosure under the generic roof), and each specific space modelled takes into account the temperature of the generic space it is exposed to (as well as the external temperature) in calculating resultant indoor temperatures.

The spaces were analysed for January and July conditions, respectively the coldest and hottest months of the year in Glasgow.[8] It is assumed that if the thermal environmental design is feasible in these relative extremes, adjustments to ventilation and permitted solar gains in the months between should provide the flexibility to fine tune the building in response to a changing seasonal climate. For illustrative purposes, the January models for the generic space and auditorium have been shown (figs. 17, 18).

One characteristic of the static model is that diurnal fluctuations in temperature are averaged out, so that the resultant temperatures only reflect the average daily internal temperature given an average daily outdoor temperature. It was therefore desirable that some form of dynamic simulation was conducted to verify the static approximations. This was conducted by computer simulation of the final design employing a Virtual Environment Model created using I.E.S. software.[9]

Figure 18.

AUDITORIUM TEMPERATURES

	Generic			Outdoor		
	A m2	U W/m2 K	AU W/K	A m2	U W/m2 K	AU W/K
ROOF	146.00	0.36	52.56	0.00	0.36	0.00
WINDOWS / DOORS/ ROOFLIGHTS	44.00	1.40	61.60	0.00	1.40	0.00
EXTERNAL WALLS (NET)	302.00	0.36	108.72	0.00	0.36	0.00
FLOOR	106.00	0.36	38.16	0.00	0.36	0.00
SUBTOTAL BUILDING ENVELOPE			**261.04** W/K			**0.00** W/K

	No. Occ	Q	Volume m3	Air changes/hour	m3/person hour	hrs/day	
FRESH AIR FOR VENTILATION	200	1.27	1320	3.48	22.94	6	**378.50** W/K
TOTAL							**639.54** W/K

Heat Gains

	No. Occ	Watts	hrs/day	24-hr Mean	
OCCUPANTS	200	75	6.00	3750.00	W
HEATING	0	0	24.00	0.00	W
APPLIANCES	12	100	6.00	300.00	W

Solar Gains

	Glass Area m2	ISun kWh/d	Obstruction	Correction Factor	Transmitted	Absorbed	24-hr Mean	
SOUTH	42	1.3	60	0.33	0.70	0.90	477.75	W
NORTH	0	0.2	0	1.00	0.70	0.90	0.00	W
EAST/WEST	0	0.4	0	1.00	0.70	0.90	0.00	W
HORIZONTAL	0	0.6	0	1.00	0.70	0.90	0.00	W
70 DEGREES SOUTH	0	0.5	0	1.00	0.70	0.90	0.00	W
70 DEGREES NORTH	0	0.1	0	1.00	0.70	0.90	0.00	W
TOTAL GAINS							**4527.75**	W

AVERAGE TEMPERATURE RISE ABOVE OUTDOOR	4527.75	/	639.54	**7.08** K

Outdoor Temperature	°C	1.0	3.5	6.0
Generic Temperature	°C	9.3	11.8	14.3
Predicted Mean Indoor Temperature	°C	16.4	18.9	21.4
Target Indoor Temperature (lower margin)		17.1	18.0	18.8
Target Indoor Temperature (upper margin)		21.1	22.0	22.8

	Inlet Area m2	Outlet Area m2	Stack Height m	Temperature Differential °C	Pressure Pa	Q	
VENTILATION FLOW RATE	1	0.5	18	15.4	11.87	**1.27**	m3/s

Figures 19 and 20 show the results of this dynamic analysis compared with the static model for the generic space, in January and July. The static model and the dynamic simulations seem to most closely accord in January *(fig. 19)*. It is hypothesised that this is because the sheer volume of the space negates much of the dampening effect due to thermal mass, so the internal temperature is much more responsive to external fluctuations. In summer, however, while the daytime temperatures appear to reflect the static model quite closely, the dynamic simulation appears to show temperatures 2-10°C warmer than the static model during the night *(fig. 20)*. This is probably a re-

Figures 19 (Top). Generic Space - January.
Figure 20 (Bottom). Generic Space - July.

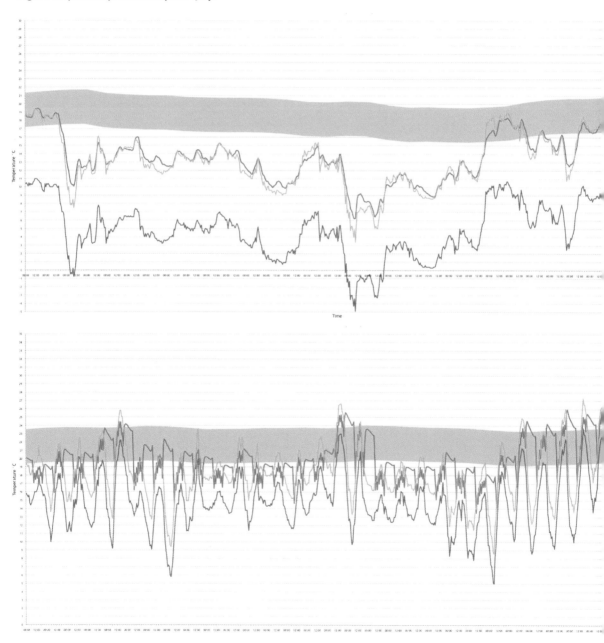

Thermal Comfort Range ———Outdoor Dry Bulb Temperature ———Indoor Air Temperature (IESve Simulation) ———Indoor Air Temperature (Steady State Model)

sult of the dynamic modelling of ventilation in the summer, which simulates 'switching' every half hour during working hours, with no adjustments at night. Overall, the suggested internal temperatures fall within the CIBSE adaptive comfort range for free running offices during the day for most of July, and only deviates from it during the day by a maximum of ±2°C in the second half of the month because of a cold snap followed by a warmer spell.[10]

In January, the space is for the most part 2-8°C cooler than the CIBSE comfort range during the daytime, and the clear diurnal rhythm of night and day present in July is somewhat more opaque. However, this is in line with the suggested architectural character of the space as an 'in-between' buffer to the more tightly controlled spaces within it, and the transient activities that do take place within it do not lend themselves to the removal of outer wear as might be expected of a fixed place of work. Instead, the space is more like an extension to the public realm of Glasgow; a forum for exhibitions, assembling large groups, or meeting individuals before moving on to another place.

Figure 21.

'THE HUMAN FACTOR'

Another great architect of the twentieth century, whose legacy Mackintosh's has been compared to on occasion[11], wrote that:

'Nowadays we use computations and prognoses in an effort to make absolutely accurate calculations about the future. But it is impossible for such systems, if that is what we must call them, to be free of the margin of human error, since it always plagues people, whatever their lifestyle. These "accurate" calculations contain just as much human error as earlier planning methods based on faith and emotion.'[12]

It is clear that Mackintosh also would have been sympathetic to this sentiment: for his architecture ultimately is one that responds to individual human desires and sensations (fig. 21). In recent times, it has again been highlighted that comfort does not necessarily equate with thermal neutrality; Nikopoulou and Steemers' research for example has focused on the definition of comfort;

'Comfortable conditions have been regarded as those where occupants feel neither warm nor cool, where ambient conditions are 'neutral'. However, it is increasingly believed that a variable, rather than fixed, environment is preferred whereas a static environment becomes intolerable.'[13]

Colin St. John Wilson went even further, stressing the importance of the experience of discomfort for psychological wellbeing:

'From the moment of being born we spend our lives in a state of comfort or discomfort on a scale of sensibility that stretches between claustrophobia and agoraphobia. We are inside or outside; or on the threshold between. There are no other places to be.'[14]

Through objective examination of the contribution of different comfort criteria towards promoting a favourable psychological response, and of the relationship between different 'specific' micro-environments within the Mackintosh building[15], this design research has proposed an idea for a radically different typology of art school based on historic examples of public space in Glasgow. This was conceived and developed intuitively, refined by static modelling and tested by dynamic simulation. The use of static modelling to inform the design process was an invaluable tool to iterate a design that performed technically as well as atmospherically. It also confers credibility to the dynamic modelling, which is all too often used to post-justify a design without a developed practical understanding of the situation being modelled.

It was proposed that a series of 'specific' micro-environments were developed using 'selective' design principles and maintained within a 'generic' macro-environment that functions technically as a thermal buffer space. Potvin describes how these kinds of spaces:

'Simultaneously engage the thermal sensations and movement of the entire body, and provide a progressive adaptation to a new environment. Whereas environmental determinism creates uniformity, environmental diversity increases the morphological possibilities of architecture and urban form.'[16]

Thermal comfort modelling did reveal some uncertainties about some of the spaces modelled, but these uncertainties are in themselves useful to inform where more flexibility for user adaptation may be required in detailed design. Aalto concluded that we can

'try, by means of careful analysis, to avoid being hurt by the human factor or, more precisely, to avoid being blinded by the short-sightedness that accompanies it.'[17]

But;

'The attempt to eliminate the human factor is a sign of helplessness, a prayer for advance pardon, a wish to replace the knowledge of life's uncertainty with absolute certainty and some kind of truth, but the result is, that the same margin of error that was inherent in emotional calculations is transferred to rational calculations. The hope to eliminate the human factor by absolutist measures remains an illusion.'[18]

Further research might explore how this 'new' 'type' of building might be appropriately deployed in other urban situations, to breathe new life into under-utilised buildings and spaces around them, to promote a more diverse and psychologically engaging kind of environmental design, as well as to suggest a more 'sustainable' alternative to our increasing dependence on ever more intensive means of mechanically regulating the warming future of our environment.

(ENDNOTES)

1   'Modern art: school wins £50m funding for revamp', Glasgow Herald (17/06/2008).

2   'Glasgow's Lighthouse gallery calls in administrators', Glasgow Herald (25/08/2009).

3   The LT method was used in this instance primarily to quantify the possible scale of improvement in energy consumption that could be brought about by altering the built form of the urban block. See Baker, N. and K. Steemers, Energy and Environment in Architecture, E & FN Spon, London (2000), p. 94.

4   Hawkes, D. and N. Baker, 'Glazed Courtyards: An Element of the Low-Energy City', in Hawkes, D., Owers, J., Rickaby, P. and P. Steadman (eds.), Energy and Urban Built Form, Centre for Configurational Studies, and the Martin Centre for Architectural and Urban Studies (1987), p. 235.

5   Potvin, A., 'Intermediate environments', in Steemers, K. and M. A. Steane (eds.), Environmental Diversity in Architecture, Spon Press, Oxford (2004), p. 122.

6   Simos Yannas, Director Of Sustainable Environmental Design, Architectural Association Graduate School.

7   Data from CIBSE, Guide J: Weather, Solar and illuminance data (2002), pp. A6-16-A6-18.

8   Data from Met Office. Accessed at http://www.metoffice.gov.uk.

9   Integrated Environmental Solutions, Virtual Environment, version 6.0.5.

10   This is a function of the exponentially weighted running mean of outdoor air temperature, so that for the lower margin for internal temperature tint = 0.33tint+16.8, and for the upper margin tint = 0.33tint+20.8. See CIBSE, Guide A: Environmental Design (2006), p. 1-17.

11   MacMillan, A., 'Charles Rennie Mackintosh – His Contribution to the Modern Movement', ptah, issue 1-2 (2007), pp. 38-39.

12   Aalto, A., 'The Human Factor', in Schildt, G (ed.), Alvar Aalto: In His Own Words, Rizzoli, New York (1997), p. 281.

13   Nikopoulou, M. and K. Steemers, 'Thermal comfort and psychological adaptation as a guide for designing urban spaces', Architecture, City, Environment: Proceedings of PLEA 2000 (2000), p. 567.

14   Wilson, Colin St. John, Architectural Reflections: Studies in the philosophy and practice of architecture, Butterworth Architecture, Oxford (1992), p. 5-6.

15   See: Lawrence, R., The Potential for Naturally Conditioned Public Buildings in the Northern Part of the UK, unpublished MPhil thesis, Cambridge University (2010), pp. 22-31.

16   Potvin, A., 'Intermediate environments', in Steemers, K. and M. A. Steane (eds.), Environmental Diversity in Architecture, Spon Press, Oxford (2004), p. 121.

17   Aalto, A., 'The Human Factor', in Schildt, G (ed.), Alvar Aalto: In His Own Words, Rizzoli, New York (1997), p. 281.

18   Ibid., p. 281.

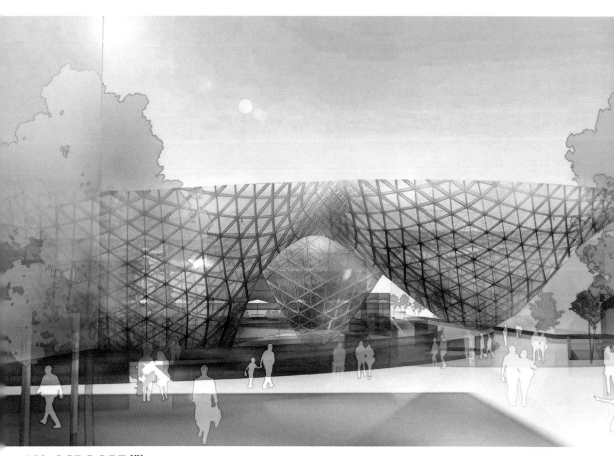

Transit-Oriented Mixed Use Development as an Urban Regeneration Strategy

by Ziyan Xing

AN INTRODUCTION TO TRANSIT-ORIENTED DEVELOPMENT

Transit-Oriented Developments (TODs) broadly categorise a range of compact, mixed-use schemes that are to be built near fast and large capacity passenger transit facilities.

The principal aim of mixed-use TODs is to boost ridership of public transportation whilst leveraging economic development. Although always project and site specific, high quality walking environments and human scale neighbourhoods are often included as common design features. Because of the potential of mixed-use TODs to address key social development objectives, and accommodate present-day market force and lifestyle preferences, they are

Ziyan Xing studied Architecture at the University of Sheffield and has just completed an MPhil in Environmental Design at the University of Cambridge.

considered a primary tool for implementing Smart Growth, originally conceived of as a reaction to what many planners believed were the undesirable features of continued 'suburban sprawl'.

In his paper *Transport: maker and breaker of cities*, Colin Clark argued that since the first industrial revolution the growth of cities has been shaped by the development of their transport facilities, which in turn has been dependent on the evolution of transport technologies. For each successive development of the technology, there was a corresponding type of city. However, activities, land uses and transport systems are all single elements in a complex symbiotic relationship.

The challenge today is to use our understanding of the relationship between land use and transportation to establish a socially equitable, economically viable, and environmentally friendly sustainable urban form, which could work effectively for the people living and working within it. The key is to concentrate residences, work areas and amenities so as to produce the shortest possible trip distances between homes, places of work and services, most being possible by bicycle and public transport.

The growth of cities has always been linked to the development of transport facilities. Patterns of land use activities generate the need for travel, and transport accessibility in turn shapes further development. Mixed-use TODs have proved to be beneficial in terms of economic, social, and environmental perspectives. While the functional divisions in modernist cities arguably caused the death of urban neighbourhoods, mixed-use developments have gradually become the preferred way forward in order to improve accessibility, the quality of life in regional communities, and the financial success of transit investments.

TRANSIT-ORIENTED DEVELOPMENT IN THE UK CONTEXT - CAMBRIDGE CB1

Over half a century of planning constraints on the City of Cambridge has, more or less, preserved it as the university town Holford envisaged in 1950. The lack of space for expansion has, however, led to high housing costs, rapid growth in small towns and rural areas outside the City's green belt, and traffic congestion, all of which are increasingly impeding the competitiveness of business in the City and the surrounding sub-region.

The problems in Cambridge are summarised in The Regional Planning Guidance for East Anglia:

'Much development in East Anglia in recent years has been in smaller settlements, and has been poorly located relative to the location of employment and services... if East Anglia is to accommodate its development needs in an environmentally acceptable and sustainable way, existing trends will need to be modified. Development for housing, jobs and services will need to be much more closely integrated with each other and much more closely related to sustainable transport provision.'

In order to facilitate appropriate and sustainable forms of growth in Cambridge, a portfolio of wide-ranging developments have been proposed by the Cambridgeshire and Peterborough Structure Plan. Growth is proposed through planned extensions and new settlements, as demonstrated by the £1.75m University of Cambridge-led SOLUTIONS Project, aimed at preventing purely market-led urban sprawl and protecting the countryside. The CB1 development aims to regenerate the Brownfield site around the Cambridge Station area.

At 158,000 square metres the CB1 scheme is the largest development ever planned for Cambridge, with the aim of improving the integration of public transport and promoting other sustainable modes of travel. It was proposed in partnership between private developer Ashwell, Network Rail and Cambridgeshire County Council to improve cross-City linkages and support the wider growth of the Cambridge Sub-Region. After an initial planning refusal, a revised CB1 scheme designed by Rogers Stirk Harbour and Partners obtained outline planning consent in October 2008.

It is the contention of this author, however, that the new transport interchange is not fully integrated, with different transport modes separated far apart from each other across only one level. The potential for an inspirational arrival point to Cambridge has not been fully realised, and there is no focal point for the urban design, with a danger that the chaotic status quo will only be replicated.

DESIGN OPPORTUNITIES FOR AN IMPROVED CB1

In the Cambridge Futures 2 report, Echenique and Hargreaves detail how extensive improvements to the public transport network have been tested as a possible means of coping with an increase in travel demand and congestion generated by the policies of the 2003 Structure Plan.

One proposed strategy is for bus tunnels under Cambridge city centre to improve public transport service levels and reduce any congestion in the centre arising from a forecasted increase in public transport routes.

The south entrance of the 2.7km tunnel would be an underground bus station at the railway station, that would then branch to emerge at ground level at two locations; one linked to the guided bus system along the disused Bedford railway line, and the other to the east of the railway tracks, connected to Davy Road and then at surface level to the Airport area and the orbital road.

The bus tunnel proposal highlighted in the Cambridge Future 2 report opens up the potential of creating a multi-level, multi-mode transportation hub at Cambridge railway station, which could lead to significant alterations to the entire CB1 scheme.

A more fitting design brief for CB1 may therefore centre on the requirement for a multi-level, multi-mode transportation hub at Cambridge railway station, to separate pedestrian movement, bicycle path, vehicular access, and fast transit (the guided buses) in order to achieve maximum efficiency and safety. A focal point could be created outside the station, connecting the station building itself, the different interchange levels, and a spacious yet human scale public square, with meaningful functions for social or commercial activities.

It is important to treat the CB1 development as a unified site, and not as a series of individual elements. It can only become a meaningful and successful development by interconnecting all of its disparate elements – the railway station building, the new bus and guided bus stations, bicycle parking facilities, pedestrian paths and the open spaces – into one urban quarter.

A NEW MULTI-LEVEL AND MULTI-MODE TRANSPORTATION INTERCHANGE

Creating a multimode transport node on different levels enables more space to be freed up at ground level for pedestrians, and provides better opportunities for commercial frontage, and public activities. Each piece of infrastructure – trains, buses, and the newly proposed guided buses – can occur at a different level. The challenge is to make these circulation patterns as simple and convenient as possible.

The interchange facility proposed by this author includes more than a new lower ground level; it creates a spacious bus station underneath the railway station building, and provides entrances to the underground platforms of the guided bus tunnels. A connecting subway is extended from this lower

Figures 1 (below).
Figure 2 (far right).

ground floor concourse level over to the eastern side of the railway tracks, establishing a shortcut to the other side of the railway lines.

This lower ground level is connected with Station Road, a tree-lined boulevard, by means of a gentle ramp. A large covered drop-off area for taxis and buses is formed with pedestrian access through stairs, escalators and lifts *(fig. 1)*.

A NEW STATION SQUARE

For the first time it is proposed that people coming out of Cambridge railway station will be welcomed by a major urban space. It is an opportunity for urban sculpture, for landscape features, and a chance to relate the movements of passengers, buses and taxis *(fig. 2)*.

As requested by local residents, green landscape features and trees are proposed across the square, providing shading in the summer, and softening the otherwise hard surface edges.

KEY:

1. Refurbished /enlarged station entrance.
2. New Ticket Hall
3. Cafe sitting area
4. Circle Markings.
5. Covered arcade
6. Entrance to CU frontage building.
7. Information desks.
8. University Offices.
9. Reception to Hotel.
10. Internet Café.
11. Sitting Area (Hotel Restaurant)
12. Storage and Loading.
13. Kitchen.
14. Canopy infront of MSCP.
15. Retail spaces.
16. Student Accomodation.
17. Commercial use (by other developer).
18. Office / Commercial with GF retail.
19. Office / Commercial with GF retail.
20. Vehicle Ramp.
21. Bicycle path bridge.
22. Pool harvesting rainwater.
23. Main footing of Canopy structure.
24. Escalators to lower ground level.
25. Bicycle parking.
26. Lifts to lower ground bus terminal.
27. Cycle ramp to lower ground level.
28. Grand Stairway.

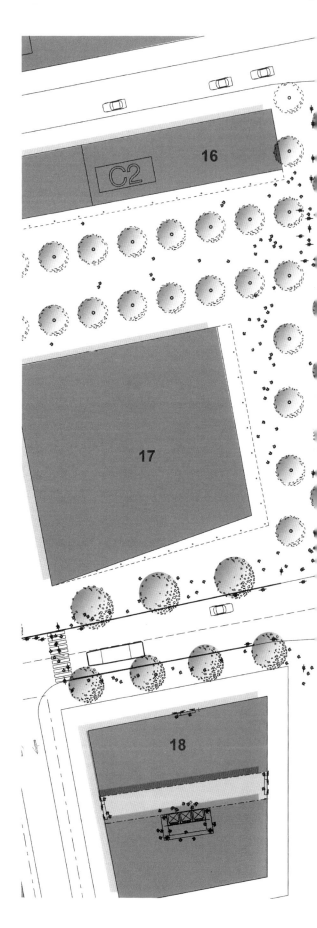

Figures 3. Plan of new Station Square.

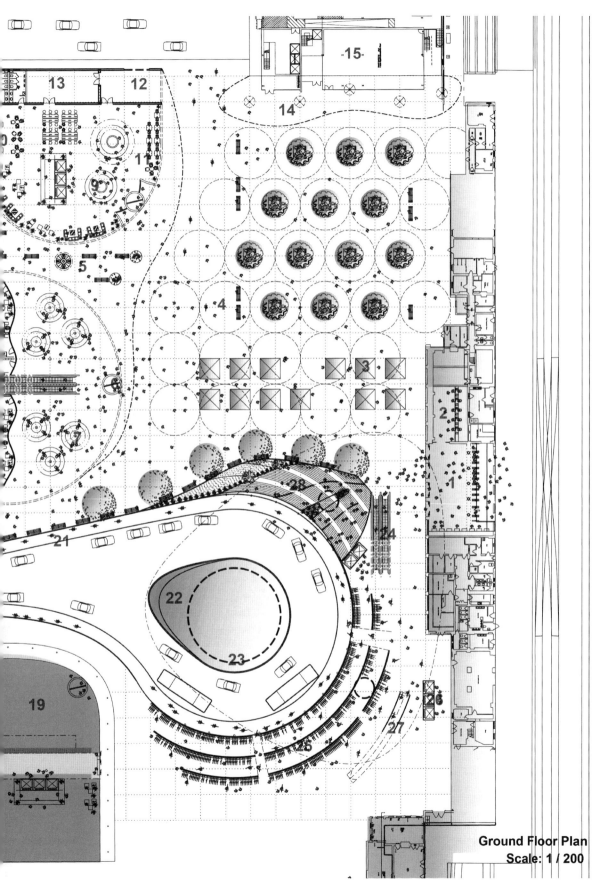

Ground Floor Plan
Scale: 1 / 200

Temporary market stalls and cafés are located outside the station entrance. This provides an opportunity for local small businesses to represent the characteristics of Cambridge, and provides people with an opportunity to spend more time in the square.

The new station square also functions as a temporary information platform for the University of Cambridge. During the summer months, and on open days or during alumni events, the public square can serve as the first information point for visitors, prospective students, and alumni alike who arrive at Cambridge by train. College or School events can be staged here without the physical constrains of the historic city centre.

There are 31 circles marked on the square with different flooring materials, which represent the 31 colleges at Cambridge University *(fig. 3)*. In addition, with the square connecting directly to the entrance of Cambridge railway station at the east end, it feeds into the newly proposed Cambridge University frontage building and a hotel building on the west side. There are permanent offices in the University frontage building to provide information and services for visitors all year round; and 6 information circles represent the 6 schools at the University, where employees from the University can greet new arrivals.

Figure 4.

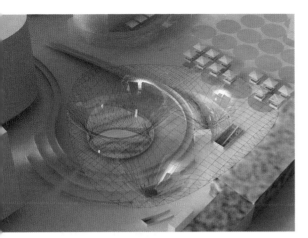

Figure 5 (above), Figure 6 (below), Figure 7 (top right), Figure 8 (right).

THE CANOPY STRUCTURE

The canopy structure establishes an elegant architectural gesture which connects different spaces, people and movement between the changing levels *(fig. 4)*. The horn-shaped canopy collects rainwater which is filtered and stored at the bottom of the structure and then used throughout the urban square for water features and irrigation purposes *(fig. 5)*.

It also generates renewable energy through solar panels installed on part of the canopy surfaces with high amounts of solar radiation; the areas with low radiation will be fully glazed to allow natural light

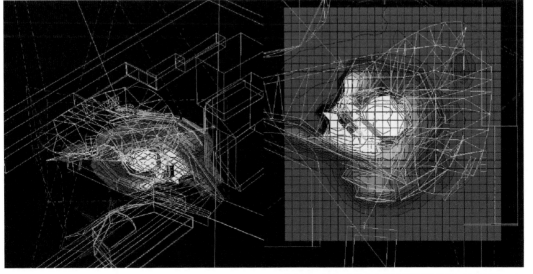

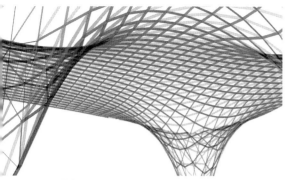

Figure 9 (above), Figure 10 (below).

penetration down to the lower ground bus station. *(figs. 6, 7)*. As well as sheltering the entrance to the station building and ramps and escalators down to the lower level bus station, the canopy's transparent nature gives it an elegant urban presence initself. It would enhance the visual image of the station area, and mark a striking end to the vista along Station Road *(fig. 8)*.

Structurally, the three horn shaped legs are integrated into one smooth canopy roof entity through a Triangular Trussed Structure network. It is simple, graceful and elegant, pared down, light-filled and transparent *(fig. 9)*.

UNIVERSITY FRONTAGE BUILDING

According to the original CB1 proposal, the two buildings adjacent to the station square are proposed to be six stories tall. This was challenged by the local residents as being too 'big'. Although there are colonnaded retail units planned on ground and first floor, the upper floors are still too dominant in comparison with the station building and its surroundings.

The proposed design is more open, with gradual set-back transitions *(fig. 10)*. Two large roof terraces are made available, providing fantastic views and recreational spaces to the upper floors of the hotel.

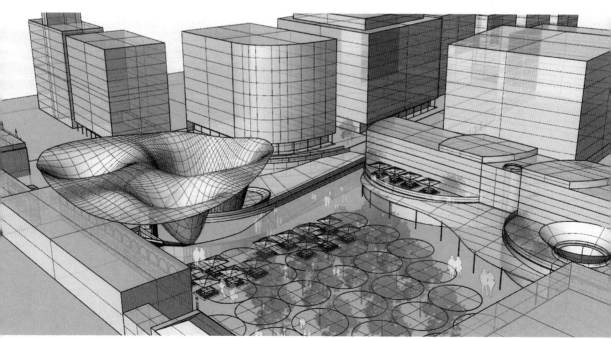

The Algae House Project

by Christopher Bowler

Algae House is a design project that origi-nated from a multi-disciplinary architect–engineer group exercise to design a small dwelling self-sufficient in its use of energy. As research worldwide explores the poten-tial for algae as a clean, renewable energy source, the potential for providing a truly 'green' solution to the ongoing global en-ergy crisis emerges. However, the majority of this research is lab-based; the interest and challenge for the design team on this project came about through the prospect of reconciling the needs of algae cultivation and human comfort in a single architectural solution – algaetecture – an integrated solu-tion that eschews the prevailing 'add-on' approach of renewable energy technologies such as wind-turbines and PV panels.

Think of algae and one might imagine a

Group project by Christopher Bowler, Daniela Krug and Karuga Koinange (with further input from Ben Taylor, Oliver Hudson, David Valinsky and Ben Sheppard).

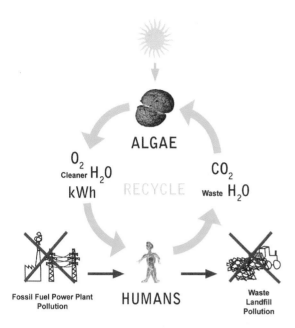

O$_2$ Cleaner H$_2$O kWh

ALGAE

RECYCLE

CO$_2$ Waste H$_2$O

Fossil Fuel Power Plant Pollution

HUMANS

Waste Landfill Pollution

Figure 1. The Algae Cycle

murky pond, a neglected swimming pool or a deserted, seaweed-strewn stretch of coastline. In any case, it's not normally associated with innovation or practical usefulness. However, this may be about to change.

Algae differs from conventional biomass crops in that useful energy can be harnessed via a variety of methods.

Like traditional crops, algae can be burned to release energy. The extraction of energy rich lipid oils presents another route. Uniquely though, algae can also be used to produce hydrogen, a far cleaner and greener method of energy production. Under certain conditions – specifically in the absence of sulphur – algae switches from the production of oxygen by photosynthesis to the production of hydrogen.

To capture this hydrogen and subsequently use it in conjunction with a fuel

cell would open up the potential for a fully carbon free energy source. It was through this mode of energy release that the team set out, through a process of experimental design, to investigate the potential for the micro-generation of hydrogen from algae within a domestic residential context.

From early on in the design process it became clear that certain environmental constraints – namely light and heat – for successful algae cultivation were analogous to those required by humans. Eukaryotic organisms, such as algae, generally thrive on exposure to high levels of light. However, the capture of gaseous hydrogen produced by the algae necessitated its housing in a sealed, transparent enclosure. Consultation with researchers in the field of algae cultivation, who had completed mock-ups of such tubes – termed photo-bioreactors – confirmed that they were highly prone to overheating. Indeed algae is killed at temperatures over 30°C. Humans of course, whilst fortunately not suffering quite so acutely, have a similar temperature comfort range.

Thus it became clear that the potential existed for the algae and domestic spaces of the AlgaeHouse to enter a symbiotic relationship, whereby one promotes the optimum environmental conditions for the other. The form of the AlgaeHouse façade was developed as a direct consequence of this constraint.

The guiding objective in the design was that, whilst temperature stability was essential, it was also desirable to obtain the maximum amount of light from the sun. Multiple, 120mm diameter cylindrical photo-bioreactors were proposed to provide optimum surface area. A fixed glazing system shaded by louvres and surrounded by a water pool was developed that independently controls solar heat gain and light throughout the day as well as across the year. To allow the algae to function efficiently, and to reduce artificial lighting, the bioreactors would need as much sunlight as possible without risking over-exposure. Therefore, through the oblique angling of the algae tubes' orientation to the sun, direct solar heat gain was allowed only during winter months and on spring and autumn

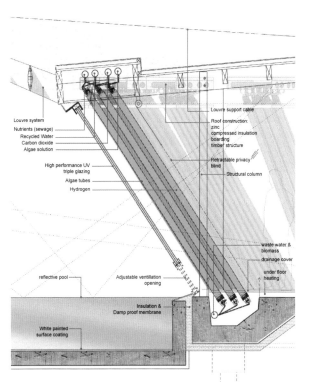

Figure 3. Detailed Section showing bio-reactors within thermal envelope.

mornings and evenings.

As the house plans illustrate, the shallow pool of water, or 'moat', that lies adjacent to the façade, is intended to perform two basic functions. Firstly, the reflective properties of water are such that the amount of light reflected increases exponentially as the angle to the surface of the water decreases.

This means that the pool reflects low angle sun up to the overhanging algae façade, whilst absorbing more of the higher energy, high angle, mid-day summer sun. Secondly, water absorbs up to a hundred times more energy from infra-red light than from visible light. As heat energy is mostly transferred by infra-red light, the water would usefully absorb much of the heat from direct sunlight before reflecting it up to the algae. The amount of reflection was optimised by

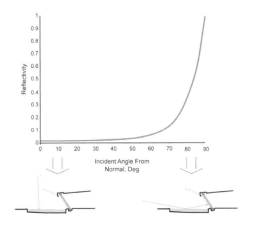

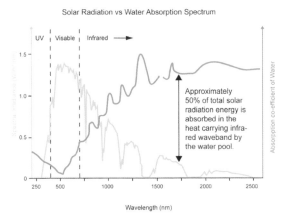

Figure 2. Water Reflectivity increases reflected light energy in Summer whilst omitting infra-red solar radiation.

the addition of a reflective surface or coating to the pool floor.

In the summer the pool also benefits the occupants of the house in providing cooling as air is drawn into the house after passing across the surface of the water. The aqueous movement of the reflected light playing across the green algae tubes and the living room ceiling would also contribute to a visually interesting and unique living space.

Working with Cambridge PhD Biochemist Ben Taylor, the total amount of energy produced through hydrogen production was estimated using anticipated rates of efficiency derived from laboratory research –

as much as 10% efficiency in the conversion of light energy to hydrogen. Based on this rate, 75 square metres of algae is estimated to produce 6570 kilowatt-hours of hydrogen per year – enough to drive an electric MINI E car from London to Beijing and back three times. To make the most efficient use of this energy, the majority of it would be converted to electricity through a fuel cell with an efficiency of approximately 50%. The associated waste heat that is produced as an inevitable consequence of this technique would be recovered to satisfy space-heating needs.

Algae and people may not present themselves as obvious bedfellows, but this

Figure 4. The geometrics and solar system developed in AlgaeHouse are adaptable to an increased urban desnity and scale.

Urban Algae

The geometries and solar system developed in *AlgaeHouse* are adaptable to an increased urban density and scale.

'AlgaeHouse'

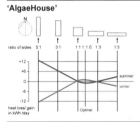

Moderate climate

Algae strain used;
Chlamydomonas reinhardtii
Favour moderate conditions

6 dwellings per hectare
= approx. 24600 kWh per annum per hectare

'AlgaeCourtyard'

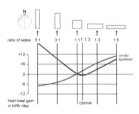

Hot, arid climate

Algae Strain used;
Scenedesmus obliquus
Tolerant of hot, arid conditions

25 dwellings per hectare
= approx. 65000 kWh per annum per hectare

'AlgaeTower'

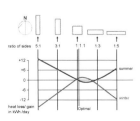

Cool climate

Algae strain used;
Chlamydomonas f-9
Marine (saltwater) tolerant

100 dwellings per hectare
= approx. 300000 kWh per annum per hectare

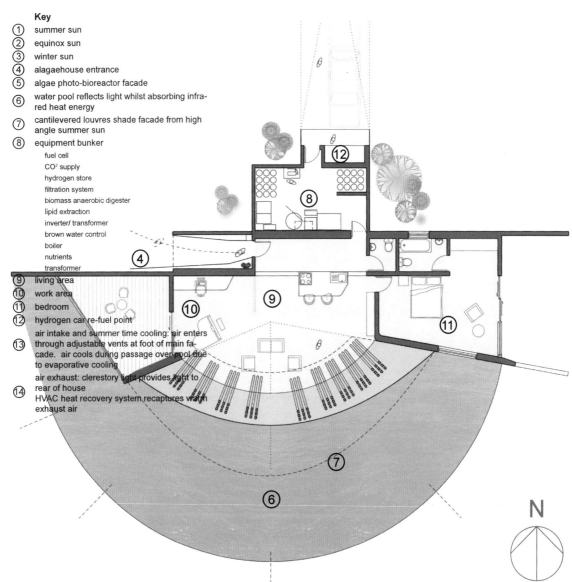

Key

1. summer sun
2. equinox sun
3. winter sun
4. alagaehouse entrance
5. algae photo-bioreactor facade
6. water pool reflects light whilst absorbing infra-red heat energy
7. cantilevered louvres shade facade from high angle summer sun
8. equipment bunker
   - fuel cell
   - CO_2 supply
   - hydrogen store
   - filtration system
   - biomass anaerobic digester
   - lipid extraction
   - inverter/ transformer
   - brown water control
   - boiler
   - nutrients
   - transformer
9. living area
10. work area
11. bedroom
12. hydrogen car re-fuel point
13. air intake and summer time cooling: air enters through adjustable vents at foot of main facade. air cools during passage over pool due to evaporative cooling
14. air exhaust: clerestory light provides light to rear of house HVAC heat recovery system recaptures warm exhaust air

N

Figure 5. AlgaeHouse Plan and Key

project shows that the use of algae as an energy generator within a house is not only feasible, but that cohabitation can result in a self sustainable symbiotic system which opens up many exciting architectural possibilities for 'green living'.

This recently concluded project, developed as part of a course module, has awoken great interest and enthusiasm within not only the algaetecture team, but from academic science publications (Wired, Common Future, Science in Society, BlueSci) and the wider popular media (BBC Radio). We feel that algae technologies could play a significant role in the future of our built environment. A web platform - www.algae-tecture.com - has been established that, it is hoped, will inspire fellow students, academics, and professionals to think of algae as a sustainable resource. We encourage you to get in touch if you have a general interest in algae or if you want to be involved in developing the algae living concept further.

Interview with Piers Taylor of Mitchell Taylor Workshop

Interview by Ranald Lawrence

Piers Taylor set up Mitchell Taylor Workshop with Rob Mitchell in 2005. Previously he studied in Australia under Glenn Murcutt. He leads Third Year Studio 3 at Cambridge with Meredith Bowles of Mole Architects, and founded the annual Studio in the Woods design charrette. Here he talks to Ranald Lawrence about the central ethos of his work: that it should engage with, and be informed by, its context. Piers's own house, Moonshine, is a self-built extension to a 1786 castellated stone building, 400 yards from the nearest road, constructed entirely out of materials that were carried to site by hand. It won the AJ Small Projects Award in 2009.

What do you think we have to do at the beginning of the twenty first century to redefine the relevance of architecture to society? Is 'sustainability' just a fashionable gimmick?

As a culture, we need to rethink our attitude to sustainability, away from quick fix bolt on solutions, reclaiming terms like intelligent design from the creationists. By intelligent design, I mean optimising a building to take advantage of where it is, developing a new typology about place, and reclaiming the 'local' from the nostalgiaists and the neo vernacularists.

What were the most important lessons you took from studying in Australia and how did you apply those lessons in your approach to practice in the UK?

I studied in Australia before words like sustainability and energy efficiency were commonly used. What was discussed at length, however, were issues of ecological sensitivity, issues of sustainability that were implicit rather than explicit. Words like 'place', in Australia, didn't mean forever mimicking vernacular traditions, but harnessing the intrinsic qualities of a site.

I first saw this when I went to visit Glenn Murcutt's Magney House (fig. 1) *on the south coast of New South Wales. Murcutt had given the first lecture I went to in the first week of my undergraduate degree, and in a sense, he gave me the road map for what we did when we started Mitchell Taylor Workshop. Murcutt's Magney House had a strategy that allowed the first chink of sunlight to enter the building on the day after the winter equinox (21st March in the southern hemisphere), and allowed, by the middle of winter, the sun to reach right to the back of the narrow plan and saturate the exposed thermal mass with heat. In summer, no direct sunlight was allowed to enter the building, and the building was clad in cheap, locally available, reflective corrugated metal. The roof form was pushed out to encourage air flow underneath it like an aerofoil and to allow a maximum surface area to collect that precious resource in Australia – water.*

How important do you think the precedent of simple agricultural buildings is to the sort of modern vernacular architecture Murcutt is now renowned for?

The agricultural reference was incidental; Murcutt is utterly unsentimental about an agricultural vernacular. What he does acknowledge, though, is that farmers have an instinctive knowledge of how to site

Figure 1. Glenn Murcutt - Magney House

a building so that rain is kept out, but light and ventilation allowed in.

What about the 's' word – what do you think it means to design sustainably? Can there be such a thing as truly 'sustainable' architecture?

When I set up the practice and began teaching, I never really used the word sustainability – my intention was that it was implicit in what we did. We never marketed ourselves as a practice that specialised in environmental design – but of course it just seemed to us that there was no other way of designing than intelligently. To be intelligent a building should have no option other than to engage with where it was and to adapt accordingly. It surprised us when clients came to us wanting a

Figure 2. Moonshine.

so called sustainable building, and their eyes would glaze over when we would talk of correct orientation, passive design, shading, day-lighting – to the point when one client said "you just don't get it – I want to feel smug. I need a solar panel even if it won't work."

Tell us about your work at Moonshine – was that born out of your experiences in Australia? How did the design evolve?

When we designed Moonshine, we attempted to demonstrate what I'd learned in Australia from masters like Glenn Murcutt. The site had no car access, and was on a sloping woodland site 7 miles outside Bath (fig 2).

There was a delicate eco system in that there was a mature moisture hungry ash tree night next to where we wanted to build, as well as rare bee orchids. We had to build in such a way that meant the water table remained undisturbed. We designed the glazing to respond to seasonal shading from the Ash. We examined prevailing winds, and designed spaces that were sheltered from these. The entire building section directed wind some distance from the house. We worked out where the morning sun came through the canopy, and located bedroom clerestory glazing to capture this. We measured rainfall, and the direction that it came in from, and worked out how we could open spaces up to the outside even in a gale (figs. 3, 4). We also looked at how farmers in the valley had built, and how they had responded to the local climatic conditions.

So what is the environmental strategy at Moonshine – is it a particularly technical building to live in or something much more intuitive?

At Moonshine, there are no solar panels, ground source heat pumps or PVs, but the building consumes precious few resources. It needs no artificial light in daylight hours whatever the weather. Because of capturing and retaining of heat when we want it, the heating season is very short, and when it does need heating in the severe winter months we use wood grown on site. The building used so little material in its construction (fig. 5)*, all of which had to be carried down a woodland path by hand, that in severe storms, it has guy ropes anchoring the building down. Conveniently, the building is sited so that we can watch, and predict, the weather coming in* (fig. 6).

Perhaps most importantly – recognising James Wines maxim "there's no sustainability without art" – the joy of the site is maintained: the building is completely transparent at ground level to allow uninterrupted views down through the site, through the house, to the bottom of the valley (fig. 7). *Similarly although utterly distinct from the site (it is a building ON the ground, not OFF the ground), the building merges with the surrounding canopy* (fig. 8).

And your teaching at Cambridge – is that informed by a similar concern for properly understanding the environment and integrating aspects of it into a design?

With my teaching partner Meredith Bowles in Studio 3, this is how we work. Our students begin each year by constructing 'tools' that allow them to gather data relating to the landscape in which their major project will be set. These tools meas-

Figure 3. Sketch Section.
Figure 4 (below). Sketch Plan.
Figure 5 (right) lightweight construction.

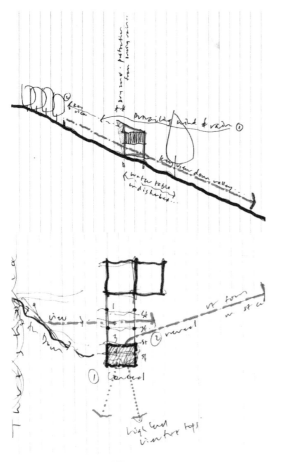

ure, for example: porosity, topography, wind quality and sound frequency. Armed with this, they design buildings that have an intelligence to how they are located, meaning that few need bolt on quick fix eco-bling solutions to make them perform.

For the last two years, we have been working on the edge of Ely where the city joins the fens. Roger Deakin described this area as one of the most mysterious in Britain. It is a landscape defined by water and is in part below sea level. It depends on a complicated series of man made drainage ditches, pumps and dykes to keep the water at bay. Questions of how to site a building, how it meets the ground, where ground level is, how rainwater is collected, become critical.

What about Studio in the Woods – is that also about the exploration of local environmental characteristics and how they inform what to build?

We set up the Studio in the Woods (with Feilden Clegg Bradley, Mole Architects, Gianni Botsford Architects, Kate Darby, Ted Cullinan and Erect Architecture) five years ago to explore issues of site specificity (fig. 9). Whilst of course there was an overriding architectural preoccupation and a desire to test idea through making at 1:1, there was also, embedded in the programme, questions of where materials come from, how we could use them, how we could fix them with no mechanical fixings, how much we could do with a finite set of materials.
In addition to this, Gianni Botsford's work at Studio in the Woods has been largely to do with issues of light – exploring how a building volume can be optimised to take advantage of natural light conditions, as evidenced in his Light House on a back land site in Notting Hill, and

Figures 6, 7 & 8. Moonshine and its connection with its external envrionment.

the self shading *Casa Kike* in Costa Rica. It was rewarding to see how a student from one of his workshops went on, in my studio at University (fig. 10), *to design a sublime light-weight structure that was floated into the site (meaning nothing was disturbed), sat on the ground using several slender poles, had a strategy for light penetration developed from his work with Gianni, and that ranged from qualitative and experiential to knowing exactly where to locate the (woven copper) water tank to collect maximum solar gain.*

What do you think the future holds for architecture? Does a drive for greater 'sustainability' imply a return to an earlier, simpler, way of building?

The past is very definitely not the future. I'm a great believer in technology and modernity. I am resolutely un-nostalgic, but I wonder sometimes whether as a society we've lost the ability to recognise where we are. *I'm always surprised when I ask a group of students where north is, how few know. If perhaps we discovered an instinct for where we were, we'd have no option but to design accordingly.*

Figure 9 (below). Building in the landscape.

Figure 10 (right). Studio 3 questions the nature of sustainability, permenance and the experiential qualities of space.

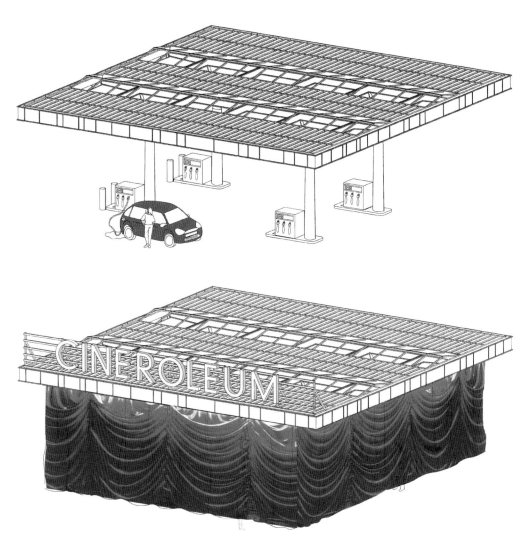

The Cineroleum (cinema + petroleum)

by The Cineroleum Team

A TEMPORARY CINEMA BUILT IN A DISUSED PETROL STATION ON CLERKENWELL ROAD, LONDON

The Cineroleum was collectively designed and built to re-imagine a traditional cinema in an unusual setting. Conceived as a riff on the decadent interiors of the 'golden age', the Cineroleum took its formal inspirations from cinema's rich history of ornate and decorative symbols.

This combination of a concern to use salvaged materials and yet to capture some of the extravagance of what cinema-going once was delivered a strangely timeless total experience: a combination of the classic, the unusual and the downright seedy: a stand-alone ticket booth in the middle of the old supermarket, flip-up seats fashioned from

Figure 1. As a petrol station / as a Cineroleum during screening.

Figure 2. Entrance door to cineroleum foyer, Tyvek uniforms.

reclaimed scaffolding boards, a large festoon curtain made entirely out of silver Tyvek hanging from a petrol station forecourt roof, and neon flickering above a knackered old fire escape. These were some of the unexpected adornments to Clerkenwell Road's infamous deserted petrol station.

The Cinema Museum lent fourteen red velvet seats, which sat interspersed amongst their scaffolding-board descendants. The wooden sign that was fixed to the fore-court roof to face the street was made out of some shelving found at the back of the service station shop. Not only were materials recycled, but also motifs: the foyer furniture's marquetry was inspired by images of intricate old projectors, elegant

sign boards, ticket stampers and curtains from the *House of Cinema Knowledge*. Their miniature size was down to the fact that they were adapted from some Key Stage 1 furniture, donated by The Lonesome School in Mitcham.

A COLLABORATIVE DESIGN PROCESS

Suddenly confronted with some of the mundanities of conventional architectural practice, the initial progenitors of the Cin-eroleum sensed that a temporary, self-build project might be the antidote to the lengthy and often alienated process of making build-ings.

Figure 3. Cineroleum with Tyvek curtain up (Image: Morley von Sternberg).
Figure 4 (below). Seating design.

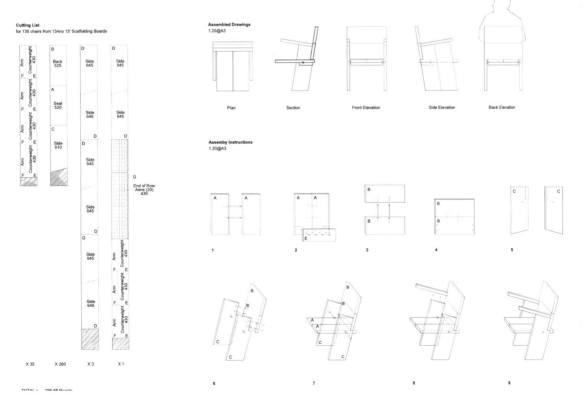

This group soon grew as friends, acquaintances and members of the public seized the opportunity to be involved. The remarkable generosity of individuals and organisations we have encountered attests to the power of the not-for-profit project: many of these groups have been crucial to the Cineroleum's realisation: The Cinema Museum, Flint's Theatrical Chandlers, Ken Creasey Ltd. and Studio Dekka being just a few.

Working collaboratively has allowed us to be involved in aspects of a project usually beyond our remit; the boundaries between design, construction and the planning and running of the event becoming blurred. At least twelve people were needed to raise the curtain at the end of each performance; many more to run the bar, allocate the tickets and oversee the projection. Work was certainly not finished after opening night.

Figure 5. Cineroleum model.
Figure 6 (below). View to Clerenwell Rd.
Figure 7 (right). Cineroleum empty.
Figure 8 (right). Interior screening.

Occasional sirens or motorbikes acted as reminders of the proximity of the road; thus it was Duel that turned out to be the most fitting choice of the programme. It was only on the raising of the curtain each night that many audience members even realised that the pavement was little more than a few metres away, Clerkenwell Road continuing like any other night save a regular stream of baffled passers-by.

A PILOT PROJECT

The Cineroleum acts as a protest not only against the bland homogeneity of the contemporary cinema-going experience, but also as reminder of the need for flexible, open urban spaces and an open-minded attitude towards their use. Now is the time to take advantage of the recent postponement of so many large developments. With 4,000 petrol stations lying derelict in the UK, this pilot project demonstrates the potential for their transformation as exciting and unusual spaces.

Image: Richard Bryant

Frank's Café

by Paloma Gormley & Lettice Drake

Frank's was designed through a series of sketchup models bounced between Cambridge and London while Paloma was finishing her third year and Lettice was working full time at Cotteral and Vermulen. The cafe was commissioned to accompany the sculpture show Bold Tendencies. From July to September each year the top four floors of a disused multi-storey car park becomes a new public space in Peckham.

Paloma and Lettice assembled a volunteer workforce and together constructed the café over a period of three weeks, with a budget of £5,000. The monolithic concrete car park became the host for a small temporary cafe strapped parasite-like to its uppermost deck. Constructed primarily from reclaimed scaffolding boards, it was designed in order that it could be removed without a trace, to be resurrected each summer. The simple design provides just enough protection from the elements without obscuring the visitor's experience of, and relationship to, the site itself: the huge exposed top deck and the breathtaking views over London.

Paloma Gormley and Lettice Drake studied Architecture at Cambridge University. They founded Practice Architecture, a design-build practice working primarily in London, in 2009.

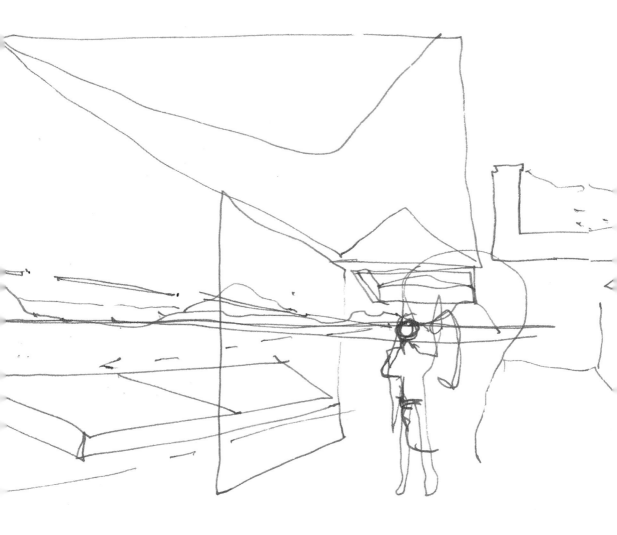

Architecture as Medium, Environment as Object, User as Subject

by Kevin Fellingham

Kevin Fellingham is a Design Fellow at Cambridge University who jointly leads the MPhil in Environmental Design Studio. Kevin worked at Rick Mather Architects and Arup Associates, before forming his own practice, Kevin Fellingham Architecture + Urbanism, in 2006. He is a graduate of the University of the Witwatersrand in Johannesburg and of MIT, where he won the Ralph Adams Cram Award for outstanding interdisciplinary research. His House J in South Africa won the World Architecture News House of the Year Award in 2007.

INTRODUCTION

I want to talk about a very general way of thinking about architecture and its relationship to the broader environment and a very specific response to a particular place and programme. I would also want to question the often antagonistic relationship between two fundamental ways of thinking about the way architecture mediates our relationship with the environment. One is experiential and symbolic – the construction of a meaningful relationship to a particular place. The other is a technical response to the environment, using built form to reduce the impact of the environment on ourselves. I have chosen to explain the use of architecture as a medium for understanding and working in the environment – through a project carried out for my family near the southern tip of my native South Africa – in order to move from the general to the specific, the objective to the subjective, from the landscape to the interior.

OBJECT

Anything that is visible or tangible and is relatively stable in form.
A thing, person, or matter to which thought or action is directed.
The end toward which effort or action is directed; goal; purpose.
Anything that may be apprehended intellectually: objects of thought
The thing of which a lens or mirror forms an image.
Something toward which a cognitive act is directed.

The drive to reduce the energy consumption of buildings is an aspect of the latter – if we do not do so, the environment will self adjust to the detriment of our current political economy. That we should build fewer, smaller, naturally lit and naturally ventilated buildings closer together, using locally sourced, low embodied energy, carbon sequestering materials, internally organised to promote pleasure of use and social interaction, externally massed so as to combine sensibly together into urban ensembles that on a broader scale promote social interaction, and constructed using socially equitable or enabling labour practices should be taken as read. It really shouldn't be that difficult, should it? Except that it is.

There is no necessary connection between these two kinds of response to the environment – a building might well offer a feeling of intimate connection with the natural world whilst causing irreparable damage to the ecosystem, or equally may have a carbon negative footprint and provide a niche environment for an endangered species whilst being a wound in the flesh of the earth and a source of psychological distress to all who experience it. This is not to say that a way of building which satisfies both a phenomenological and a technical agenda is impossible, just that there is no natural connection between the two. Architecture has a dual structure, metaphoric, and physical, and it is very rare for those two ways of thinking to map directly onto one another. When this occurs it is either the result of a long refined vernacular knowledge or as a result of working with an intimate and fluent understanding of the medium of architecture, and is in the latter case (almost) always likely to be a fiction that appears for a while to be real. The current focus on the energy embodied in and expended by buildings is a necessary corrective, but offers very little by way of architectural significance or environmental richness – it says almost nothing about topography, hydrology, biodiversity, landscape, urban form, and very little about architectural form, structure or use. Taken along with a much broader set of technical constraints and cultural aspirations it might however contribute new material, physical and metaphoric to the medium of architecture.

MEDIUM

An intervening substance through which something else is transmitted or carried on.
An agency by which something is

accomplished, conveyed, or transferred.
    A method or way of expressing something.
    A substance that something grows in, lives in, or moves through.

Architecture mediates the relationship between ourselves and the environment. It can be seen as a medium for interacting with the environment, natural or man-made, rather than as a thing in itself. Like any medium, it is resistant, it has its own characteristics, its own history, which must be acknowledged and understood if one is to be able to make use of it. Architectural significance lies in the relationship between the subject and the medium, the medium and the environment and the intended relationship between the subject and the object – the person and the natural environment.

A work of architecture can be both a result of work within the medium of architecture, and an element of a larger work producing a (largely) man-made environment, or a device (technical, social, functional or aesthetic) constructing or communicating a relationship between a person and the environment.

Architecture can make use of the raw material provided by the environment technically (as building material, as light, air or water) or experientially (as space, as view, as cooling, heating or ornament) or more usually in combination.

Architecture is essentially a conservative discipline; it is too subject to the vested interests of users, owners, clients, con-tractors, craftsmen, lawyers and insurance salesmen to be otherwise. It will change in response to a new societal framework centred on a low carbon, low energy, under-capitalised economy. Those changes will be incremental, pragmatic, technical, piecemeal, compromised and contingent.

All building is already all of these things, but the best architecture somehow makes a coherent narrative of these conditions. More environmentally sound buildings will eventually become the norm, becoming invisible, just as structurally sound and pre-dictable buildings have become the norm. Structural stability creates interest only when it is not present. If more sustainable buildings do not become the norm (as part of a more sustainable social settlement), buildings will contribute to societal collapse due to conflict over resources, and archi-tecture will by default become less intensive in material and energy use.

Architecture only changes fundamentally when one or more of the of the funda-mental factors determining the way it is produced changes. The modern move-ment saw a dramatic shift brought about by a radical change in aesthetic possibilities, structural potential and social needs. More recently, the representational possibilities of computation have enabled a shift in the aes-thetic and structural bravura of architecture allied to an economic bubble, itself brought about by increased computational power. In this context, possible architectures have seemed endless, yet really significant build-ings less so. This would seem to be a result of the ability to generate and construct forms that cannot be imagined without the mediation of visualisation software, and a severing of the relationship between form, use and structure seen to be fundamental to architectural meaning. It may well be that the Vitruvian triad is not essential, but rather a habitual way of thinking which has come to an end. If this is the case, then self generating formal experiment will be limited only by economic limits – including sustainable use of resources or not. That is one end for the humanist tradition in architecture.

SUBJECT

That which thinks, feels, perceives, intends, etc., as contrasted with the objects of thought, feeling, etc.
The self or ego.
A person or thing that undergoes or may undergo some action.
A person or thing under the control or influence of another.

The experience of a building or environment as architecture, that is to say something meaningful or significant, is not a characteristic of the built object, it is a subjective experience dependent on the person experiencing or using the building. That some architects are able to consistently produce environments seen as significant is best understood by their ability to understand their own response to an existing situation and to imagine a new situation in which another person is likely to experience a similar response. Architecture acts here as the medium for an inter-subjective communication about an objective situation outside of language, and even outside of visuality. The relationship between the technical and experiential at the scale of building and body is where the architectural event can occur. The accumulation of aesthetically, structurally and functionally integral results forms a typology of pre-existing solutions that form the disciplinary memory of architecture.

The realisation that human action cannot transcend the laws of nature, nor in all useful likelihood the limits of our planet, is another end of the anthropocentric worldview. Humans are not the measure of all things, but are part of nature, capable of reflection on their position within nature. Their perceived subjectivity is an attribute of nature, a function of a mind evolved to understand and operate within the natural environment, to read the landscape, and the patterns of growth of fauna, the patterns of use of other animals, human and non human, in order to make productive use of the environment. This evolutionary relationship to the environment in no way presupposes that our use of the environment will be wise or sustainable.

Architecture is a way of mediating our relationship to the environment, be it natural, manmade or a composite of the natural and the manmade. Architecture is an all encompassing medium, we are within it and so its mediation tends to become invisible to us. The relationship between the environment as object, architecture as medium and ourselves as subject can operate at a number of levels. At its most basic, there could be a relationship between us and nature which is entirely unmediated – as there is between a jellyfish and the ocean, or a relationship where a natural object might serve, unmodified, to our advantage. The occupation of caves by the San people of Southern Africa as a place of refuge and of prospect is a case in point. The idea of making use of a situation is in this case the architecture *(figs. 1, 2)*.

One could modify an existing feature to make it better serve ones needs, as in the Anasazi settlements, where landscape features and built features are merged to produce a composite environment *(figs. 3, 4)*. More usually, we transform natural materials into products that we arrange into buildings sitting on the ground, arranged so as to produce maximum return on investment. These are not differences of principle, but differences of degree. For all the close relationship between the Anasazi settlements and their surrounding environment, their society collapsed due to over-exploitation of the resources provided by that environment.

It might well be possible to imagine a way of building in which we have no contact with the natural world and yet are able to use nature sparingly enough to carry on ad-infinitum. And so a close relationship with the land is no guarantee of a sustainable relationship with the environment. I would like to think though, that living in a close relationship to the natural environment might encourage a relationship of respect for the environment, and in turn an understanding of the need to avoid unnecessarily damaging the environment.

WORK

The relationship between building and landscape has always been at the centre of my thinking about architecture. Growing

Figure 1.

up on the fringes of a developing city, as the veld was built over into suburbia and the indigenous vegetation replaced with lawns and flowerbeds, I was conscious that something was being lost while something else was being gained: I loved to watch things being built, or later to build things myself, but regretted that access to the wide horizons was always moving further away. For those who grow up in cities, or in countryside where everything has already been hedged in, reshaped and softened; the sense of identifying oneself with a topography might seem anachronistic, or romantic, or worse.

The South Africa of my youth was not a place of which to be proud – identifying oneself with the dominant culture was unthinkable, but not identifying oneself with the landscape was impossible. That identity was not, however, simple – the apparently natural world was marked all over with the signs of disputed ownership: barbed wire fences, Boer War blockhouses, abandoned villages, San rock art, erosion due to over-grazing, mine dumps, electric fences, towns split into two with a wasteland where the centre should be.

The conflict over land and belonging meant that any simple identification with a landscape could never be innocent, and yet the sense of connection with place is

Figure 2.

undeniable, yet irresolvable. Conflict over land is of course not just a conflict over identities, it is first and foremost a conflict over the right to exploit the resources of a place, with culture used to construct an apparently natural relationship to the environment: the right to ownership.

Nobody, however, really owns the world. All places have existed before us, and will continue to do so without us. The sense of identifying with a place is not that a place belongs to us, but that we belong to a place. Human consciousness evolved in response to the natural environment, of which it is an attribute, and it is unsurprising that we find beauty, meaning, consolation and pleasure in nature: it is in our nature to do so.

Figure 3 (left).
Figure 4 (above).

 We designed a house above Simon's Town in-between an architectural conservation area and a national park. Due to a fold in the east facing coastline around the massif of the Simonsberg, the site slopes due north, looking out past the layered headlands of the striated sandstone topography towards the rest of Africa *(figs. 5, 6)*. The topography means that the bay below is sheltered from the prevailing south-westerly winds which give the place one of its names: The Cape of Storms. The town below consists of small white buildings with flat or low-pitched roofs, stepping up the slopes with steep alleyways and stairs between them. The buildings generally have a formal face to the street, and break down into thin spans of construction, determined by the span of a simple trussed or lean-to roof. The mountainside behind the settlement is a scree slope with sandstone overhangs, which once gave shelter to the earliest human occupants of the land. It was once covered in the characteristic fynbos vegetation of the Cape, hugely diverse in species and subspecies – each differentially evolved for a specific environmental niche. This vegetation had been largely destroyed by invasive species, but the landscape is now slowly being modified to encourage the regrowth of the indigenous vegetation.

The house is located within this context, but also represents this context, and of course modifies it *(fig. 7)*. The relationship to the land and to the landscape is multivalent. The house frames a view of the bay, screening out the foreground and the glare of the sky to construct a picture of the environment *(fig. 8)*. The rear of the house is cut into the slope, the sandstone scree extending onto the terraces, the replanted fynbos slowly merging with the recovering flora, the boundary between built and deposited becoming blurred through natural and artificial processes *(fig. 9)*.

At the beginning of the design process the decision was made to leave out everything we didn't like about most buildings.

The house consists of four terraces cut into the scree slope of the Simonsberg, three blocks, the spaces between the blocks, and the spaces between the blocks and the walls of the excavation. The first space is a forecourt, the second space is a terrace 4.5 metres wide, and the third space is 300 mm wide, forming a skylight that brings light into the centre of the plan on two levels. The fourth space is a wild garden formed between the house and the mountain.

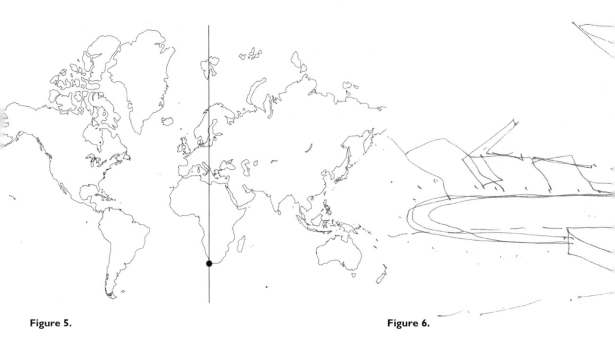

Figure 5.

Figure 6.

Many of those things are necessary – meaning that design and detail problems had to be solved from first principles. A set of proscriptive rules were developed, rules which state what cannot be done, rather than rules that define what can be done. The intention was to find a rigorous and systematic way of working which would lead to unexpected creative decisions.

A dialogue between solid and void is developed at all scales of the design, beginning with the layered view of headlands receding to the north, which is echoed in the layers of building and courtyards receding to the south. This analogy is resolved as a reality, when turning towards the view, the layers of the house form the foreground to the layers of the landscape beyond.

The interaction between blank surfaces, experienced close up, which foreground the material character of the house, and frameless openings which allow the eye and the space to reach out to the horizon, is carefully organised by the routes through the house. These routes are in places narrow and steep, in others they are part of the spaces to which they give access. The compression and expansion spaces allow the body to experience architecture directly, through the ears, the hands and the

– respecting the difference between what is structural and permanent and what is useful and subject to change of use.

Absences, blanks and gaps are used throughout the house to articulate experience – the view is hidden in places to make it stronger in others, shadow gaps allow each material to be independent of others, windows slide on the outside of walls so that no detail intrudes between the interior and the exterior.

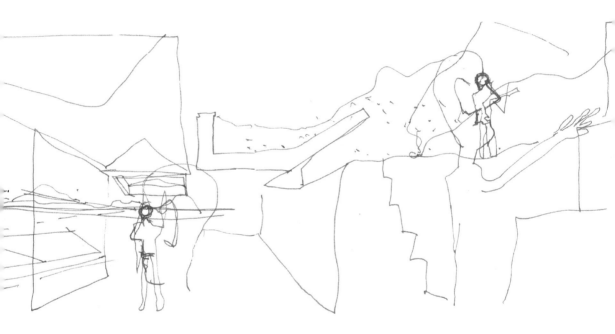

feet. The visual and physical systems are juxtaposed to create the richest possible variety of experiences, approaching vertigo or claustrophobia at one extreme, and extreme calm at the other.

The spaces of the house are domesticated through the use of built in furniture and sliding screens in the same way in which we would fit out an old building for a new use

Every detail was thought through from first principles so as to reduce it to it essentials. The dwelling and the site are coextensive – there is no left over space.

The house exploits natural ventilation, using the stair tower to draw air through the house from all levels. A careful study of the microclimate was made in order to find a site sheltered from the cape winds,

with a variety of outdoor spaces ensuring there is always a quiet corner. The house references the old buildings of Simon's Town in its colour, the simplicity and scale of the main rooms, its direct use of material, and the use of square and golden section proportions; it is accessed up an alleyway like those of the old part of the town, the steelwork is painted the grey of the naval vessels, and the overhangs echo those of the hillside above the house. The landscaping has been designed as if the house were a part of the hill, with restia on the flat roofs and fynbos retaining the slopes.

Figure 7 (opposite, top).
Figure 8 (opposite, bottom).
Figure 9 (above).

The Form of Light: Sverre Fehn's Norrköping Villa

by Katia Papkovskaia

INTRODUCTION

Parallels may be drawn between the ideas of Martin Heidegger and Sverre Fehn. The language both Heidegger and Fehn employ in their writings is strikingly similar – themes of life and death, the horizon and the boundary, and the house and the dwelling are examined by both the architect and the philosopher, showing Fehn's regard for Heidegger's teachings. In his introduction to 'The Thought of Construction', Kenneth Frampton proposes a link between the work of Fehn and the ideas of Heidegger:

'For Fehn, as for Heidegger, the ultimate sense of place is bound up with man's presence in the land and his literal inscription in the earth's surface.'[1]

Katia Papkovskaia studied the MPhil in Environmental Design, Option A, researching the environmental qualities of plan typologies in domestic architecture. She studied Architecture at University College Dublin, graduating in 2009.

Sverre Fehn's writings reveal the poetry of inhabiting and pay homage to vernacular tradition, craft and landscape, which constitute the perfect dwelling as envisaged by his contemporary Christian Norberg-Schulz. Fehn's story of a dwelling evolves from the past, builds on precedent, and reconciles the inhabitant with his space, making him the *dweller*. The metaphysical element always present in Fehn's work resists the transient essence of modernity, becoming part of the *'eternal and immutable'*. Heidegger's fourfold exists in the narrative of Sverre Fehn's work – in 'The Thought of Construction' the earth, the divine, heaven and mortal unite. Yet Fehn can also be described essentially as a Modernist – his architectural point of departure is more akin to the work of Mies van der Rohe[2] than the Norwegian vernacular tradition.

Despite this, symbolic meaning, especially in his handling of light, is an integral part of Fehn's work. I am going to discuss the Norrköping Villa *(fig. 1)* as a manifestation of Fehn's ideas of dwelling, a house where his poetic language and a technological spirit of the epoch merge in a modern vernacular form.

Norrköping Villa was designed as a competition entry in 1963 for a Nordic House Parade in Norrköping, Sweden. The villa was one of the five villas being exhibited; Sverre Fehn's design representing Norway. Unlike his Boedker Houses, or Villa Schreiner, the Norrköping Villa was not constructed for a specific client, and is the only house designed by Sverre Fehn for a competition. It was to be a representation

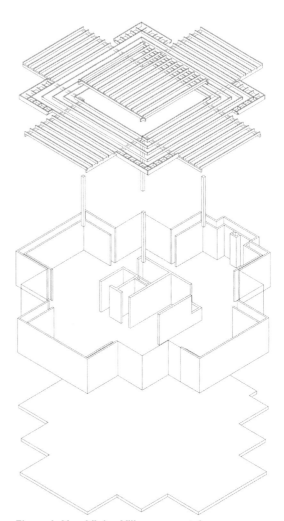

Figure 1. Norrköping Villa axonometric.

of a house for a generic family of four, with an area of 150 square meters.[3] The villa represents the architect's attitude towards dwelling in the epoch of modernism, taking into account the values of society in general, not a specific owner with his individual needs. It symbolises the progress of modernism and Fehn's regard for its ideas, which he reinterprets in a Nordic tradition.

THE VILLA

Sverre Fehn's poetic musings on the Norrköping Villa begin his written work,

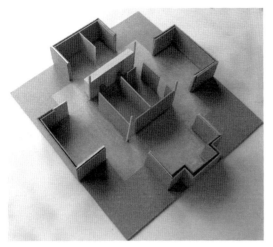

Figure 2. Norrköping Villa model and aerial of site (right).

'The Thought of Construction', which consists of a series of conversations held between the architect and Per Olaf Fjeld. The plan of the Norrköping Villa is proof of his thesis:

> **'The corners of the house are sources of light. At this point the structure separates and creates a discourse of illumination. The corners reflect the activity of the day. At night a child's display on a window-sill reminds us of a fading day, while potted plants await the sunlight of the morning. Thus the corner is where the day begins and ends.'[4]**

Relationship to the given site appears to be less significant here than in Fehn's other houses. Norrköping Villa is situated on a flat piece of land on the crossing of two roads with other Nordic villas, which include the Finnish villa by Kristian Gullichsen and the Swedish villa by Lennart Kvarnström, as well as other houses in close proximity. The site lacks the expansive Norwegian landscape of the Bødtker Houses or the private suburban woodland shielded by the Schreiner House. The poetry in Fehn's other houses lies within the site, they are spaces for which a room has been made for. Norrköping villa is introverted; it creates a world within itself (fig. 2).

The entrance faces north and as Kenneth Frampton notes, the point of entry is determined solely by site considerations.[5] A cruciform plan based on a 2.5 metre grid wraps around a toplit core (fig. 3). Four glazed corners, the cyclopean eyes, are recessed and open to the surrounding landscape. They fit precisely to the module of the timber beams carrying the roof. Four windowless alcoves form rooms in between the corners that are shrouded in shadow, denied any direct light. These complete the plan and create within the house eight distinct areas – four brightly lit and four enveloped in darkness around a central network of service spaces. The alcoves are places of silence, of the night, of time when activity within the four eyes of the house subsides. The plan is symmetrical, the niches almost identical, except where one is recessed again to create a niche within a niche for

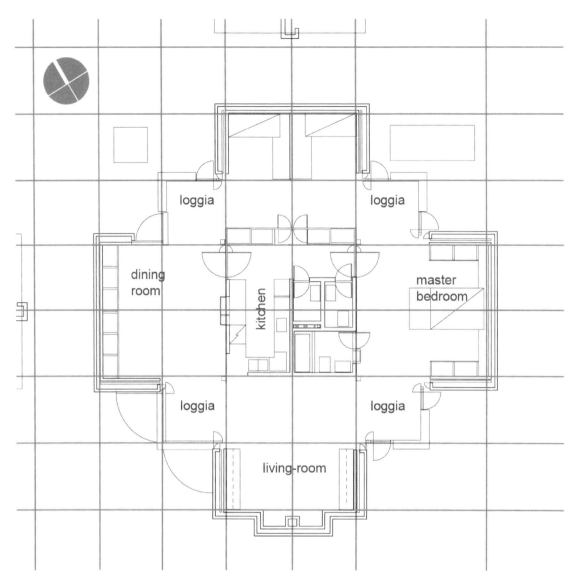

Figure 3. Norrköping Villa plan on 2.5m grid.

the fireplace, layering the shadows.

The wooden partitions that slide out of the brick cavity walls and rotating glazed panels transform the house according to the needs of the dweller:

'Where the house of isolated rooms is restricted to a singular mood, the house at Norrköping displays, through its openings and changing enclosures, shifts in mood and pattern of behaviour. The sliding walls regulate the light and secure the silence of the night. The house is a reference in relation to each day. The door mechanism is a challenge to make the place coexist with one's temperament.' [6]

The four alcoves villa the more private spaces: the living-room to the south-west, master bedroom to the south-east, dining room to the north-west and two children's bedrooms separated by a timber panel to the north-east.

The glazed corners are loggias – there, the activity is not prescribed and when all partitions are drawn back one can walk around the core through the continuous space that is created (*fig. 4*). This flexibility of space adopts the house to the daily rhythm of occupation:

'When the son leaves, his room dissolves the loneliness of separation. Only the objects will be left behind, for his room will revert to the totality of the house'.[7]

THE PLACE

In 'Nightlands', Christian Norberg-Schulz explores light as a phenomenon that characterises the north. He compares the qualities of the light in Italy and Greece to that of Scandinavia. Southern sun, rising in the morning and reaching its zenith, defines the landscape and gives it identity. Horizon is clear and thus boundaries and spaces attain their unity. The light in Scandinavia is quite different:

'Here in the North, the sun does not rise to the zenith but grazes things obliquely and dissolves in an interplay of light and shadow.'[8]

The Nordic light blurs the horizon; ever-changing weather and fragmented landscape generate a world that is hardly complete but rather unfinished and disjointed.[9] Norberg-Schulz proposes two approaches to the architectural interpretation of a space in landscape, one where the landscape of which the space is a part is complimented, and another where features that the environment lacks are added. In the south the quality of light defines a Eucledian whole; it implies unity and geometry in architecture and hence the architecture pays tribute to the existing topography.[10]

Nordic space is given identity through its light and is proposed by Norberg-Schulz to be indefinitely more complex than in the south.

Figure 4. Image left, partitions opened to create one spcae, image right, partitions colsed to make five enclosed rooms.

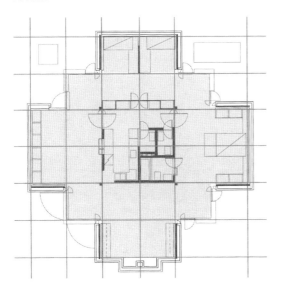
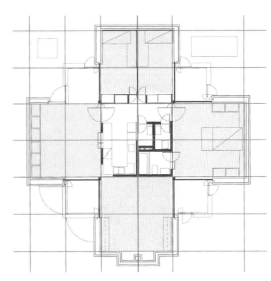

Here, with the presence of the summer night, it is only on winter's nights that the sky becomes large, whole.

'Over the snow-covered earth it vaults, saturated with a peculiar "dark light".'[11]

Horizon and continuity are questioned and the Nordic psyche is shaped by this – the Norwegian term *rom* (space, room) derives from *rydning* (clearing).[12] Nordic space can thus be compared to a clearing in a forest, where the light and the landscape blur the boundary.

Sverre Fehn muses on the difference in light quality from the north to the south:

'In Greece light creates your architecture. It suffices that you scratch the marble with your fingernails, and the scratch remains visible. Up here in the North, light is weak and we would not have seen anything. Here our architectural world is a world without shadow. The shadow of a stone is different from that of an autumn leaf. The shadow penetrated the material and reveals its message. Through our skin, ears and eyes we communicate with the material.'[13]

He is responsive to the Northern light and its ability to give identity to his architecture. The Norwegian Pavillion creates in Venice the 'shadowless' world of Scandinavia[14] *(fig. 5)*. Southern sun is diffused by closely-spaced beams that support translucent gutters lined by fallen leaves which form the roof cover. The space created beneath the canopy of the pavilion represents the architect's acute awareness of light as a giver of distinctiveness to Norwegian archi-

Figure 5. The Norwegian pavillion in Venice (model: Ranald Lawrence).

tecture. There is a stark contrast between the Venetian light outside the pavilion and the gentle muted light inside; the light inherent to its source is calmed.[15]

It is as if the qualities of the north embodied in the landscape are rooted in Sverre Fehn's architecture and emerge in his designs intuitively, almost on a subconscious level:

'I have tried all my life to run away from the Nordic tradition. But I realise it is difficult to run away from yourself.'[16]

And the Norrköping Villa exemplifies this: the band of windows raised above the central core is a lantern in the night sky, it pools the summer's night light into the central core *(fig. 6)*. Glazed loggias illuminate themselves during the day, maintaining a shadow in the remaining rooms. Light does not cut through the villa – its diagonal path is broken by the central core allowing only obscured visual connection between the corners. The temptation to play with the possibilities of a free façade – to open the alcoves housing the living and the dining areas to the landscape, and provide relief from the overpowering shadows – is resisted.

Both Norberg-Schulz and Sverre Fehn refer to a dwelling as a 'cave'; the earth as a common 'room' and a place of security. In Norrköping the four alcoves are cavern-like rooms that wrap around the central service core of the villa. The mortar joints of the brickwork trap shadows in the alcoves, and subtly diffuse the light.

The fireplace is recessed into the brick fabric of the living space and private seating is built into the brick wall. It is a physical reminder of a time when daylight was the only source of illumination and fire the sole giver of light in the night:

'The night taking over with a 'room' that had no limit. Its nature was that of silence. The open fire yielded points of light in the night.'[17]

The darkness around the fireplace is in itself an embodiment of the metaphysical, of man's way of primitive dwelling before the coming of electricity. Shadow carries with it a personal scale, and the room has no limits or boundaries. Sverre Fehn beautifully describes the fading of the fire and the change in the perception of the room that comes with it: as the flame grows, the room

Figure 6. Norrköping Villa plan demonstrating light entering the house.

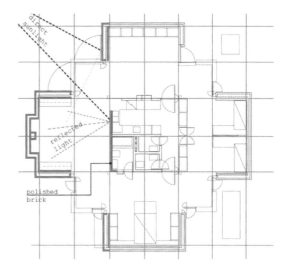

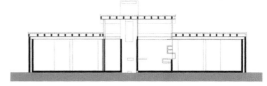

becomes larger, as it diminishes, the room shrinks with it:

'At that time the light one carried defined the 'room' around the body, the body participated in the light and was inseparable from its source. As the fire ebbed, the point of light withdrew until the 'larger' room was complete.'[18]

The darkness is perceived as a welcome guest; rather, the electrical light is the enemy. Fehn celebrates the timeless quality of the open fire: the alcove keeps the flame, unbroken brick walls embrace the fire and gather the dwellers. The night is content with the light from the fire and the repose of its inhabitants.[19]

A ROTONDA OF THE NORTH?

After the Norrköping villa was built, Sverre Fehn acknowledged similarities between it and Villa Rotonda (fig. 7). He draws on this coincidental resemblance to compose a lyrical conversation with the master himself and examine the formal rigour present in both villas:

'In this house I met Palladio. He was tired, but all the same he spoke:

"You have put all the utilities, bath, toilet and kitchen in the centre of the house. I made a large room of it, you know, and the dome with the opening was without glass. When I planned the house it was a challenge toward nature – rain, air, heat and cold could fill the room."

"And the four directions", I replied.

"Oh yes, you know," and he became smaller. "At that time we were about to lose the horizon. You have opened the corners," he stopped a little. "You are on the way toward losing the globe."

"Tell me more," I said. His voice began to weaken, but he whispered:

"All constructed thoughts are related to death." And then he was gone.'[20]

Villa Rotonda stands proudly on the Italian hilltop, raised on a pediment. The setting is theatrical; the sharp horizon of the Italian countryside is glorified and Palladio admires it in his Quattro Libri:

'The four fronts are dictated by the hilltop site, it is atop a little mountain (Monticello) of very easy ascent, and is washed on one side by the navigable river, Bacchiglione, and on the other side is surrounded by other very pleasant hills, which create the appearance of an enormous amphitheatre.'[21]

This conforms to Christian Norberg-Shulz's description of the built environment in the south, 'the southern world constitutes a lucid whole where each thing 'knows' what it is'. The landscape and the architecture do not merge, they coexist. The Norrköping Villa sits humbly in its site; its scale and materiality relates to the surroundings. Spaces within respond to the size of a man and are without hierarchy. The outside is always within reach – whether through large sliding panels in the summer or smaller pivoted openings in winter. The boundary between enclosure and the exterior is blurred; the house sits in the landscape like a clearing in a forest.

The orientation of the two villas is similar. In Rotonda, in order for each room to receive sun, the design is rotated 45 degrees from each cardinal point of the compass. Norrköping Villa is also shifted similarly, allowing the sun to enter the corners throughout the day. Sverre Fehn distributes the functions within the villa so that the living-room receives reflected light at the beginning and end of the day for most

Figure 7. Villa Rotunda - Plan and Section.

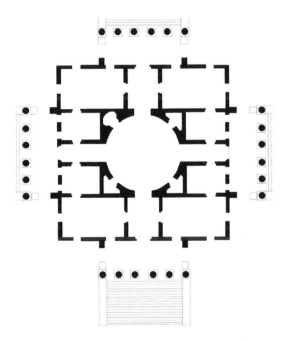

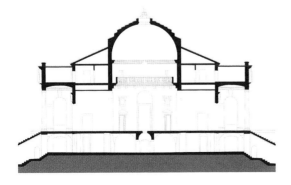

of the year, and the two glazed loggias on either side of the children's room benefit from the afternoon sun. Palladio, however, assigns the same functions to the spaces around the central dome. In Villa Rotonda, the dweller's daily routine is not accommodated to the path of the sun, if he wishes to follow the light tracing its way around the villa, this would be done for sheer enjoyment, not necessity.

Where Fehn places loggias, Palladio creates rooms, and the glazed corners in Norrköping become apartments in Rotonda; but both buildings contain four private rooms and four places to provide relief to the outside. Villa Rotunda's central space is the 'living-room'; in Norrköping, this room is shifted to one of the alcoves to become a more intimate space in the villa *(fig. 8)*. A memory of the Villa's lifted dome remains in the form of a lantern raised above the service core.

In Norrköping, it is the light that rules. It pierces the villa selectively, and the generous clerestory windows above the central core serve only the spaces beneath. The light dictates the character of the spaces, and from the owner's account, it also shapes the way the villa is occupied.

THE EXPERIENCE OF LIGHT

The Norrkoping Villa was bought straight after construction in 1964 by Professor Bo Sylvan, who was the former director of the Art Museum in Norrköping. He has lived there with his wife and children to this day, and it is interesting to learn how the house has fulfilled the expectations of the architect and its dwellers.[22] The inhabitants use the house the way Fehn had imagined it, and the sliding panels are used by both adults and children to establish their own boundaries within the free-flowing space. They connect with the landscape through opening the glazed corners when needed:

When going to bed we close the walls to the bedroom, so did once our children in their rooms (and also when they wanted to be for themselves at daytime)... During the day all the sliding walls are hidden in the brick construction so that the daylight may take up the whole house. Some of the glazed doors in the corners are often opened in summer time. (There are also special airing doors to be used all the year).[23]

Bo Sylvan attributes the atmosphere of the house to the quality of light created by Sverre Fehn, and the way he describes the way the sun moving through the spaces is telling of its significance to the lives of the dwellers. The darkness is embraced at night and during the day the glazed corners are inhabited:

In daytime, when the house is fully opened, there is a bright light sweeping through the front part of the 'alcoves' reflected through the wooden parts in the 'fourth' wall, whose bricks are varnished in a limpid way to reflect the light into the duskier parts of the room. Usually we are staying in the glazed bays ('karnap') during the light hours in contact with the nature outside. In the evening we move to the living room with reading corner, TV and – now in winter – fire.[24]

When examined under a daylight simulator with the lighting conditions of Norrköping through the year, the light inside the house appears truly unique *(fig. 9)*. The architect, whether intentionally or intuitively, creates an environment that emphasises its Nordic location. The sun traces the time of day on the floor of the loggias as the light sweeps across the sky. Direct sunlight does not penetrate the alcoves – the rooms see only the rays reflected off the brick of the service core and the fire from the fireplace at night, a reminder of the dim interiors of the past.

In March sun enters the west corner between the living-room and the dining-room and sweeps across it and deeper into

Figure 8. Norrköping Villa Living room studies under artificial sky simulating swedish lighting ccondtions. Left - Overcast sky in June, Right - Midday June.

the house. It leaves at 2pm to turn around the children's room and at sunset sunlight just grazes the east loggia. In June, on the longest day of the year, just before the sun leaves the living-room it touches the brick edge of the seating around the fireplace but does not enter the alcove. In December, because of the 6 degree angle of incidence of the sun at its lowest point on the winter solstice, direct sunlight does not enter the loggias. Lighting conditions are similar on days when the sky is overcast and during the Nordic summer nights *(fig. 8)*. The house becomes transparent when viewed through the corners, as the reflections of the sun disappear. In the long winter's night, the loggias glow with the artificial light and the villa becomes an abstract lantern in the landscape.

CONCLUSION

Sverre Fehn drew on vernacular and classical architecture to compose the Norrköping House. Designing the villa for the House Parade, Fehn exhibited a work based on his own philosophy, a rigorous building unmarred by the requirements of a specific client.

The strictness of his compositional elements – the alcove, the core, and the corner – is uncompromising and the architecture inflicts Sverre Fehn's vision of poetic dwelling upon the inhabitant, but the flexibility of the house allows the dweller to adapt it to his needs, to connect with the outside at will or to shut out the surroundings entirely.

Fehn accepted the direction of modern architecture and its unavoidable influence; he also welcomed the logic of construction it brought forth. A structural clarity characteristic of the architect is evident in Norrköping; its language represents a continuity of tradition. Each element displays a linear thought – the poetic weaves into the vernacular which is in turn interlaced with the material to prompt the structure.

Francesco Dal Co describes Sverre Fehn's works as architecture that does not succumb entirely to the genius loci or attempt to interpret architectonically Heidegger's ideas.[25] Fehn recognised that poetic thought is not enough in the creation of a dwelling, and this is evident in all his work. Constructive logic, always so clear in his projects, stems not from the vernacular but from the modernist elements which Fehn picked up during his architectural upbringing in Oslo and Europe in the fifties. His architecture confronts the vernacular with the thought of construction:

'The view gives the space, the space gives the light, the light gives the structure, the structure gives the material, the material gives the dimensions, the dimensions give the joints, the joints give the technique... in Fehn's early houses, these linkages describes circles and loops, which can be followed forwards and backwards, forming closed, self- referential systems.'[26]

The villa is a Nordic counterpart to Palladio's Villa Rotonda, reinterpreted by Sverre Fehn in a domestic context. It sits in the landscape as an addition, complementing its surroundings, comfortable in its context. Its dialogue with the dweller allows a close relationship with the outside, and this substantiates the reasoning of Christian Norberg-Schulz that Nordic light is a giver of identity to Scandinavian architecture.

The sun sweeping the glazed corner in the July morning manifests Sverre Fehn's architectural poetry – the rays of the sun dance with the activity of the day whilst the alcove remains silent in preparation for the night and the fire (fig. 9).

Figure 9. Norrköping Villa - studies of the loggia under Artificial Sky simulating Swedish lighting conditions, light travelling through the corner over the course of a day in June, living room (top) and service core (bottom).

(ENDNOTES)

1   Fjeld, P.O., *Sverre Fehn on the Thought of Construction*, Rizzoli International Publications, (1983), p. 14.

2   Gronvøld, U., 'Norwegian Contemporary Architecture: Fehn and His Legacies', *A+U Architecture and Urbanism* (December 2004), p. 8.

3   Norberg-Schulz, C. and G. *Postiglione, Sverre Fehn, Works, Projects, Writings*, 1949-1996, The Monacelli Press, 1997, p. 105.

4   Fjeld, P.O. (1983), p. 64.

5   Kenneth Frampton as quoted by Fjeld, P.O. (1983), p. 12.

6   Fjeld, P.O. (1983), pp. 64-65.

7   Fjeld, P.O. (1983), p. 67.

8   Norberg-Schulz, C., Nightlands: Nordic Building, The MIT Press (1993), p. 1.

9   Norberg-Schulz, C. (1993), p. 2.

10   Norberg-Schulz, C. (1993), p. 3.

11   Norberg-Schulz, C. (1993), p. 6.

12   Norberg-Schulz, C. (1993), p. 9.

13   Norberg-Schulz, C. 'The Poetic Modernism of Sverre Fehn', A+U Architecture and Urbanism, (January 1999), p. 168.

14   'Nordic Pavillion, Biennale, 1958-1962', A+U Architecture and Urbanism (January 1999)

15   Fjeld, P.O. (1983), pp. 64-65.

16   Sverre Fehn as quoted in 'Sverre Fehn – Above and Below the Horizon', A+U Architecture and Urbanism (January 1999).

17   Sverre Fehn as quoted by Fjeld, P.O. (1983), p. 50.

18   Sverre Fehn as quoted by Fjeld, P.O. (1983), p. 50.

19   Sverre Fehn as quoted by Fjeld, P.O. (1983), p. 50.

20   Sverre Fehn as quoted by Fjeld, P.O. (1983), p. 9.

21   Palladio, A. *I Quattro Libri dell'Architechtura,* facsimile edition, Hoepli, Milan (1980)

22   Personal correspondence between the author and Ann-Charlotte Hertz, the curator of ancient monuments in Norrköping (November 2008).

23   Personal correspondence between the author and Professor Bo Sylvan, the current owner of the Norrköping house (December 2008).

24   Personal correspondence between the author and Professor Bo Sylvan, the current owner of the Norrköping house (December 2008).

25   Norberg-Schulz, C. and G. Postiglione (1997), p. 8.

26   Norberg-Schulz, C., 'The Poetical Modernism of Sverre Fehn', A+U Architecture and Urbanism (December 2004), p. 94.

The image on Page 170 is by Sebastian F, reproduced under the terms of the *Creative Commons Attribution-Share Alike 3.0 Unported License*, the full terms of which can be viewed at: http://creativecommons.org/licenses/by-sa/3.0/deed.en.

Figure 1.

Climate, Comfort and Control in the Developing World

by Matthew French

Matt French is currently studying for a PhD supervised by Professor Koen Steemers. In 2010 he was awarded a RIBA Research Trust Award for his research project 'Responsive slums: participatory methods and bio-climatic design in Nairobi, Kenya.'

UNFASHIONABLE AND UNCOMFORTABLE SELF-BUILT ENVIRONMENTS?

When we think of global construction activity today, we think of the large scale activity in Dubai and China. By far the majority of new construction activity today, however, is taking place in self-built residential environments of the developing world. Consequently, most development in urban settings is being driven by the consistent and dispersed activities of onsite lay-people in countries such as Brazil, India and Kenya, not by the highly trained and coordinated activities of professionals.

These self-builders are designing and building their homes in urban environments that have traditionally been called slums or squatter settlements, but are now commonly referred to as informal settlements. These urbanites are engaged in an ongoing struggle to obtain land, collect and buy building materials, and design and construct their homes, all within severe social, political and economic constraints *(fig. 1)*.

Informal settlements are not a fashionable topic. Throughout the gradual retreat from high modernism, architects have – along with mass housing in general – increasingly kept away from such environments. Apart from the occasional exception, housing has come to mean bespoke, expensive homes. Architects have not concerned themselves with the self-built housing, infrastructure, or the urban organisation (or apparent disorganisation) of informal settlements. Our peers from other disciplines, for example sociology, anthropology, economics, and political studies, have been the leaders in understanding this dominant settlement approach.

However, as the sustainability agenda increasingly takes prominence in built environment discourses, many are beginning to place serious doubt over the energy intensive nature of current Western urban environments. Within the context of such doubt, alternate models of urban structure and form are being sought and it is timely that informal settlements are being reappraised. Is it radical that informal settlements could provide the West with lessons? Most would say yes. Is it impossible that they have something positive to say? Surely not.

It is from this position that a refined ar-

chitectural and environmental understanding of informal settlements is sought. This article focuses on one aspect: the thermal performance and comfort of dwellings in such contexts. How do self-built dwellings perform in terms of climatic responsiveness, and thus energy use? How thermally comfortable are these dwellings perceived to be by their occupants?

Self-built dwellings are by far the dominant, but not the only dwelling approach for people from lower socio-economic groups. Some governments have initiated programmes to design, build and supply houses to their poorest citizens, often in partnership with the private sector. This seems a particularly Latin American phenomenon, especially evident in the case of the larger economies of Chile, Argentina and Brazil. So, how does the housing designed and built by governments – 'social housing' – compare in terms of thermal performance and comfort with the self-built houses often located next to them? Specifically, this article explores how the method of housing procurement affects the resulting occupant thermal comfort.

LOS BARRIOS

This article draws its findings from an ethnographic study of three adjoining barrios (neighbourhoods) in the San Fernando municipality of Buenos Aires, Argentina, conducted between September 2008 and August 2009.[1] The housing in *los barrios* can be categorised into three generalised typologies: incipient, consolidated and government houses. The typologies are primarily differentiated by two characteristics: their physical quality, and occupant design and construction control.

In terms of their physical quality, incipient houses are constructed from timber and corrugated iron sheeting *(fig. 2)*. Consolidated houses are constructed from reinforced concrete frame with clay brick infill walls and timber and iron roofing *(fig. 3)*. Government houses are also constructed from reinforced concrete frame with clay brick infill walls and are plastered and painted both inside and out *(fig. 4)*.

The second way the housing typologies differ is through the level of occupant control. Occupant control is broadly defined as the level of involvement in decisions related to the design (spatial layout, room quantity and size, orientation, etc.) and construction (material selection, phases, etc.). In the case study *barrios* the three types have varying levels of occupant *initial* control. The basic incipient and consolidated houses generally have the highest levels of design and construction control. Residents in these houses either designed their houses or chose the design (plan) that they liked, and in many cases were involved in the construction either entirely, or as a help to a building contractor. Residents in government houses received their houses upon construction completion and thus had no input into design or construction.

Figure 2.

OCCUPANT CONTROL AND COMFORT

A central tenet of adaptive thermal comfort theory is the positive influence of occupant environmental control on thermal comfort.[2] The occupants' ability to modify the environment (either through passive means such as opening a window or active systems such as altering a thermostat) psychologically influences thermal comfort responses. This article attempts to expand adaptive thermal comfort theory. The adaptive control described above can be considered 'operational control'. While operational control is influential to comfort, it does not account for the initial design and construction of the built environment. Current theory does not account for the development of the environment, only the operational control once it is occupied.

Figure 3 (above).
Figure 4 (Right).

INITIAL AND SUBSEQUENT CONTROL

Stemming from the ethnographic research in los barrios, this article proposes two new categories of control, namely initial and subsequent control.[1] These have been found to be significant psychological adaptive mechanisms that influence occupant comfort. Initial and subsequent control is loosely defined as the occupants' involvement in, and ability to influence decisions on the design and construction of their houses. It is important to note that control does not necessarily mean building one's house with one's own hands, but rather control of dwelling decisions. A revised model with three levels of occupant control is proposed:

Initial control refers to the primary stages of house building. This is a common phase for squatters, who occupy a piece of land and build a core house. Likewise, it is common for houses built in *asentamiento* developments: where people form a collective, secure a piece of land, and start building a structured neighbourhood of similar urban form to the formal city, with the aim of future legal integration with the formal city.

Subsequent control is when the built environment exists but is modified by the occupants. For example, houses that are extended, where additional rooms are added to an existing house.

Operational control is when the occupant is free, on a daily basis, to change elements in the house: for example opening the window or door for ventilation.

Initial and subsequent control create a psychological attachment to the built environment. This attachment positively influences environmental evaluations, thermal comfort being one evaluation. Within the adaptive framework, it is now accepted that thermal comfort is influenced by more than just objective environmental conditions, such as air and globe temperature, humidity, and wind speed.[3] Recent advances in comfort theory have demonstrated the importance of adaptive actions on thermal comfort and it has been further suggested that the psychological aspects also have a significant influence on comfort.[4] The central argument of this article is that self-builders have a *psychological attachment* to their built environment because they have controlled (designed and constructed) it, and this influences their evaluations of their environment, particularly in relation to thermal comfort.

Kowaltowski et al. (2005) found a similar psychological attachment in lower socio-economic houses in Campinas, Brazil. When evaluated in terms of satisfaction and environmental comfort conditions, occupants who had a role in the initial and subsequent design and construction of their houses rated their performance positively. This contrasted with thermal comfort analysis of measured environmental conditions, which predicted that the majority of occupants would be dissatisfied. Although the authors do not directly attribute these evaluations to occupant design and construction control, they note the evaluations are 'a normal reaction to the situation in which these families found themselves, having just gained their own home through relocation, tenure of an urban lot and the self-building process.[5]

Why do those who design and build their house rate it as more comfortable than if they were not involved in its design and construction? Why is initial and subsequent control influential in thermal comfort assessments? From the case study in *los barrios*, there are two main influences on initial and subsequent control: dwelling attachment and performance expectations.

DWELLING ATTACHMENT

In *los barrios* self-builders are not critical of their own design and construction efforts. For many years they have fought to secure a piece of land, saved money to buy materials, spent time collecting materials and over time gradually built their house. For these marginalised urban residents, housing is a long-term struggle and thus self-builders have a strong emotional attachment to their dwellings. This attachment is, in part, generated by their control of dwelling processes. They control dwelling decisions such as the timing of construction phases, material choices, and design decisions such as room layout, size, and spatial organisation. Initial and subsequent control influences their attachment to, and assessment of, the product – an observation that the influential housing theorist John F. C. Turner highlighted in his Peruvian fieldwork in the 1970s.[6]

Self-builders are driven by a belief that the future will be better; that the time, energy and money that is put into their housing projects will provide them with a more comfortable, controllable environment in which to live. They have a great deal of faith in their house-building projects and often take considerable pride in the results. Compared with government housing, then, it appears that tolerance to a wider range of thermal conditions is higher in self-built houses than government houses, due to the occupant's greater emotional attachment with the former.

PERFORMANCE EXPECTATIONS

Initial and subsequent control also influences performance expectations. When professionals, such as formally trained and accredited architects, engineers, and urban planners are involved in developing a housing project, occupants have higher expectations of the built environment's performance. Professionals are usually engaged to ensure a high quality result and when the performance of the final house does not match occupant expectations, sympathy with environmental discomfort decreases.

The government houses in the case study site were designed by a local architecture practice and built by professional building contractors. Such formally procured buildings are presumed to perform to a higher and more acceptable standard than if a layperson designed and built them in the informal sector.

Formal design and construction carries with it higher performance expectations than informal self-build design and construction. Self-builders are conscious they are not formally trained in architecture, building science or services, so thermal performance expectations reflect their non-expert skills. It is not that self-builders drastically reduce their expectations; rather their sympathy towards the cause of discomfort, and their perceived lack of knowledge of technical skills, moderates their expectations to make slight discomfort bearable.

REFINING INITIAL AND SUBSEQUENT CONTROL

There are several limits to this control theory. Firstly, some residents have control, but not the economic or spatial capability to exercise such control. This is the case with one interviewee, Mariela. She has security of land tenure and 'owns' her incipient house so, theoretically, she can design and build what she wants. But, as a single mother with three children and only informal, intermittent employment, Mariela lacks the economic capability to exercise control as much as she would like. While all residents in lower socio-economic residential environments have plans to develop and expand their houses, for many residents the economic ability to realise such control is limited. Thus, the ability of lower socio-economic people to manipulate their environment and improvise within its constraints is limited by economic conditions.

Secondly, is actual (hands-on) construction necessary to create dwelling attachment and thus increase the comfort zone? Many residents in *los barrios* do actually build their dwellings with their own hands. However, many residents also contract out construction tasks to local informal builders, often friends or relatives, who are employed in the formal construction sector and thus knowledgeable about construction materials and methods. So, is it necessary for the occupants to build their own house? Or, if it is built by someone else but is still controlled by the occupant, does this result in the same sort of attachment as if they built it themselves? While such a question is still under investigation, it appears that while actually constructing the dwelling oneself is not a requisite for having a high level of attachment, it does help strengthen dwelling attachment.

Thirdly, residents in government houses are so pleased to finally have, among other things, piped running water, a roof that does not leak and a legally recognised address, that for some it does not matter if they did not control their dwelling design or construction. What is important is they have control *now*: subsequent control. They can expand, add rooms to the rear, re-paint the interior any colour they wish, add a front fence and garden. In fact, most residents in the case study government houses have carried out such alterations, demonstrating a high level of exercised subsequent control. Tipple argues that *subsequent control* is essential for the occupants of government housing schemes to feel at home and satisfied with their dwelling environment.[7]

Fourthly, although initial control positively influences occupant comfort, many people may not want initial control. For some, the prospect of designing and physically constructing their dwelling is a daunting task for which they have no desire to undertake. It is typically a long process that takes many years, or even decades, during which time the living conditions may be very challenging. Instead, for some urban poor families, a government procured house, finished and complete with all services, is more attractive than self-build even though there is no scope to influence the initial design.

QUANTIFYING DIFFERENT LEVELS OF CONTROL

Which is more influential in comfort assessments: initial, subsequent or operational control? In this pioneering study it was not possible to quantify the relative benefit of each level of control, only to highlight these as influences on domestic comfort. All three control mechanisms are advantageous for thermal comfort and they are not mutually exclusive. Through design, initial and subsequent control improves the congruence between the physical environment and the occupants' needs and preferences. Operational control tailors the house to occupants' daily, weekly and seasonal lifestyles.

What is important is that the exercised control is seen to influence the thermal conditions. For psychological benefit from an exercised action, occupants must consciously link their action with the resultant thermal conditions. In the predominantly passive buildings in *los barrios*, residents understand that thermal conditions relate to the dwelling's primary construction materials and design. Residents understand that, for example, the laying of kitchen tiles or the repainting of an interior wall (considered here as subsequent control) are not so influential on the *thermal conditions*. Therefore, it may be that initial control, control of the major dwelling design and construction decisions, is more influential than subsequent and operational control.

CONCLUSION

This article sought to contribute to adaptive thermal comfort theory concerning occupant control. Drawing from ethnographic fieldwork in lower socio-economic residential environments in Buenos Aires, the article suggests initial and subsequent control are two positive influences on occupant thermal comfort. These extend the existing adaptive theory, which only considers operational control. The study finds that when occupants have initial and subsequent dwelling control they are more sympathetic to thermal discomfort and they appear to have a wider comfort range than those who had no initial and subsequent control. Furthermore, comfort assessments are not only based on physiological responses to environmental conditions as comfort also has psychological dimensions.

The self-built environments that characterise urban areas in the developing world – where occupants design and build their own houses – is an understandable context from which such findings have emerged. Importantly, in terms of housing in developing countries, the findings challenge assumptions that finished and 'respectable' housing forms (of which the government housing most closely resembles) have the highest levels of comfort and satisfaction and, conversely, the rough, seemingly chaotic, slum environments are uncomfortable and inadequate. An important factor in the comfortableness of an environment is the degree to which the occupant controls it. Perhaps, then, self-build should be supported, rather than considered a housing approach that produces poor-quality, uncomfortable environments. In this sense, the findings support Hardoy and Satterthwaite's assertion that:

'Rapid growth of illegal settlements in and around cities can be viewed not as the growth of slums but, in a very real sense, as the development of cities which are more appropriate to the local culture, climate and conditions than the plans produced by the governments of these same cities.'[8]

The findings highlight larger theoretical and practical concerns. Should researchers and designers focus on models and simulations to predict optimum comfort conditions, or should design principles and strategies be developed that enable occupants to have more control? Rather than developing comfort models and designing to narrow energy intensive comfort temperature ranges, perhaps built environment professionals should widen the base of design control so that the occupants, whether in workplaces or the domestic context, can have an input

in the design and production of their environment, and not just the operation of it.

(ENDNOTES)

1   This article draws from the author's current PhD research project that explores the culture of thermal comfort in lower socio-economic residential contexts, using a case study from Buenos Aires.

2   Brager, G. and R. de Dear, 'Thermal adaption in the built environment: a literature review', Energy and Buildings, v. 27 (1998), pp. 83-96.

3   Humphreys, M., 'Thermal comfort temperatures and the habits of hobbits', in Nicol, F., Humphreys, M., Sykes, O. and S. Roaf, Standards for thermal comfort: Indoor air temperature standards for the 21st century, Chapman Hall, London (1995).

4   Brager, G. and R. de Dear, 'Thermal adaption in the built environment: a literature review', Energy and Buildings, v. 27 (1998), pp. 83-96.

5   Kowaltowski, D. et al, 'A house design assistance program for the self-building process of the region of Campinas, Brazil: evaluation through a case study', Habitat International, v. 29 (2005), p. 106.

6   Turner, J., Housing by people: towards autonomy in building environments, Marion Boyars, London (1976).

7   Tipple, G., Extending themselves: user initiated extensions to government-built housing in developing countries, Liverpool University Press, Liverpool (2000).

8   Hardoy, J. and D. Satterthwaite, Squatter citizen: life in the urban Third World, Earthscan, London (1989), p. 8.

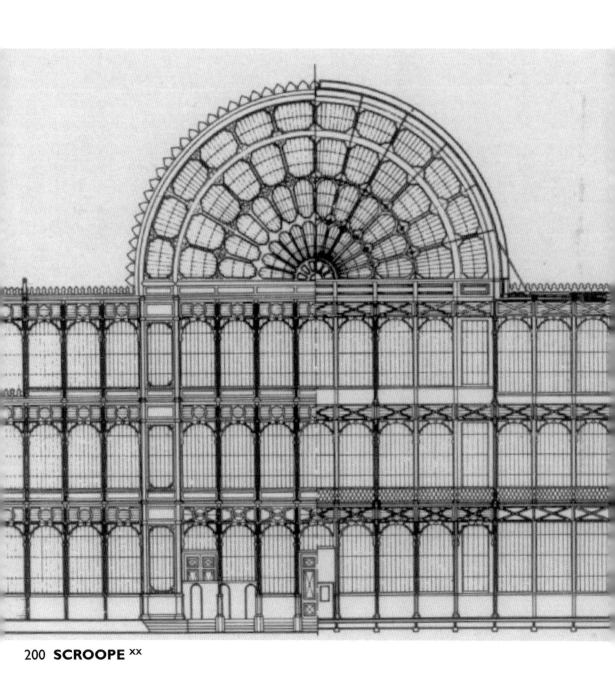

Paxton's Experimental Glasshouse at Hyde Park

by Henrik Schoenefeldt

Henrik Schoenefeldt studied at the Prince's Foundation, Portsmouth University and TU-Wien. In 2007 he was awarded an MPhil in Environmental Design at the University of Cambridge, where he is currently studying for a PhD on the History of Glass Architecture supervised by Professor Alan Short. Since 2007 Henrik has been the co-organiser of the Martin Centre's Wednesday Research Seminar Series.

SYNOPSIS

Contemporary records show that the temporary building for the 1851 Great Exhibition at Hyde Park, based on a design by the horticulturist and glasshouse designer Joseph Paxton, represented a pioneering effort to appropriate the horticultural glasshouse for human occupation.[2] The objective behind Paxton's design, apart from exploiting the modular construction systems and mechanised production processes previously developed to surmount the excessive cost and labor associated with glasshouse construction, was to appropriate the climate and lighting conditions inside the exhibition building to the specific environmental requirements of the exhibition.

The project correspondence reveals that the Royal Commissioner's decision to adopt

Paxton's design in favour of the Building Committee's scheme was significantly influenced by the successful reconciliation of important functional aspects, in particular lighting, ventilation and the control of humidity and temperature. In extensive disputes among members of the Royal Commission and various committees the Building Committee was fiercely criticised for having failed to address these issues in their own design.[3]

For Paxton, analogous to the design of horticultural glasshouses – where the manufacture of artificial climates for the nurturing and preservation of tender plants was the chief design objective – the guarantee of adequate environmental conditions for the display and preservation of artifacts and for the comfort of the building users was a critical functional aspect of the exhibition building. While the executed building was clearly the outcome of Paxton's successful collaboration with the contractors, suppliers and structural engineers, contemporary sources reveal that the design builds extensively on Paxton's experience with the design, construction and the environmental performance of horticultural glasshouses.[4] The contractors and engineers admitted that they were highly dependent on Paxton's specialist knowledge and experience as a glasshouse designer, in particular in terms of the detailing of the glass envelope and the control of the indoor environment.[5]

Commentaries in the contemporary press reveal that Paxton's idea of adopting a glasshouse as a model for the exhibition building was widely criticised as a very risky and untested design experiment. Referring to the Palm House at Kew and the Conservatory at Regent's Park as examples, prospective exhibitors and critics in the media warned that success of the building depended on the facility to successfully manage the interior environmental conditions, a prerequisite for protecting vulnerable exhibits from exposure to excessive sunlight, heat and humidity, as well as for ensuring the comfort and health of staff and visitors during the period of the exhibition.[6]

Paxton, however, stressed that his idea was not without precedent, but that it was informed by his extensive experience with managing the environment inside glasshouses, and referred to a number of his earlier conservatories as precedent cases which provided evidence of the feasibility of his proposition.[7] Contemporary horticultural literature, which contains detailed accounts of the working methods, design criteria and issues underlying Paxton's experimentation with glasshouses in the period 1833-50, illustrates that the glazing employed at Hyde Park was the outcome of extensive experiments with glazing systems which Paxton had conducted to improve the environmental performance of glasshouses.

TEMPERATURE IN THE GREAT EXHIBITION.—We have been favoured by Mr. Bennett, clock-maker, Cheapside, with the mean result of one hundred readings, taken five times a day, from twenty thermometers, placed in various parts of the Exhibition, at intervals of two hours from ten a.m. to six p.m. :—

	Ten o'clock.	Twelve o'clock.	Two o'clock.	Four o'clock.	Six o'clock.	Daily Mean Temperature.
July 28, Monday......	65	69	71	69	63	67·2
July 29, Tuesday......	67	75	76	75	72	73
July 30, Wednesday ...	65	70	73	73	67	69·3
July 31, Thursday	61	67	72	73	71	68·4

Figure 1. Sample of Temperature readings published in the Morning Chronicle 1st August 1851 (Image: CU Library).

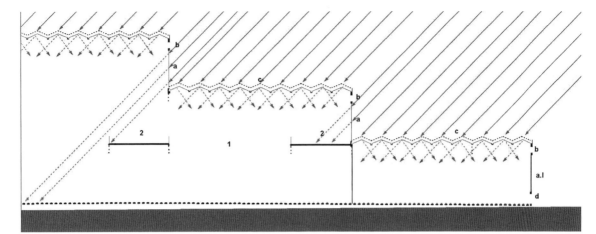

Figure 2. Cross section.
Key: a. Vertical boarding b. Top Ventilators c. Ridge & furrow glazing with external canvas shading d. low level ventilators 1. Light Court, 2. Galleries.

Paxton's chief objective was to improve the performance of glass envelopes in terms of weather tightness, internal condensation and heat conservation.[8] The development of this innovative glazing technology represented a first step towards appropriating the glasshouses environmentally for the purpose of an exhibition building. Although Paxton had conducted a small-scale experiment to demonstrate the effectiveness of his ventilation and passive cooling strategy, the Executive Committee remained sceptical and requested that the temperature inside the building, like in horticultural glasshouses, be systematically monitored and recorded.[9] Large parts of the temperature data, collected during the period of the exhibition between May and October 1851, were published in various newspapers *(fig. 1)*.[10]

The anxiety among the public and the Executive Committee was not unjustified, since the environmental design issues at Hyde Park, in particular the issue of cooling, which was required to keep the interior temperatures at comfortable levels for human beings during the summer, had no precedent in horticulture.[11] Furthermore, Paxton proposed an entirely passive system of environmental control, constituting of shading, evaporative cooling and natural ventilation, which, apart from the small-scale demonstration at Chatsworth, had not been tested before.

The objective at Hyde Park was to keep the interior atmosphere not only very dry but also to maintain low interior temperatures during periods of excessive heat in the summer.[12] A detailed study by the author of the environmental design objectives and strategy underlying Paxton's design, which can only be discussed very briefly in this article, was the subject of an MPhil Dissertation and a recent journal article by the author published in *Architectural Research Quarterly*.[13]

This article goes on to discuss the post-occupancy history of the building, revealing the process by which the environment inside the Crystal Palace was monitored, and how the ventilation system of the building was retrospectively modified to improve its performance. It reveals that Paxton and the Executive committee were confronted with the serious difficulties of making fully glazed structures climatically suitable for human purposes. The finding of Paxton's pioneering experiment at Hyde Park, however, had a significant influence on the design of the Crystal Palace at Sydenham, which has to be understood as a second step in Paxton's effort to transform the horticultural glasshouse prototype into an environmental design model for architecture.

PAXTON'S ENVIRONMENTAL DESIGN STRATEGY AND OBJECTIVES

An overarching environmental design strategy, as contemporary sources illustrate, had been an integral and important part of the design from the very beginning.[14] The aim was to provide good lighting conditions for the display of the exhibits through diffuse top lighting, to provide adequate levels of ventilation, and to maintain a comfortable indoor temperature during the period of the exhibition. The objective was to keep the indoor temperature lower than the external temperature during periods of extreme heat.[15] A very brief summary of Paxton's environmental design objectives and strategy is given in the following two sections.

LIGHTING CONTROL

One of the major environmental objectives behind the design of the Crystal Palace was the creation of a uniformly lit interior space, using daylight as the only source of light.[16] To maintain the transparency of the iron and timber space frame, used to create a flexible open plan interior space, the roof and vertical elevations were almost completely glazed, using two glazing systems. The ridge and furrow glazing used to glaze the horizontal part of the roof made it possible to enclose, drain and adequately daylight an extremely deep floor plan on the ground floor of 408 by 1,848 feet.[17]

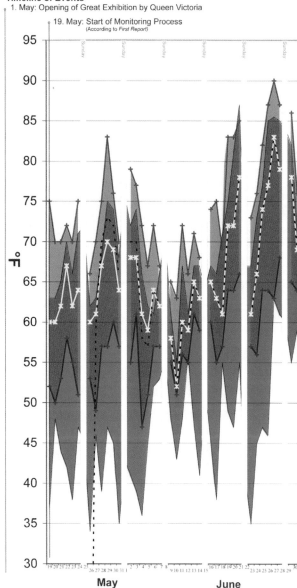

Source: Graph Compiled by author based on data published in the *First Report* [average outdo and minimum outdoor temerature]

Timeline of Events
1. May: Opening of Great Exhibition by Queen Victoria
19. May: Start of Monitoring Process
(According to *First Report*)

In order to subdue the intense sunlight, the entire horizontal part of the ridge and furrow roof was covered with translucent calico screens, so that the interior was illuminated by a relatively uniform diffused top light *(fig. 2)*.[18] The lighting strategy also governed the internal layout. While the central aisle, the transept and first floor gallery had direct access to top light from the roof, the deck was punctured by a se- quence of courts to bring top light down to the ground floor spaces below. As a consequence, the galleries were reduced to a network of shallow bridges 24 feet in depth. Since the daylight regime limited the extent to which multiple floors could be inserted inside the volume of an extremely deep plan building it was practically a single storey building with a secondary level of shallow bridges. Its volume was divided into three

Figure 3. Maximum, Minmum and Average Indoor and Exterior Temperatures recorded by the Royal Miners and Sappers between May and October 1851

d indoor temperature + maximum and minimum indoor temperature] and the *Gardener's Chronicle and Agricultural Gazette* between 24th May and 18th October 1851 [maximum

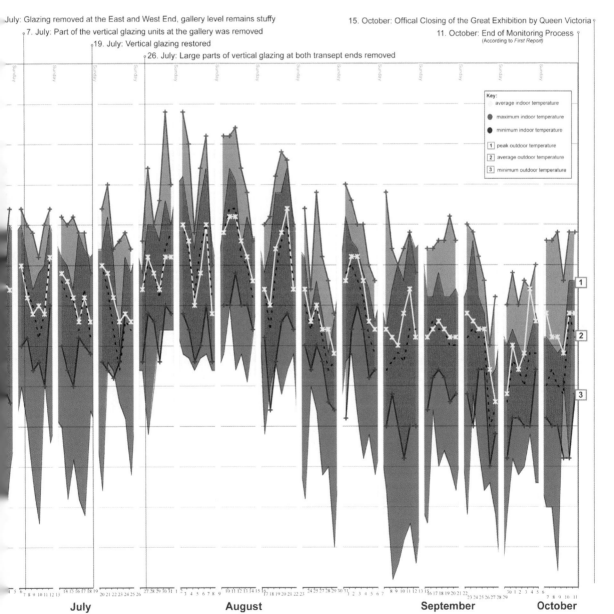

July: Glazing removed at the East and West End, gallery level remains stuffy

7. July: Part of the vertical glazing units at the gallery was removed

19. July: Vertical glazing restored

26. July: Large parts of vertical glazing at both transept ends removed

15. October: Offical Closing of the Great Exhibition by Queen Victoria

11. October: End of Monitoring Process
(According to *First Report*)

Key:
- average indoor temperature
- maximum indoor temperature
- minimum indoor temperature
- 1 peak outdoor temperature
- 2 average outdoor temperature
- 3 minimum outdoor temperature

July August September October

tiers of diminishing width, forming the shape of a stepped pyramid in cross section.

THERMAL ENVIRONMENT

In order to control the thermal environment, Paxton adopted a combined shading and ventilation strategy. Calico screens were used to cover the entire surface of the ridge and furrow roof externally to exclude excessive solar gains.[19] The purpose of the ventilation system was to prevent the stratification of hot air and sustain an adequate supply of fresh air in a building occupied by up to 90,000 visitors at any one time. The ventilation apparatus constituted of continuous rows of ventilators in the upper wall section of each of the three tiers. Rows of low-level ventilators were installed at ground floor level.[20] 300 feet of ventilators could be operated simultaneously. The S-shape cross-section of the louvre blades prevented rain entering the building when the ventilators were open, and thereby permitted continuous ventilation.[21] The ventilators were regulated by the Royal Sappers and Miners, who kept a two hourly register, and systematically monitored the internal temperature in the whole building by means of fourteen thermometers installed in different parts of the building (fig. 3).[22]

However, the environmental design strategy that was implemented in the final design excluded a number of features of Paxton's original proposal. It included additional canvas shades in front of the glazing in the south elevation to further reduce solar gains, and internal punkha fans, large sheets

Figure 4. Average Temperature recorded at two hourly intervals on a selected number of days.

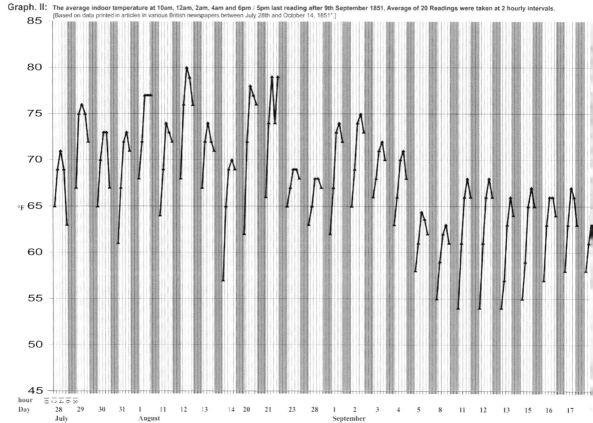

Graph. II: The average indoor temperature at 10am, 12am, 2am, 4am and 6pm / 5pm last reading after 9th September 1851. Average of 20 Readings were taken at 2 hourly intervals. [Based on data printed in articles in various British newspapers between July 28th and October 14, 1851*.]

of canvas that were made to move up and down to expose visitors to an artificial breeze.[23] Aware that ventilation and shading alone were not capable of effectively lowering the indoor temperature below the potentially high outdoor air temperature during the summer, Paxton proposed to employ a passive evaporative cooling system which was composed of canvas sheets installed in front of the ventilators which were periodically moisturised to cool down the incoming air stream by evaporation.[24]

THE GREAT EXHIBITION BUILDING AS A LARGE SCALE ENVIRONMENTAL DESIGN EXPERIMENT

Contemporary sources reveal that an extensive post-occupancy analysis was conducted inside the Exhibition building on behalf of the Commission's executive committee during the period of the Exhibition, demonstrating that the interior temperature was systematically monitored and recorded. Various contemporary British newspapers reported the detailed temperature measurements inside the building during opening hours *(fig. 4)* and a summary of this post-occupancy study was included in the First Report of the Commissioners of the Great Exhibition.[25] This appears to be one of the first systematic post-occupancy studies ever conducted inside a building for non-horticultural use. Horticultural glasshouses were monitored, in some cases sporadically, in others systematically, to ensure that vulnerable foreign plants were kept in an adequate artificial climate.[26] In the Great Exhibition building, the first full-scale environmental design experiment with glasshouses intended for exclusively human purposes, the monitoring process facilitated an objective evaluation of the interior environmental conditions with respect to human comfort. The monitoring data provided objective feedback for the regulation of the ventilation apparatus during the opening hours and was used for a critical analysis of the building's overall environmental performance after the exhibition.

POST-OCCUPANCY STUDY

Following the Executive committee's decision in March 1851 to monitor the performance of the ventilation system during the period of the exhibition, 40 thermometers were installed throughout the interior on

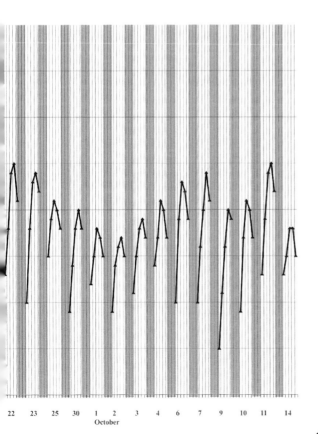

22   23   25   30   1   2   3   4   6   7   9   10   11   14
October

Figure 5. View of East elevation, showing two of the ventilators that had been retrofitteed ith retractable canvas screens (Image: London Metropolitan Archives).

two levels of the building by a thermometer maker named Mr Bennet of Cheapside, although no information was given on their exact position.[27] The Royal Sappers and Miners, who were responsible for regulating the ventilation, monitored and kept register of the interior temperature.[28] Between 19th May and 14th October readings were taken daily from each of fourteen thermometers at two hourly intervals between 9 am and 6pm except from the period after the 9th September when the last reading was taken at 5pm. Three additional thermometers were installed outside the building to monitor the corresponding external temperature.[29]

HISTORICAL CLIMATE DATA COLLECTED INSIDE THE CRYSTAL PALACE

While the evidence from original temperature log sheets had been lost, large parts of the data collected during the Exhibition were documented in various contemporary British newspapers and in the First Report for the Commissioners of the Great Exhibition, forming the basis of a reconstruction

of the actual environmental conditions that occurred inside the building.[30] The First Report included a summary and a brief analysis of the post-occupancy study, listing the daily maximum, minimum and average indoor temperatures (based on 56 readings) and daily average external temperature (based on 12 readings) recorded between 19th May and 11th October 1851. In addition a large quantity of the original monitoring data was printed in various contemporary British newspapers such as the Times, Daily News and Morning Chronicle, which frequently reported on the temperature conditions inside the building between 18th June and October 14th 1851. These articles included more detailed records of the original temperature recordings than the First Report, including reports of the temperature change measured across the period of a day at two hourly intervals. In order to illustrate the relationship between the indoor and outdoor temperatures, minimum and peak temperatures, outdoor temperature data of the Horticultural Gardens Chiswick, published in the Gardener's Chronicle during the same period, was added by the author.[31] The following section is a reconstruction and analysis of the building's environmental performance based on the temperature records discussed above.

THE ENVIRONMENTAL HISTORY OF THE GREAT EXHIBITION BUILDING AND ITS ANALYSIS

On the 27th June 1851, for the first time since the opening of the exhibition in May, the Times gave an account of the climate inside the Crystal Palace, reporting the unprecedentedly high temperatures inside the building: intense direct solar heat of 104°F, at an outside air temperature of 83°F in the shade. It caused even greater extremes of heat in the interior of the Crystal Palace, with a maximum air temperature of 97°F in the afternoon and a daily average of 78.7°F.[32] This extreme heat, which continued to occur inside the building on the following days, was perceived as extremely uncomfortable by both visitors and the staff and the Times gave several accounts of people's desperate attempts to find ways of adapting themselves to these conditions.[33] The management, having consulted visitors and exhibitors about the extreme heat in the building, removed the glazing units of the East and West elevation on 2nd July (fig. 5), with the intention of reducing the indoor temperature and 'to secure a refreshing thorough draught from end to end of the interior.'[34] It reported that it lowered the indoor temperature at ground level, but hot and stuffy air continued to accumulate at the upper part of the building.[35] To improve the climate at gallery level parts of the glazing in the north and south galleries were removed on 7th July. It resulted in a more uniform temperature across both levels. Around the 19th July, when the minimum indoor temperature had fallen to 59°F, the glazing was restored and the ventilators were used to regulate the indoor temperature in response to varying degrees of solar gains.[36] The problematic temperatures reported between late June and early July were part of the first of two periods with distinctly higher indoor temperatures. In the first period temperatures ranged between 80°F and 90°F on nine days, followed by a period with notably lower indoor temperatures, ranging between 70-80°F. In the second period, occurring between the 1st and 22nd August, the peak indoor temperature exceeded 80°F on fourteen days.

Considered in the whole the measurements demonstrate that the temperature inside the Crystal Palace was highly variable both across the day and between individual days. On 2nd June the indoor temperature ranged between 47°F and 78°F and on the 1st August the average indoor temperature rose from 68°F at 10am, to 72°F at noon, peaking at 77°F at 2pm, which prevailed until 6pm.[37] Strong temperature variations between daily average temperatures were recorded, for example in the period between 22nd August and 3rd September. The average indoor temperature dropped from 73°F on 22nd August to 58°F on 30th August, but rose to 69°F on 3rd September.

The peak indoor temperature consistently exceeded the peak outdoor temperature by a minimum of 2°F and a maximum of 15°F, demonstrating that the shading and ventilation strategy employed was not sufficient to prevent the indoor temperature from exceeding the outdoor temperature, the aim of Paxton's original strategy. While the highest indoor temperature was recorded on 27th July the most extensive heat period and the highest excess temperatures were recorded between the 1st August and the 11th October. Also the daily minimum indoor temperature, ranging between 45°F (25th September) and 69°F (13th August), constantly exceeded the daily minimum outdoor by between 3°F to 20°F.

FIRST REPORT OF THE COMMISSIONERS

The First Report of the Commissioners, published in April 1852, illustrates that the collected temperature data was used for a scientific analysis of the building's overall environmental performance after the Exhibition. It included data tables with the maximum, minimum and average indoor temperature and the average outdoor temperature for each day between 19th May and 11th October. It shows that out of a total of 126 days on which the temperature was recorded, the average indoor temperature exceeded the outdoor temperature by between 1° F to 9°F on 70 days, while the average internal temperature was recorded to be between 1-4°F lower than the corresponding external temperature on 26 days only.[38]

The report also included a chart comparing the daily number of visitors with the daily mean indoor temperature (fig. 6). It concluded that variations in the number of visitors inside the building had only had a marginal effect on the indoor temperature. It reported: 'On 79 days on which the Visitors were more than 40,000, the mean excess of the interior over the exterior was 1.11 degrees; on 40 days that the Visitors were less than 40,000, it was 0.85 degrees.'[39] The main cause of the

Figure 6. Graph showing visitor numbers and corresponding daily indoor peak temperatures (Image: First Report, British Library).

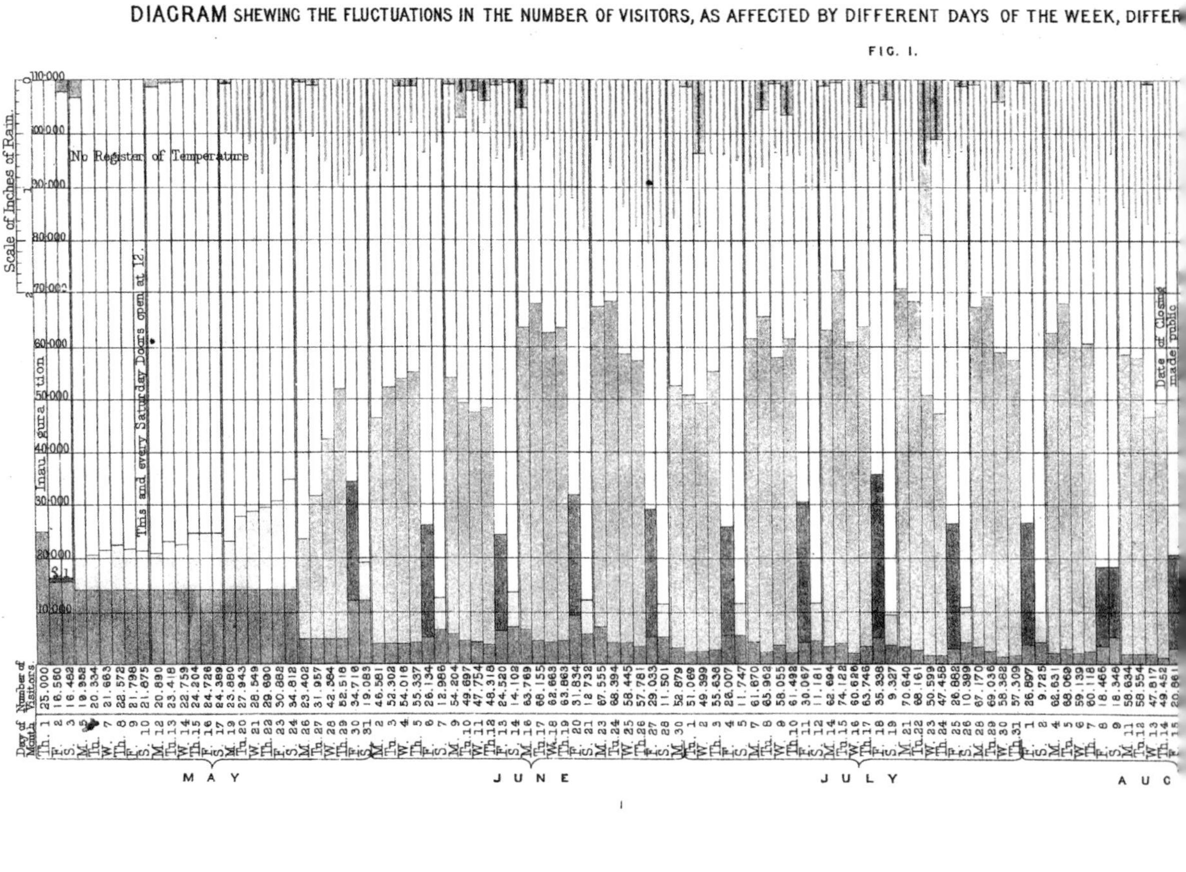

DIAGRAM SHEWING THE FLUCTUATIONS IN THE NUMBER OF VISITORS, AS AFFECTED BY DIFFERENT DAYS OF THE WEEK, DIFFER

FIG. I.

extreme interior temperature, it concluded, was insufficient ventilation. However, the proper operation of the original ventilation strategy was inhibited by the large quantities of exhibits and partitions on the ground floor along the north elevation that were obstructing the air flow in the building. In order to compensate for the restricted air-flow it became necessary 'to remove about 90 sashes, each about 20 feet high by 8 feet wide, in different parts of the building, the openings being closed when necessary by canvas blinds.'[40]

CONCLUSION

This paper has shown that aspirations to maintain ideal lighting conditions for the

display of artifacts, and to provide fresh air and thermal comfort inside a large-scale building with thousands of visitors, had been an integral part of the design of the Great Exhibition building. It also reveals that it represented a pioneering experiment on adopting a large scale 'glasshouse' for exclusively human purposes. To achieve these objectives a completely passive environmental design strategy was proposed, and the building management conducted a post-occupancy study during the opening hours of the Exhibition to objectively evaluate its thermal performance. Various contemporary newspapers report that excessive temperatures, humidity and reduced levels of oxygen had occurred inside the building over extended periods of time and had lead to complaints by staff and visitors about discomfort, drowsiness and headaches.[41] In response to these issues the management took measures, with some effect, to improve the ventilation. This included the temporary removal of glazing units and the installation of operable canvas screens.[42] A statistical analysis of the data, and an inquiry into the building's problematic performance and its causes, was subject of a final post-occupancy study included in the Commissioner's First Report.[43] The inquiry into the appropriating of glasshouses for human occupation, which started at Hyde Park, continued after the exhibition. Contemporary records show that Paxton had critically re-evaluated his own design and had made several proposals for a second prototype.[44] This was finally realised in his design for the Crystal Palace at Sydenham, the subject of the author's current research.

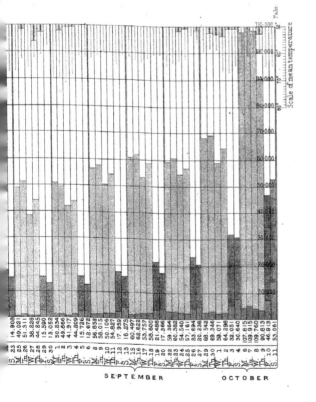

LE OF PAYMENT, RAIN AND HEAT OF THE BUILDING.

(ENDNOTES)

1   The main body of this paper is a reproduction of a short paper read by the author at the PLEA Conference 2008: 'The Building of the Great Exhibition of 1851. Environmental Design Experiment', in Kenny, P., Brophy, V. and J.O. Lewis (eds), Proceedings of the 25th Passive and Low Energy Architecture International Conference, School of Architecture, Landscape and Civil Engineering, University College Dublin (2008).

2   The author's work is based on extensive archival research. Apart from the study of contemporary Journals and Newspapers, the author studied contemporary source material, such as diaries, letters, drawings, reports and photographs held at Chatsworth, the British Library, the Metropolitan Archives, the National Art Library and the RIBA Drawing Collection at the Victoria and Albert Museum, National Archives, Archives of the Royal Commission of 1851, Imperial College, and the Archives at the Royal Botanic Gardens Kew.

3   Memorandum on the Advantages of Paxton's Plan, dated 4th July 1850, and Francis Fuller's diary, held at the Victoria and Albert Museum.

4   While Robert Mallet emphasised the contribution of the contractors and engineers towards the resolution of structural issues, extensive reports in the contemporary Architecture and Engineering Journal illustrate that the resolution of the environmental design issues was equally important to making the use of a glass structure feasible for an exhibition building: Mallet, R., 'The Record of the International Exhibition', William Mackenzie, Glasgow, Edinburgh, London (1862), p. 60.

5   'Public Dinner at Derby to Mr. Paxton', The Times (7th August 1851), p. 8.

6   The Times (15th July 1850); 'National Exhibition Building', Architect and Building Gazette (20th July 1850), p. 344; 'Building for the Exhibition of 1851', Builder (27th July, 1850), p. 358; An Architect, 'Exhibition Of 1851', The Times, (17th July, 1850), p. 8.

7   Anonymous, 'The Palace of Industry: a brief history of its origin and progress, with a descriptive account of the most interesting portions of the machinery employed in its construction', Illustrated London News (16th November 1850), p. 385.

8   Detailed Accounts of Paxton's glasshouse experiments were published in the Gardener's Chronicle, Paxton's Magazine of Botany, Horticultural Register, and Loudon's Gardener's Magazine.

9   Henry Cole's Diary (1850); The Times (29th March 1851), p. 5; Illustrated London News (16th November 1850), p. 385.

10   Large quantities of data was published by The Times, Daily News, Morning Chronicle and the Illustrated London News.

11   Illustrated London News (16th November 1850), p. 385.

12   Detailed accounts of his environmental design objectives and strategy were given by Paxton in various lectures between August 1850 and August 1851.

13   Schoenefeldt, H., 'The Crystal Palace - Environmentally Considered' in Architectural Research Quarterly (2008), pp. 283-94; (2007).

14   'Memorandum', llustrated London

News (6th July 1850).

15 Gardener's Magazine, v. 9, pp. 303-317.

16 The Times, 14th November 1850, p. 4.

17 Downes, C., The Building for the Great Exhibition of the Works of Industry of All Nations, John Weale, London (1851) pp. 39-41.

18 Paxton, J., 'The Victoria Regia House, Chatsworth', Civil Engineer and Architect´s Journal (October 1850), p. 324.

19 Illustrated London News, (16th November, 1850), p. 386.

20 Commissioners of the Exhibition of 1851, First Report of the Commissioners for the Exhibition of 1851, London (1852), pp. 67-89.

21 Anonymous, The Palace of Industries, John Olivier, London (1851).

22 Commissioners of the Exhibition of 1851 (1852), pp. 67-89.

23 Illustrated London News (6th July, 1850), p. 13; 'Exhibition of 1851, Monthly Report of
Progress', Journal of Design and Manufactures (1850), pp. 29-32.

24 Illustrated London News (16th November, 1850), p. 386.

25 Commissioners of the Exhibition of 1851 (1852), pp. 67-89.

26 Gardener´s Magazine, v. 9, pp. 303-317.

27 The Times (16th September 1851), p. 5, The Times (29th March, 1851), p. 5.

28 Commissioners of the Exhibition of 1851 (1852), pp. 67-89.

29 Ibid.

30 Ibid.

31 Gardener´s Chronicle, May 24th 1851, p. 328 to Gardener´s Chronicle, October 18th 1851, p. 664.

32 Times, September 16th, 1851, p. 5.

33 Times, June 30th, 1851, p. 5. & Times, July 1st, 1851, p. 5.

34 Times, September 16th, 1851, p. 5. & Times, June 27th, 1851, p. 5.

35 Times, July 1st, 1851, p. 5 & Illustrated London News, October 11th, 1851, p. 471.

36 Illustrated London News, October 11th, 1851, p. 471.

37 Times, August 2nd, 1851, p. 5.

38 Commissioners of the Exhibition of 1851 (1852), pp. 67-89.

39 Commissioners of the Exhibition of 1851 (1852), pp. 67-89.

40 Commissioners of the Exhibition of 1851 (1852), pp. 67-89.

41 Numerous accounts of people's perception of the environmental conditions inside the building were published in The Times, Examiner, Daily News, Morning Chronicle.

42 The Times (27th June, 1851), p. 5; Illustrated London News (11th October, 1851), p. 471; The Times (1st July 1851), p. 5.

43 Commissioners of the Exhibition of 1851 (1852), p. 67.

44 Accounts of Paxton's proposal were given in various, interviews, pamphlets, letters, newspapers and journals between summer 1851 and spring 1852.

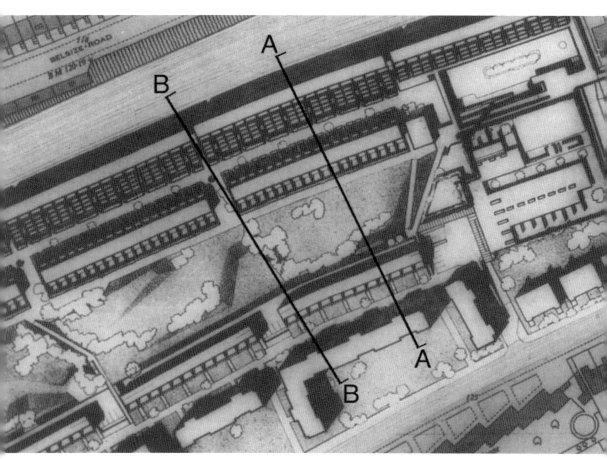

The Radiant Walls of Alexandra Road

by Lefkos Kyriacou

Lefkos Kyriacou is a researcher for Conflict in Cities and the Contested State, an ESRC funded project based in the Department of Architecture in Cambridge, and Director of Studies at Fitzwilliam College, Cambridge. He is a practicing architect at Cottrell and Vermeulen Architecture in London. He has lived on Alexandra Road since 2006 and is a member of the Alexandra and Ainsworth Tenants and Residents Association.

INTRODUCTION

Since 2007 the district heating and hot water system of the Alexandra Road estate in North-West London[1] has been the focus of an impassioned tussle between a multitude of officers from Camden council, local politicians, architects, services engineers and local residents. It may seem unusual for a prosaic issue like heating to arouse high emotion. However many of the problems that have been encountered on this Camden estate reveal the difficulties that government is facing in its attempt to tackle the problem of drastically reducing carbon emissions from the existing housing stock in the UK.[2]

An analysis of this case could belong to a wider discussion of sustainable design but it also touches on how communities are consulted on changes to the environment of their homes. It also provides an historical insight into the shift in attitude of local government to environmental design, in this case Camden Council, from the highly imaginative (some would say gung-ho) approach of the post-war, pre-Thatcher era[3] to the present day culture of risk aversion coupled with a desire to deliver on environmental promises.

When Camden engulfed Holborn, St. Pancras and Hampstead, during the redrawing of London's borough boundaries in 1965, it soon gained a reputation as one of the more progressive boroughs. Sydney Cook had just been made Borough Architect and Director of Housing, and he was constantly challenging the government's push for high-rise and industrialised schemes, with feasibility studies based around low and middle rise solutions. Cook started by appointing the architect Neave Brown who, supported by Cook, set out on a journey to deliver a series of low rise high density housing projects in Camden, which would include one of Europe's great social housing projects: Alexandra Road, designed in 1968 and taking the best part of the next decade to complete.

The 6.47 hectare site of Alexandra Road near South Hampstead station lies between the railway line into Euston to the North and the point blocks of the Ainsworth estate to the south. The key elements of the estate are two parallel pedestrian streets separated by a park, one a kilometre long, formed by two rows of terraces against the railway, and the other by a further row of terraces forming a street against the existing point blocks. The two streets, Rowley and Ainsworth Way, provide 520 homes for over 1,600 people (fig. 1).

THE RADIANT WALLS

The context of the decision on how Alexandra Road was to be heated is important: the 1961 Parker Morris report on space, heating and services (Homes for Today and Tomorrow) gave local authorities the option of applying for extra funding to centrally heat entire estates for the first time. Brown and Max Fordham, the Services Engineer on the design team, decided on a centralised district heating system in view of the disastrous history of heating dwellings individually in deprived areas.[4]

The decision to choose the heating scheme was taken following an investigation by the design team into several possible options.[5] Any electrical heating system would have been too costly to run and radiators were both expensive and would have cluttered the tightly planned dwellings. Underfloor heating had many advantages – it was unobtrusive and produced comfortable radiant heat – but it would have necessitated many expensive movement joints when applied across the long concrete blocks. So the innovative decision was made to embed steel coil pipework that would carry hot water within the cross-walls of the flats: a radiant wall heating system (fig. 2).

Radiant walls were not only less costly

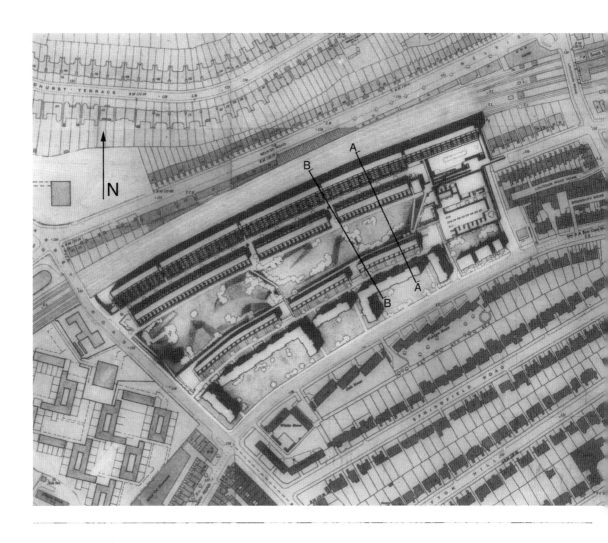

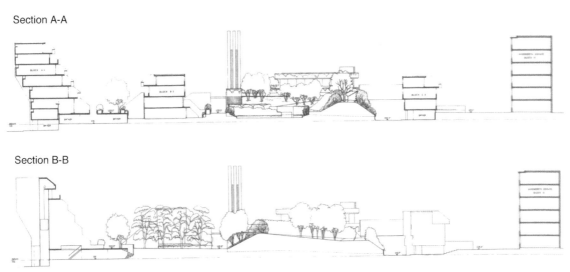

Figure 1. Original Site plan and sections of Alexandra Road, showing Rowley Way to North, Ainsworth Way to South and Central park (Neave & Brown).

and spatially discreet but two dwellings could be heated at the same time (fig. 3). As well as not requiring further movement joints, the radiant wall heating system had another advantage over underfloor heating: the surface temperature of the walls could be higher than for a heated floor system, thus achieving higher room temperatures.

For all the positive aspects of such a system there were two problematic issues that the design team had identified at the time and which reappear in present-day discussions.

Firstly how do residents control a shared system? According to Max Fordham, during design development, the brief set by Camden's Housing Manager swung from limited tenant control to asking for complete control of the heating within flats; in the end a compromise was reached that called for 'some measure of tenant control.'[6] At about the same time that controllability was integrated into the brief, there was also an additional requirement for the environmental design of the flats to help with the significant acoustic challenge of the railway, along which the largest block of the estate was to run. The solution was to minimise the need to open windows along the facade against the railway[7] and incorporate mechanical ventilation in the form of fans that could draw in cool or warmed air – thus acoustically attenuating the air path across the noisy railway façade and introducing a degree of heating control for residents.

The second major issue was that the steel coil pipework was embedded in structural

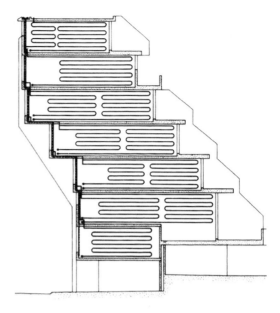

Figure 2. Diagram showing typical Radiant Wall (Max Fordham).

concrete walls, so any mechanical failure within the cross-walls would be extremely disruptive and costly to repair, but Max Fordham's view of this issue at the time was that failure would not be likely:

Some people find that surprising, but the decision to embed the pipework in the concrete walls was taken in the expectation that corrosion would not be a problem any more than the decision to embed steel reinforcement in the concrete walls. Everybody who was involved expected the pipework to last as long as the building.[8]

Certainly part of the reason behind using steel reinforcement bars is that the alkalinity of concrete coupled with its dryness prevents corrosion of the steel; logically the radiant wall pipework made of the same steel should last as long as the structural integrity of the building (fig. 4). Of course, pipework can corrode from the inside out

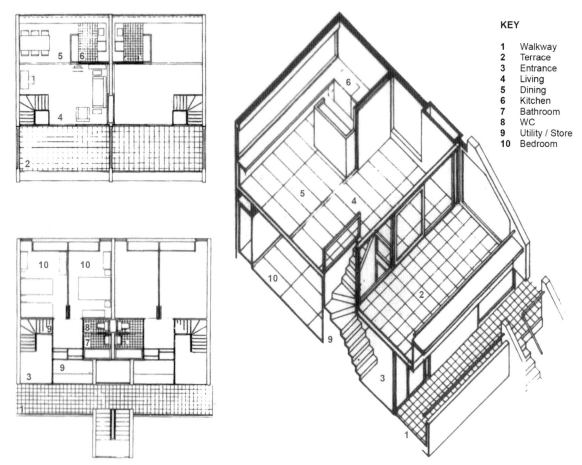

KEY

1   Walkway
2   Terrace
3   Entrance
4   Living
5   Dining
6   Kitchen
7   Bathroom
8   WC
9   Utility / Store
10 Bedroom

Figure 3. Typical Plan and Axonometric note Radiant wall is cut away through section (Neave Brown)

as well, but basic management of the heating system's water supply[9] should limit this happening.

Despite the design team's reasoned logic for adopting a radiant wall system, it was still a very unusual and ambitious proposal to implement.

As Alexandra Road approached completion in 1977/78, Neave Brown recalls that the handover of the flats from the contractor to the new tenants was moved forward and that insufficient time was allowed to balance out the vast district heating system.[10] Consequently the initial cases of too much or too little heating within the

Figure 4. Radiant wall during construction showing heating coils (Max Fordham).

brand new flats were bad publicity for what had become a very expensive and lengthy building contract.[11] But it is also true that a survey by Camden of their new tenants' homes showed that the heating scores for Alexandra Road were the best that they had received.[12]

TIME FOR A CHANGE?

In the 1980s, with the arrival of Thatcher and rate capping, the appearance of Alexandra Road, conceived as a building that would require regular maintenance, deteriorated rapidly. With repairs and maintenance funded by revenue, and revenue reduced by rate capping, the public areas, concrete and other elements became dirty and unkempt.

In 1989 a group of residents who had lived there from the beginning, dissatisfied with insensitive and inadequate repairs being carried out by Camden, began a petition to return the scheme to its original glory. This campaign headed by resident Elizabeth Knowles and supported by Christopher Dean of DOCOMOMO succeeded in 1994 in getting a Grade 2-star listing for the estate. English Heritage announced that Alexandra Road would join Foster's Willis Faber building and the Smithsons' Economist building as an exemption to the rule that a building must be thirty years old to be listed. So Alexandra Road became not only the youngest and largest building ever to be listed, but also the first modern housing estate.

In this period, the management of the estate switched to a tenants' managed co-operative (the largest in London at the time), before returning to being managed by Camden Council, but retaining an active and experienced Tenants and Residents Association (TRA) as a legacy from the cooperative years.

During this time of upheaval, the district heating and hot water system was still operational, feeding the radiant walls and heating the estate. The heating system would be turned on from late autumn to early spring and be completely off for the warmer months; as a result there were some balancing issues with its seasonal activation.

On the whole, the radiant walls worked well and were liked by residents. In a way, they worked too well. Bearing in mind that the original design intention was that the radiant walls would be background heating, the residents were to retain some control of the environment in their flats by switching between warmed or cool air through the mechanical ventilation system. But given that radiant walls could achieve quite high surface temperatures, they produced more than enough heat to function as the only source of warmth for the flats. As a result over years of use and management, the de facto heating of the flats came to be solely from the radiant walls, with the mechanical ventilation system largely falling into disuse.

In 2007, this was the context in which Camden Council officers involved in the borough's Mechanical and Electrical Capital Investment Programme[13] approached the estate's TRA with serious reservations about the state of the radiant walls and advised the residents that they were planning major changes.

The officers perceived the heating system as expensive to run and maintain, unsustainable in that it used excessive amounts of energy to power, and feared that the system was approaching the end of its expected lifespan. Having secured the multi-million pound funding required to potentially install a brand new heating system across the estate, Camden's officers instructed a design team to carry out feasibility studies. The appointed group of consultants was led by Services Engineers and included an architect to draw up the spatial impact of the mechanical proposals on the estate.

The feasibility studies looked at life-cycle costs of various systems over a thirty-year period, primarily financially but also taking on board energy consumption. Initial findings indicated that a centralised system was still preferable for a dense housing estate and installing boilers and ventilation flues into Grade 2-star listed flats would also meet with difficulty from English Heritage. Within the flats, it soon became apparent from the feasibility studies that the cheapest, most sustainable (according to the scope that the consultants were working within) and therefore preferred option for Camden was to decommission the radiant walls and install radiators connected to an upgraded district heating system. It seemed straight forward to the council: the money was in place to achieve a complete over-

haul of an antiquated heating system that would give tenants complete control of the environment of their flats, reduce energy consumption and provide a reliable modern system that would cut maintenance costs. There was only one problem: the residents hated the idea.

'HANDS OFF OUR HOT WALLS'

The problems that the residents had with Camden's proposals fell into two areas: firstly, they were not convinced that the radiant walls were indeed failing, and secondly, they were not happy with the quality of the proposed radiator design.

As a result of these concerns the TRA decided to approach consultants to obtain professional advice regarding the questions they had over Camden's reasoning. Over the course of eighteen months, a series of reports were commissioned by the TRA from Fulcrum Consulting[14], and also from Max Fordham himself. The TRA was able to fund these reports because it had generated some money from shooting fees paid by television and film production companies who have long been fascinated with Alexandra Road as a dramatic urban location. Neave Brown also supported the residents in this process at meetings, wrote letters and issued a press release.

The first major concern held by the residents was that there was no hard evidence that the radiant walls were failing. Camden's reasoning behind its proclamation that the radiant walls were approaching the end of their expected lifespan was based upon guidelines by CIBSE[15] for underfloor heating systems with similar construction to the radiant walls. However, there had only been three recorded failures of radiant wall coils on the estate over a thirty-year period in 520 flats, and these failures had not taken place in recent years.

Camden's officers were not willing to carry out physical testing of the pipework because they felt such work within residents' flats would be too disruptive. However, Fulcrum Consulting were able to identify a method of non-destructive testing[16] of the radiant walls using ultra-sonic detectors to establish the thickness of the metal pipework and to establish whether corrosion was occurring. Camden did eventually carry out some testing following this specification, albeit within a limited scope. The results of this work remain the only hard evidence on the current condition of the radiant walls and as the following extracts indicate, no evidence of failure was identified:

The visual examinations conducted during the period on site indicate that the majority of the pipework exhibits good external condition.

The Heating Coil pipes that were tested show a surprising consistency in wall thickness.

The current wall thickness of the larger pipes... is very similar to that specified... for new, heavy grade pipe.[17]

The council officers were not swayed by these findings, citing the limited scope of the tests as not being sufficient evidence to warrant saving the system. This resulted in an intransigent position on both sides: the residents felt the burden of proof lay with the council to show that a system that showed no outward signs of failure was indeed in need of replacement; whereas the council officers felt it was too great a risk to retain a system of that age, and that a significant amount of further testing would be needed to allay their concerns, which they were reluctant to do for reasons of cost and disruption.

In parallel to the question of whether the radiant walls should be retained, the TRA was challenging the Council's preferred alternative to the radiant walls: the installation of radiators in every flat. The TRA carried out a survey of residents on the estate in June 2008 asking whether they would prefer radiators to the existing radiant wall system. A strong response to the questionnaire[18] indicated that 89% of residents wanted to keep the radiant walls over a new radiator installation. It appeared from the responses that the residents valued the spatial benefits of the existing system, as Neave Brown explains 'without the radiators which clutter up and limit furnishing in small dwellings' there is 'a gain in individual freedom and choice'[19] over the benefits of a fully controllable system (fig. 5). Other contributing factors would have been the costs incurred for the leaseholders on the estate and of course the anticipation of major disruption from building works within the dwellings.

It also became apparent from architectural designs for the proposed radiator system that significant amounts of surface mounted pipework and boxing would have been needed to supply the radiators. Such alterations inside people's homes had wider implications in that the interior of the flats as well as the exterior are Grade 2-star listed. Unsurprisingly, the prospect of these changes angered many of the residents, some of whom had been involved in the push to have Alexandra Road listed in 1994.[20] To allay these concerns, the Council used a void flat on the estate to mock-up the proposed installation and also organised a trip for residents to visit the Brunswick Centre in Bloomsbury, where a similar design was approaching completion within the existing flats. These efforts did not appear to change the view of the residents and their concerns were exacerbated by the fact that the Council had not meaningfully consulted English Heritage within the design process.[21]

Coupled with the concerns over the impact of radiators on the architecture of the estate, serious questions were raised over the credentials of Camden's proposals with regards to sustainability. In a press release by the TRA that set out their objections to the proposals, they questioned the logic of bettering the energy efficiency of the building through a new radiator installation by comparing such a scheme to 'pumping air into a flat tyre without fixing the puncture.'[22] The argument, which had been developed with Fulcrum Consulting and Max Fordham, was that Camden's proposals were only focused on the replacement

Figure 5. The living room of Alexandra Road and campaginer Elizabeth Knowles in 2009. The image shows a well preserved block B, Rowley Way (Matthew Rosenberg).

of a heating system and did not engage with a holistic approach to the environmental design of the estate. Most notably, it was felt that ways of reducing heat loss from the building fabric had not been sufficiently examined; as a result the opportunity was being missed to reduce the heat load of the estate, which would also have a significant impact on alternative proposals for heating the flats.

This approach to environmental design within Camden is likely to have its roots in the structure of the council's departments, in that officers working on mechanical and electrical schemes are in a separate department to those dealing with sustainability projects and less surprisingly are separate from planning and conservation officers. This compartmentalisation of responsibilities may be very efficient on more straight-forward and smaller projects but in the case of Alexandra Road where pipes and hot water are intrinsically linked with listed interiors and draughty, single-glazed windows then it seems that a multi-disciplinary team working closely together would have been more appropriate.

By the autumn of 2009, both sides had become entrenched in an unyielding position. So on the 14th October 2009, the Council officers who had worked on the proposed changes to the heating at Alexandra Road submitted a report to the Executive committee of councillors to seek approval to decommission the radiant walls and install radiators throughout the estate. At this meeting of the Executive, a crowd of residents from Alexandra Road gathered at Camden's town hall in Kings Cross with banners proclaiming 'Hands off our hot walls' and '90% say no to radiators.' Inside the chamber, the officers put forward their position, followed by a deputation from the TRA setting out their concerns and ultimately urging the councillors to reject the proposed changes.

Unanimously the councillors voted to not accept the proposals of their officers, but neither did they wholly reject them. The major issues voiced by the politicians in the Executive committee were that further investigative work was needed in partnership with local residents into finding an economically and environmentally acceptable solution that would respect the architectural integrity of the estate's listed status. This reinforced similar recommendations made at an earlier council meeting of the Housing and Adult Social Care Scrutiny Committee, which also stated that there was not enough evidence that the radiant walls were failing and that further testing would be required.

While it may appear that the councillors were significantly swayed by the Alexandra Road TRA's arguments, it must be mentioned that the politicians' decisions were taken a few months before an election and that there may have been concerns amongst the Liberal Democrat majority Executive Committee that supporting an unpopular proposal would be potentially damaging with the electorate.

An important factor in the politicisation of the heating issues that also characterised the resistance of local residents to the council's proposals was the role of the media. The TRA were prepared to approach journalists and issue press releases, which led to local newspapers reporting on this story in the build-up to the Council Executive meeting which doubtless highlighted the unpopularity of the proposals to local politicians.[23]

CONCLUSION

Following the decisions of the political committees, Camden councillors and officers decided on a new approach to developing the proposals and have suggested the formation of a heating steering group for Alexandra Road. This group would potentially be made up of residents from the estate, the original designers Max Fordham and Neave Brown and officers from the Mechanical and Electrical delivery team as well as from sustainability and conservation, with local councillors as neutral observers.

The following statement is an extract from a report commissioned by the Alexandra Road TRA from Fulcrum Consulting that summarises a vision for the future environmental design of the estate of which the radiant walls remain a part:

Radiant walls can achieve comfort conditions at lower air temperature and lower flow temperatures than radiators. Direct control of the temperature of the building fabric is an important concept in the design of modern energy efficient buildings... The inclusion of radiant walls within the Alexandra [Road] Estate was an achievement ahead of its time. If money could be spent on improving the thermal performance of the building fabric the radiant walls would allow the use of other energy sources and deliver an exemplar estate improvement with improved occupant conditions and lower fuel use.[24]

One suggestion for how the environmental experience of the residents could be further improved is through the resuscitation of the mechanical ventilation system in the flats, possibly utilising heat recovery technology and allowing the radiant walls to return to their original design intention as background heating. If managed correctly, this could give the residents a reasonable amount of control of the temperature in their homes.[25] There has also been a call for feasibility studies into Combined Heat and Power or geothermal energy as potential alternatives or supplements to the gas boiler that currently supplies the district heating and hot water system. But the biggest challenge will probably be upgrading the windows and uninsulated external walls in a manner that does not adversely change the character of the building.

It remains to be seen whether there is a will within the council to engage with the residents' vision in a meaningful way. Of course there are many issues that council officers will have to negotiate to do this, such as being liable for retaining a thirty year old heating system or trying to deliver an exemplar scheme within tight financial constraints, exacerbated by a recession. Maybe a common ground will emerge from a shared desire to deliver a genuinely sustainable future for the estate.

Reviewing such a case reveals the complexity of trying to engage with and alter the environment of people's homes in a large community. On the surface the renewal of a heating system may appear to be the primary concern of a services engineer, but in the case of Alexandra Road, it has been drawn in to the realm of politics, sustainability, conservation and community consultation.

I would like to thank Max Fordham and Neave Brown for taking time to give advice and provide invaluable images of the radiant walls and the estate and the many helpful comments and corrections from the residents of Alexandra Road.

(ENDNOTES)

1   'The Alexandra and Ainsworth Estate' is its official name, used by Camden Council and local residents. Architects have come to know the estate as 'Alexandra Road' and for brevity I will use this name here.

2   Technology Strategy Board, Retrofit for the Future (2009): 'Housing in the UK accounts for 27% of carbon emissions. More than 60% of the houses we will be living in in 2050 have already been built. To meet the UK's target of an 80% reduction in carbon emissions by 2050, we must dramatically improve the performance of our existing housing stock.'

3   During this period, Councils employed in-house architects to build mass social housing.

4   People suffering from economic hardship, living in individually heated rooms, not only avoided using the provided systems (often coin-fed) but also clogged up any ventilation gaps, in an attempt to conserve heat and save money which resulted in rot and condensation destroying vulnerable fabric.

5   For an overview of the heating system at Alexandra Road that describes the brief, investigation into different solutions and how the chosen option was developed and delivered, see: Fordham, M. 'Radiant wall heating for flats', Building Services Engineer, vol. 46, (1978), pp. 23-25.

6   Fordham, M. (1978), p. 24.

7   With regards to the orientation of the building's fenestration, it is important to mention the influence of Sainte Baume, Cap Martin and other schemes by Le Corbusier for the slopes of the Mediterranean, which guided Neave Brown's concepts of low rise and high density into the physical form of the stepped section block. In effect the building's elevation against the railway has limited fenestration and puts up a cliff-face that forms an acoustic wall against the train noise; whilst the stepped southern elevation (away from the tracks) is heavily glazed.

8   Fordham, M. (2009) 'Comments on Camden Council reasons for replacing the heating system at Alexandra Road', press release, (September 2009).

9   Corrosion from the pipes is limited by keeping the closed water system free of oxygen and slightly alkaline, for more details see: Fordham, M. (1978).

10   Author's interview with Neave Brown (January 2000).

11   Alexandra Road remains the one of the most expensive social housing projects

ever constructed in Europe: 'Social Experiment', Building Design (10th March 2006)

12   Author's interview with Neave Brown (January 2000).

13   A programme of investment agreed by the council's Executive Committee in 2005.

14   Fulcrum Consulting are an international firm of consulting engineers who have had previous experience of working on Alexandra Road.

15   Armstrong, J., CIBSE concise handbook, Chartered Institution of Building Services Engineers (2003).

16   The use here of the term 'non-destructive' when applied to testing a heating system refers to the continued operation of that heating system during the testing process. It may however necessitate some opening up and making good of the building fabric to access the pipework for testing.

17   Focus NDT Ltd., 'Report on non-destructive examination of heating coil pipes installed at the Alexandra Road estate, Camden', report prepared for the London Borough of Camden (April 2009)

18   Alexandra and Ainsworth tenants and residents association, 'Summary of residents' questionnaire on heating situation' (June 2008), 'Report on Open House petition' (September 2008): around 25% of residents responded to the survey, a better response rate than most local authority surveys on the estate.

19   Brown, N., 'Alexandra Road heating', press release (August 2009).

20   Alexandra and Ainsworth tenants and residents association, 'Report on Open House petition' (September 2008): a petition that objected to the proposals by Camden was set up by the TRA during the 2008 Open house event on the estate, and was signed by over 70 visitors.

21   Camden Council's Executive Committee (2009): council officers advised at this meeting in November 2009 that one 'informal' conversation had taken place between Camden's consultants and English Heritage but no further information has been made available.

22   Alexandra and Ainsworth tenants and residents association, 'Written deputation to the executive regarding proposed works to the heating system at the Alexandra and Ainsworth Estate' (October 2009).

23   This political element may have been exacerbated by the support given to the TRA by the opposition Labour party in Camden and local newspapers such as the Camden New Journal were generating publicity around the story, for an example see: Chambers, C, 'Why radiators offer leaves us cold', Camden New Journal, (10th September 2009).

24   Fulcrum Consulting, 'Alexandra Road', press release (October 2009)

25   The majority of complaints regarding the heating system at Alexandra Road received by Camden are that the flats are too warm. This is likely due to the heating levels being adjusted locally across the estate in clusters of up to ten flats, resulting in the temperatures being set to the requirements of the most sensitive residents thus making it too warm for others. The upgrading of the existing cool or heated air system would allow for some resident control and reduce the heat load on the radiant walls.

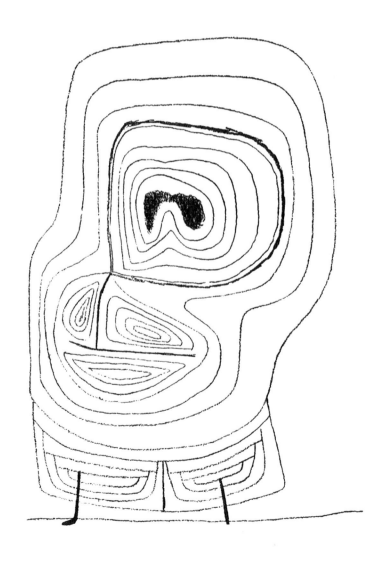

Maximum Cities: Let's Expand the Human Footprint!

by Alistair Donald

Alistair Donald is a PhD candidate at the Martin Centre. His studies involve developing a critique of localism through an investigation into the trends towards greater integration of contemporary metropolitan regions. He has worked within the private and public sectors including as an advisor to CABE, and is a regular contributor to a number of architectural publications.

SYNOPSIS

In recent decades criticism of growth, development and urbanisation has rapidly been gaining momentum in western societies. The Optimum Population Trust, whose patrons include prominent figures such as Sir David Attenborough and Sir Jonathan Porritt, argue that the destabilising impact of population growth requires the UK population to be reduced by half. The think tank, New Economics Foundation, were invited to the World Economic Forum 2010 in Davos, Switzerland, to launch their report *Growth isn't Possible* which promotes the value of a 'stationary state'. The burgeoning *Transition Towns* movement argue for a retreat from the expansive metropolitan networks synonymous with 20th century growth. The future, they contend, requires society to 'power down' and 'relocalise'.[1]

Underlying these visions is the belief that

the recent period has been one of human excess, and that environmental and moral limits undermine the case for further growth. Yet an alternative case can be presented: the problem today is not that society is too growth oriented or too dynamic, but that it *lacks* any real dynamic. Exemplified by sluggish productive growth and a dearth of infrastructure investment, the absence of a dynamic actually hinders society's capacity to deal proactively with issues such as a changing climate. Problems which we might have taken in our stride now consume many individuals with anguish and guilt. Worryingly, many solutions currently offered represent a retreat from the ambitions that have served humanity well, including the architectural and urban project of extending human control over the natural world, and in the process, transforming it to our advantage.

This provocation piece presents three main arguments. Firstly, the 'too much growth' approach reflects a pessimistic and often misanthropic view of humanity as merely consumers, rather than the talented creators that we actually are. Secondly, design solutions increasingly attempt to constrain human activity and individual freedoms, rather than striving to overcome limits and accommodate choices. Finally,

a dedicated approach to *expanding* the human footprint provides a means of securing growth, extending freedoms, *and* bringing environmental problems under human control.

HUMANITY: FORTUNATE... OR TALENTED AND CREATIVE?

Given a Google search on 'Peak Oil' currently returns over 14 million hits, it's clear that fears over resource depletion have captured the imagination. According to Rob Hopkins, co-founder of the *Transition Towns* movement, we are 'extremely fortunate to live at a time in history with access to enormous amounts of energy and a range of materials, products and possibilities our ancestors couldn't have imagined'.[2] Hopkins' assertion appears to be given credence by the narrow oil spike or 'petroleum interval' that spans but a couple of centuries in four millennia *(fig. 1)*.

As it is central to the manufacture and operation of many modern materials, products and transport systems, society has clearly benefitted enormously from oil. But what is less clear is whether we have been 'extremely fortunate', a choice of words intended to emphasise luck or chance.

Figure 1.

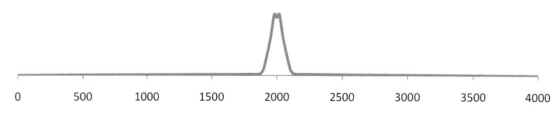

Society's ability to utilise oil is actually much better understood as a tribute to human talent and creativity. After all, oil as a raw material has been around for millions of years, only becoming a significant human resource in the late 19th century, when society advanced far enough to acquire and then use it. Without the likes of Edwin Drake who led American drillers in learning to extract oil, the German genius Nikolaus Otto who invented the first internal combustion engine, and Henry Ford who commercialised car production, oil would not be nearly so directly relevant to the lives of millions of people.

Rather than viewed in isolation, oil is more usefully located within broader developments in which society gained the ability to discover and exploit a series of new fuels (fig. 2). By advancing scientific knowledge, then using it to develop new industries and technologies, we ensured that engines – like the type of fuel they utilise – would evolve generation after generation. The trajectory has been to burn richer fuel, faster, hotter, and in less space. Given the medium term possibilities for growing fuels through high-tech farming, it is this ongoing process of discovery and advance that represents the reason why, eventually, oil will no longer be required.[3]

It's clearly the case that not only does human society draw on natural resources, but in some circumstances may run them down – although, as the saying goes, the Stone Age did not end because we ran out of stone. Yet given our ability to understand and creatively exploit the natural world, humanity should, first and foremost, be considered the creator of resources. Substances such as oil or more recently uranium become resources because we constructed a world in which they can be put to use. Given a commitment to research and development, there is no reason why advances will cease. Neither will gains

Figure 2.

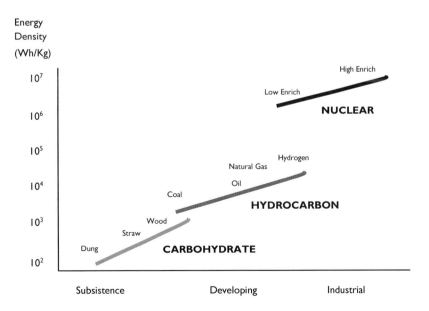

be limited merely to creating energy efficiencies or new production techniques which cut CO_2 emissions. There is every possibility of vastly expanding energy supplies which in turn could help revitalise growth and urbanisation.

RETURN OF THE HUMAN TIME-BOMB

In recent times 'creativity' has become a much used word. Yet unfortunately the notion of human beings as the creative producers of their own future enjoys little credibility. Indeed as people are increasingly viewed as merely consumers of goods and emitters of waste, our role as creative producers is increasingly ignored in favour of the idea that humanity is a burden on the natural world. In this spirit, the environmentalist Paul Ehrlich argued that 'giving society abundant energy at this point would be equivalent to giving an idiot child a machine gun'.[4]

In his earlier infamous book *The Population Bomb*, Ehrlich promoted the idea that there are too many people in the world, a view which is becoming relatively uncontroversial.[5] The London Mayor Boris Johnson, for example, argues we replicate too fast, and compares humans to bacteria multiplying in a petri dish.[6] As Martin Amis' controversial comments on euthanasia booths as a solution to a 'silver tsunami' show, sections of society no longer feel comfortable with advances in life expectancy.[7] According to one article in a mainstream magazine 'the worst thing that you or I can do for the planet is to have children' because 'they will emit some 11 tonnes of carbon dioxide (CO_2) every year of their lives, and they are likely to have more carbon-emitting children who will make an even bigger mess'.[8] Once a source of hope for the future, children are now viewed in some quarters as objects who create a 'mess', and given emission ratings in the same way as a fridge or a car engine.

The tendency to view people as a resource problem has a long and disreputable history that stretches back at least as far as the Reverend Thomas Malthus.[9] In 1798 Malthus published his famous tract on the principle of population arguing the impossibility of society growing enough food for an exponentially increasing population. Presentationally the arguments on population have been subject to change over time. While Boris Johnson might be fairly open with his misanthropic beliefs, such views are often presented indirectly, and in recent times, with what appears to be scientific justification. In the 1970's the Club of Rome report *Limits to Growth* used the then relatively new process of computer modelling to present an apparently neutral, quantitative analysis of the way resource limits are said to impose growth limits. When a team from the Science Policy Research Unit at the University of Sussex examined the report, they concluded that this was merely 'Malthus with a computer' with little basis for its 'sweeping conclusions'.[10]

Anti-growth arguments have been given a further makeover in *Growth isn't Possible*, the recent report from the New Economics

Foundation. Again a statistical approach is employed, this time to rule out growth on the basis of a changing climate and excessive demands for energy. In a damning review, Matthew Lockwood of the Institute of Public Policy Research concluded the report fails to engage with the nature of the growth problem, and opts for easy, self-indulgent posturing over rigorous reflection.[11] Or, put another way, like much advocacy research in this field, the New Economics Foundation offer a series of fanciful justifications for pre-existing prejudices against growth.

A CULTURE OF RESTRAINT

Underpinning Malthus' focus on population growth and food production was his concern about the consequences of social reform. As a conservative writing in the aftermath of the French Revolution, Malthus opposed enlightenment arguments for social change predicated on the idea of human perfectibility. He was convinced that welfare measures such as the Poor Laws would hinder the quest for improvements in society by undermining the curbs against what he perceived as the irresponsible, imprudent behaviour of the feckless poor who he viewed as lacking moral restraint.

In recent years, ideas related to the unchecked behaviour of the masses have been reworked within contemporary 'therapy culture'.[12] As well-being, self-esteem and addiction become the central motifs through which society explains itself, individuals are increasingly viewed as fragile

beings, powerless to exercise restraint without external intervention and support. Some commentators argue an urge for instant gratification has led to addictions to work and 'binge' shopping; others view modern 24 hour urban lifestyles as encouraging urban psychosis; healthy cities or slow cities are prescribed as a remedy to the so-called 'obesogenic' environments associated with eating disorders or a fast food culture; car free neighbourhoods are diagnosed as the treatment for supposed addictions to automobility and even 'hypermobility'. The Transition Towns planning methodology is explicitly based on a therapeutic model where communities are helped overcome their state of 'denial', with '12 point plans' to treat 'oil dependency' and 'post petroleum stress disorder'.

In the past, a desire to work hard, eat conveniently and cheaply, and increase mobility would have seemed sensible. Yet at a time when society is perceived as paying the price for its various excesses, these 'conditions' seem to signify a world out of control, to symbolise a lack of values and clear moral boundaries. Hence why designers now increasingly view their role as establishing codes of conduct, or what one architect calls creating 'a way of life that is ethical, feasible and good'.[13] But is it the job of designers to be creating values?

When design becomes a project aimed at shaping ethics, inevitably behaviour modification becomes the priority. This trajectory is perhaps clearest in the sphere of transport planning. For example, Government design advisors CABE pay lip service to the idea that urban infrastructure and services should be based on 'personal choices by residents'. Yet in the name of promoting sustainable travel, CABE seem to view the public as naughty children, arguing travel consultants should be available to 'advise' on how to travel, promoting a reduction of infrastructure and parking spaces, and advocating that distances travelled should be officially monitored to ascertain if quotas of CO_2 emissions have been met.[14] Little surprise then that innovating, designing and developing the infrastructural solutions to accommodate individual preferences and choices are seldom mentioned.

MAKING HUMANITY VISIBLE

Half a century ago, the urban designer Kevin Lynch argued that an individual should be free to 'choose the kind of habitat he prefers' and to enjoy 'maximum control over his personal world'.[15] In contrast, the sentiment today appears to be that mankind has already acquired too much. Terms such as 'one planet living' betray a view that unconstrained human activity is something to fear rather than encourage. The environmental commentator George Monbiot campaigns 'not for abundance but for austerity' and argues not for 'more freedom but for less'.[16]

Most would probably baulk at Monbiot's cynical call for making people 'so depressed about the state of the planet that they stay in bed all day, thereby reducing their consumption of fossil fuels'. Yet mainstream organisations like the World Wildlife Fund, whose campaign 'Earth Hour' advocates switching off the city lights, seem to encapsulate Monbiot's main premise: humanity is bad for the planet. As some councils in southern England argue for dimming of streetlights within urban space, a supporter of *Transition Towns* takes this to its logical conclusion when he argues for a future in which, ideally, humanity is rendered 'largely invisible'.[17]

Surely this is a travesty. Historically cities were lauded as the places where the lights burned brightest – where humanity was at its most visible. The slogan 'big lights, big city' captures the vitality of cities as places of boundless energy which in *Delirious New York* Rem Koolhaas *celebrated* as a 'culture of congestion'.[18] Unlike today when congestion is widely frowned upon as the result of too much activity, for Koolhaas it indicated a social dynamic – one that, by implication, requires designers to constantly revisit and expand upon urban forms that only ever can prove temporarily adequate.

THE BENEFITS OF A MANMADE WORLD

According to Koolhaas, Manhattan benefitted from a design programme dedicated to creating a world totally fabricated by man, one where the real and the natural cease to exist, as the entire city becomes a factory of manmade experience. Such a celebration of the manmade reflected what was until recently widely accepted: that humanity should transform nature to its advantage and through doing so, would realise improvement upon the natural world.

In *Silent Spring*, Rachel Carson claims there was once a town in the heart of America where all life seemed to live in harmony with its surroundings.[19] Yet Carson ignores the fact that agriculture and urbanisation developed precisely as an exercise in imposing human control over the natural world, modifying it in the process. As the writer Alain de Botton remarks, 'nature's way is to corrode, melt, soften, stain', and is ultimately 'opposed to the order that we rely on to survive'. 'The drive towards order' he asserts, 'reveals itself as synonymous with the drive towards life'.[20]

This process is writ large in Chicago which in 1933 hosted a World Fair to celebrate the scientific triumphs of the telegraph, telephone, automobile, and airplane. Even in the depths of the depression, the Fair reflected the optimism of a city that had modified nature to its advantage and in doing so conquered the forces that continually threatened its existence. Constructed on swampland, when the city started to sink buildings were literally jacked up out of the quagmire; when its topography and position on the Shores of Lake Michigan resulted in flooding and the contamination of water supplies, engineers reversed the flow of the river, built expansive canal systems, and, over time, the 110 mile long Deep Tunnel System water distribution system; after the city was destroyed by the 1871 fire, architects utilised fire proofed steel and new lift technology to develop the skyscraper, the building typology that stands in determined defiance of gravitational forces.

EXPANDING THE HUMAN FOOTPRINT

Chicago and other similar success stories rebut the assertion that disasters will result if 'human society puts itself in the way of likely natural phenomena or changes the ecosystems'.[21] To my mind, genuine resilience, and, even more importantly, progress, results from expanding the human footprint. Imposing human infrastructure certainly modifies the operation of nature. But it is this very process of extending human reach and control over the natural world that can bring social benefits including integrating more people into manmade networks. This is not to promote the wilful destruction of the natural world, but to recognise that giving up on the human centred project of mastering nature will leave us at the mercy of circumstances, rather than able to benefit from controlling and exploiting the natural world.

Until relatively recently, decisions as to where and how communities lived were subject to considerable restrictions. Locating within impregnable topography might have been necessary for reasons of security, or within river plains because of the need for water and arable land. In other words, human society was forced to adapt to the natural world. Today our options have increased precisely because we have learned to adapt the environment to our needs. Aqueducts improve upon natural water systems by distributing water to exactly where we require it at the time we need it; drainage systems and protective barriers allow us to occupy flood plains if we wish;

motorways and rail networks shrink the distance between where we live and work, giving us a choice of where we live.

Indeed, by separating ourselves from nature and learning to master it, it is clear that we can do more than just adapt the natural world; it can now be radically transformed to our advantage. China, for example, is constructing infrastructure that can store and then transfer water thousands of miles from South to North. This infrastructure provides not only water and electricity to emerging megacities, but controls the regular floods that have claimed a million lives in the past hundred years.

The current reverence for natural systems and the belief that the human footprint should be minimised seems to reflect a loss of belief in the efficacy of human inspired development. When new industrial plants and power stations, skyscrapers and subdivisions, airports and motorway networks are viewed as malignant growths on natural systems, this is seldom just a comment on the design quality of a particular intervention. Rather it reflects a broader view of humans as ultimately destructive, and epitomises the idea that such projects represent human follies that will inevitably rebound. In this sense, the popularity of planning solutions which favour going 'off grid' or that seek to build localised pockets of 'resilience' can be interpreted as a spatial reflection of broader social and political trends towards opting out – effectively disengaging from the human centred project of shaping the future.

By contrast, in developing megacities such as Chongqing, Mumbai or Sao Paulo, universalising urban ambitions remain. For villagers on the fringe of Chongqing, the world's fastest growing city, localisation translates to isolation. Without wishing to downplay ongoing problems related to poverty, pollution and democracy, connecting into the rapidly expanding metropolis is a matter for anticipation rather than trepidation. Ultimately, the onset of modernity offers, at the very least, the prospect of taking an active part in shaping the future: 'Life is much better... we are urbanised and have become proper citizens'.[22]

Compared to sluggish western economies, the relative dynamism of emerging economies offers exciting possibilities. For instance, to its already proliferating high speed rail network, China will not only add 13,000 kilometres of track in the next ten years, but also plug itself into the networks of 17 European and Asian countries. Such ambitious infrastructural commitments will not only help shrink and make easily traversable a geographically vast country. They also hold out the prospect that as the planned westwards migration of people occurs, they will be integrated within global networks. Rural populations can be freed from their isolation and subsistence farming replaced with industry.

However, cities might also in the future benefit from radically new ways of expanding human influence on the world. Today's extensive research on the operation of natural systems doesn't merely confirm anthropogenic climate change. It also boosts levels of human knowledge which could help ensure progress from *unintentionally* influencing the climate (as we have done in the industrial age), towards *consciously* controlling our influence. In this sense, geo-engineering and the development of new forms of energy infrastructure (whether nuclear, hydroelectric, solar, wave, wind or coal CCS), can be viewed as far more than just the means of reducing carbon emissions. Rather they represent aspects of macro-engineering advances that could help bring the natural world, including the climate, further within humanity's control.

FEAR OF THE UNKNOWN

Of course, whatever the potential advantages in terms of controlling floods or responding to droughts, in today's relatively conservative times, planetary engineering ambitions are viewed with horror. In historical terms however, such thinking is in line with the ethos of the scientific revolution, which thrived on the conviction that humankind could free itself from the constraints of nature. Not only was experimentation promoted as the source of knowledge, exploiting that knowledge to advance social progress was considered a moral imperative.

Whereas in the past conquering the unknown provided a powerful incentive to action, today, fear of unknown consequences has a paralysing effect. Futurologists no longer set ambitious targets, but content themselves with developing palettes of 'what if' scenarios. Yet given their start-ing point is often acceptance of the idea that we live in an uncertain, uncontrollable world, and that taking risks is irresponsible, then scenario planning is seldom a neutral process. Where the precautionary principle rules, the imagination seems to home in on worst case scenarios, which undermines any impetus to test out new ideas.

The New Economics Foundation provide a useful example of how this process works when they consider the potential for carbon capture developed through underground storage solutions. Rather than conduct a rigorous examination of the potential benefits and problems of this technology, instead the imagination of unknown consequences run riot. We have the spectre of possible leakages and the risks of living above a giant bubble of CO_2 which, we are told, might 'migrate through cracks and faults in the earth' causing pooling in 'unexpected places'. Apparently a 'colourless and odourless gas' like CO_2 may, perhaps, possibly, result in the 'asphyxiation' and 'immediate death' of 'both people and animals'.[23]

The fantasies of Armageddon that emerge from today's future thinking exercises have considerable potential as horror movie scripts, but they also serve as powerful incentives to play safe. They are an expression of the conservatism that grips contemporary society, and appear to take a lead from the former American Secretary of State Donald Rumsfeld who justified invading Iraq by citing 'unknown unknowns': 'the absence of evidence is not evidence of absence' he argued.[24] When the New Economics Foundation employ a similarly speculative approach, it serves to restrain human experimentation, deifying the mystical working of nature rather than promoting an approach dedicated to exploring how to exploit it to society's advantage. As Matthew Lockwood has argued, 'the prejudices of and limits to environmentalist thinking can stand in the way of the search for genuine solutions to the problem of growth'.[25]

CONCLUSION: FOR EXPLORING AND CONQUERING THE CITY LIMITS...

The aim of this provocation has been to challenge the dominant idea of our times

Figure 3.

Ingrown

EXPLORING THE CITY LIMITS...

Outgoing

– that humanity should accommodate to perceived new environmental and moral limits on growth and development. This is not to argue that there are no problems that have resulted from development in the past, nor that efficiencies are not needed or welcome, nor even that we should forgo finding solutions to many environmental problems that have been identified. Yet it seems to me that, first and foremost, more people, more growth and using more energy and resources represent not problems, but worthwhile metropolitan aspirations. In this sense, rather than kowtowing to the need for Minimum Cities where we accept less in order to reduce human impact on the planet, Maximum Cities represents the aspiration to do and achieve more through capturing the energy and creative spirit of humanity.

Writing in the late 1960s, the American designer Edmund Bacon affirmed his belief that the city was an expression of the highest aspirations of our civilisation. But, he argued, when thinking about cities, there is a danger we are losing one of the most important concepts of mankind: the future is what we make it. In his survey of cities from Athens onwards, he reviewed how, time and again, designers developed, tested and perfected ideas that led them to humanise their environments, and illustrated that 'the city was an act of human will'.

Of course there are no guarantees of success, and to promote an explorative, open ended approach, Bacon highlighted the work of the artist Paul Klee and presented the idea of Ingrown Man and Outgoing Man *(fig. 3)*. Today, we are very familiar with Ingrown Man. He is, Bacon argues, 'inward looking, self-concerned and safe. He reduces contact with the outside world to a minimum avoiding exposure and involvement'. The alternative Bacon presents is Outgoing Man, a figure who is 'ebullient, involved, exposed in both his strengths and his frailties. He reaches for more than he has or knows, he leaps into space, aware of the possible consequences of a fail.'[26]

What Bacon seems to suggest is that the biggest barrier to be negotiated on the way to realising a better future is a cultural one – the collapse in belief that humanity has the capacity to experiment with, and then implement new ideas, and through doing so, to impose its vision. Strange as it may seem, the lesson that can be drawn from Outgoing Man is that we need to rediscover the confidence to fail. To leap into space aware of the possibilities of failure signifies confidence that whatever the problems, humanity can emerge on the other side and reflect on the lessons, before trying again.

(ENDNOTES)

1   See: www.optimumpopulation. org; New Economics Foundation, *Growth isn't Possible* (2010); Sustainable Development Commission, *Prosperity without Growth* (2009); Hopkins, R., Transition Handbook, Green Books, Totnes, (2008).

2   Hopkins, R. (2008).

3   Huber, P.W., and M.P. Mills, *The Bottomless Well*, Basic Books, New York (2005).

4   Ehrlich, P.R., *'Machine guns and idiot children'* cited in Wolfe, B., *'Is the energy debate really about energy?'*, IAEEA Bulletin, v. 24, no. 4, p. 28.

5   Ehrlich, P.R., *'The Population Bomb'*, Ballantine Books, New York, Revised Edition (1971).

6   Johnson, B. cited in Cecil, N., *'Stop having babies to save the world says (father of four) Boris'*, London Evening Standard (14th December 2009).

7   Amis, M., cited in Chittenden, M., *'Martin Amis calls for euthanasia booths on street corners'*, The Times (24th January 2010).

8   Renton, A., *'The Human Timebomb'*, Prospect Magazine (October 2009).

9   Malthus, T.R., *An Essay on the Principle of Population*, Oxford University Press, Oxford, Reprinted Edition (1993).

10   Meadows, D. et al, *'The Limits to Growth"* London, Potomac Associates, 1972. Freeman, C., "Malthus with a computer" in "Thinking about the future" Eds Cole, H.S. D., et al Sussex, University Press, 1973

11   Lockwood, M., *'The limits to environmentalism Pt 1'*, politicalclimate. net/2010/02/25/the-limits-to-environmentalism-part-1 (2010).

12   Furedi, F., *'Therapy Culture: Cultivating Vulnerability in an Uncertain Age'*, Routledge, London (2003).

13   Steel, C. *'Architects must lead the revolution'*, Building Design (8th January 2010).

14   BioRegional & CABE, What makes an eco-town?, CABE (2009)

15   Lynch, K., *'The Pattern of the Metropolis'* in Lynch, K., Banerjee, T. and M.Southworth, City Sense and City Design, MIT Press, Cambridge, Massachussets (1990).

16   Monbiot, G., Heat: *How to Stop the Planet Burning*, Allen Lane, London (2006).

17   Goodwin, B. cited in Hopkins, R. (2008).

18   Koolhaas, R., *Delirious New York: A Retroactive Manifesto for New York*, Thames and Hudson, London, (1978).

19   Carson, R., *Silent Spring*, Penguin, London (1962).

20   de Botton, A., *The Architecture of Happiness*, Penguin Books, London (2007).

21   Head, P. and G. Lawrence, *'Urban Development To Combat Climate Change: Dongtan Eco-city and Risk Management Strategies'*, www.ctbuh.org (2008)

22   Brown, M. *'Chongqing, the world's fastest growing city'*, The Daily Telegraph, (12th July 2009).

23   New Economics Foundation (2010).

24   Rumsfeld, D., *'Press Conference by US Secretary of Defence'*, www.nato.int/docu/speech/2002/s020606g.htm.

25   Lockwood, M. (2010).

26   Klee, P., *'The Thinking Eye: The note-*

books of Paul Klee' cited in Bacon, E., Design
of Cities, Penguin, Harmondsworth (1967).

Minimum... or Maximum Cities?

Conference Review

26 November 2009 - Department of Architecture, Univeristy of Cambridge

by Matthew French

AN UNKNOWN URBAN MIGRANT MAKES HISTORY

At some moment in the second half of the last decade, someone, somewhere, packed their belongings, bid farewell to those surrounding them, and departed their rural setting. Probably nervous and most certainly unprepared, they set a course for their new living environment: the city. Unbeknown to anyone, their arrival completed a process that has characterised our age: the move to a predominantly urban global population.

Just as impossible as it is to locate the migrant, so too is to know the exact date of the watershed. What is known, however, is that at some point in the first decade of the 21st century humanity became predominantly urban with over fifty percent of our

Figure 1.

population living in cities. This urbanisation process, initiated by the industrial revolution and continued by post World War Two urbanisation in the developing world, continues, with an estimate that by 2050 three-quarters of the world's population will live in urban areas.[1] Truly, we live in an elusive but persuasive urban revolution.

Reaction to the watershed of a predominantly urban population has been mixed. For some, it was not a moment to celebrate but further indication of the pending disaster of the urban age where our cities are on 'the edge of chaos'.[2] For others, celebration of the freedoms and opportunities afforded by cities to a widening number of people was tinged with an awareness

of the challenges that lay ahead, not just in the rapidly growing cities of developing countries such as Lagos and La Paz, but also in perceivably unsustainable and energy intensive western cities such as London and Los Angeles. Some would say that the recent recession has its roots in the spatial configurations of these megacities, and that sprawling cities point to a 'whole system of economic organisation and growth that has reached its limit.'[3] Such are the mixed beliefs about the state of the world's cities.

DEBATING THE FUTURE OF THE CITY

This confusion over the state of the world's cities is the context in which the conference *Minimum … or Maximum Cities?* took place. The conference, held at the Department of Architecture on the 26th November 2009, asked: what is the future for cities? Anxieties over urban space within Western cities, and fears over the dynamic growth of megacities in the developing world have altered the way that we see the benefits and drawbacks of urbanisation. Are cities polluted, overcrowded and anonymous, or are they dynamic centres of innovation and culture? Do they foster beneficial social relations? Or do they encourage social alienation?

Central to the conference aim was opening up debate on the future of cities. Should the priority be to dampen expectations and settle for minimising potential problems? Or should we be more ambitious and experiment with new ideas and technologies that could maximise future gains? Are our creative talents best employed in seeking a 'minimum' city as a means to retrench, rethink and rebuild? Or is a 'maximum' urbanism the answer, based on expansive cities for a dynamic and globalised planet?

The conference format was developed to support the aim of open debate. Rather than hosting an event dedicated to the presentation of substantial papers, the aim of this conference was to provide a forum for debate and discussion on the future of cities. The day was organised around four

Figure 2.

panel sessions on key urban discussions *(figs. 1, 2)*. Each session included between three and six speakers (listed at the end of this article) who represented a range of different opinions on four themes: urban fear and anxiety, urban mobility, energy, and future city proposals. Fitting for a department of architecture, the last theme was explored in 'crit' format, and included three presentations of the future city. It was a means to draw together some of the ideas discussed throughout the day, and to provocatively make the case for returning vision and imagination to a central position within city building.

Throughout the day the focus was firmly on examining and critiquing ideas. In distinction to many conferences, the aim was to generate dissent or disagreement amongst both the speakers and the audience as a means of clarification. Like the speakers, the audience was very diverse – in age, discipline and interest – and included students, researchers, and professional practitioners. Such diversity proved an important challenge for speakers in terms of communicating their ideas.

Figure 3.

The exhibition *Paper City: Urban Utopias*, redesigned for the Department of Architecture after spending the summer at the Royal Academy in London, was hosted in the adjacent gallery space *(figs. 3, 4)*. The exhibition was composed of a series of images commissioned for Blueprint magazine with the aim of exploring the image of the future city. Blueprint Editor Vicky Richardson noted *Paper City: Urban Utopias* helped the magazine 'widen the debate about what form cities should take' by encouraging new ideas and 'thinking big, and outside the framework of official debate.' It was therefore a valuable part of the conference.

THE ANXIOUS CITY: THE DILEM-MAS OF GROWTH

The first session of the day focused on urban anxiety around space use, risk and security. The key debate centered on the current preoccupation with risk and whether these indicted cities are now more dangerous, environmentally degraded and anti-social places. Are we vulnerable to new perils, or merely more uncomfortable with the congestion and contestation that are longstanding features of urban life? Are cities today too dynamic and spiraling out of control? Or do they suffer from a surfeit of controls?

Lively debate ensued between the four

Figure 4.

speakers, Anna Minton, Richard Williams, Jon Coaffee and Penny Lewis. Alastair Donald productively chaired the session. Anna Minton, first to present, set-up the debate. Minton drew heavily from her book *Ground Control: Fear and happiness in the twenty-first century city* arguing public space within the city is now highly regulated, with people's behaviour limited by spatial and technical influences.

Two positions emerged. Williams, more controversially, asked: so what can we do? Williams suggested risk can never be excluded, and new risks always emerge, so there seems to be two options. We can continue to perceive the world as a threat, or acknowledge the risks and use this knowledge creatively to reduce them. In line with this, Penny Lewis suggested the dilemma of the modern subject. On the one hand we are told a small action like recycling a plastic supermarket shopping bag will have a direct influence on saving the planet (an almost in-surmountable challenge) but on the other hand we are told we have no control over larger social forces, especially those associated with risk and security.

Although the response to risk and conflict in public space was less clear, all speakers agreed that a climate of fear characterises western society, especially in the United Kingdom. Two attitudes to public space emerged, pessimistic and optimistic: do we perceive ourselves as vulnerable or do we in fact have agency to shape our urban experiences?

THE AGILE CITY: LOCAL TIES VERSUS GLOBAL REACH

The second session dealt with questions around mobility. Should we expand our mobility at local, national and international scales or constrain and moderate it? Understandably, the conversation led into a discussion of urban structure, size and appropriate types of future urban growth: concentrated, compact cities or more dispersed smaller cities. The panel included four speakers: Joseph Simpson, John Adams, Steve Melia and Timandra Harkness. Austin Williams, the director of the Future Cities Project, chaired the session.

In line with environmental concerns, Steve Melia suggested that we need to reduce our current level of mobility as it relies on high levels of non-renewable energy. Joe Simpson argued that we should consider new forms of connection, using the 'iphone' as an example. In this sense he argued for digital connectivity rather than physical connectivity. In contrast, it was suggested that we are already highly globalised, and therefore should not limit physical connectivity; increasing geographic limitations on individuals would place undesirable constraints on individual freedoms. In response to these concerns of the consequences of increased mobility in terms of energy consumption, Timandra Harkness suggested that increased mobility can lead to new, improved, more efficient technologies. Dedication to the project of mobility will inspire new solutions. However, overall, the audience was generally pessimistic about the suitability of narrow technologically focused 'solutions'. The session was well chaired by Austin Williams who promoted debate, solicited clarification from speakers on their points, and engaged the audience in the key lines of inquiry.

POWERING THE CITY: INNOVATIONS IN ENERGY

The third session explored the role of energy in the future city. It asked: is energy efficiency an ambitious enough starting point for designing the future city? Are urban layouts best determined as a consequence of energy efficiency criteria? How should designers view the elevation of energy efficiency as one of, or perhaps even the defining criterion of, design quality? Dr Ying Jin chaired the speaker panel of Rob Lyons, Peter Guthrie and Spencer de Grey.

Rob Lyons opened the session with an energetic and controversial critique of the sustainability agenda. With diametrically opposed beliefs, Peter Guthrie followed with his often-articulated position that sustainability is the central concern for our society. The audience responded energetically. Overall, there was a desire to critique the central tenets and importance of the sustainability debate. The response seemed to be a desire to see sustainability in a holistic sense, rather than a narrow energy efficiency sense. Such a response appeared to put Peter Guthrie in an unusual position: one where he was not preaching to the converted, but actively having to recruit new disciples, or at least work hard to maintain those who had traditionally ascribed to the sustainability paradigm. Indeed, during informal conversation during the afternoon coffee break Guthrie noted his surprise at the audience's response, a response he didn't think he would receive in a department of architecture. Spencer de Grey, head of design at Foster and Partners, noted sustainability is a dangerous word as it is simply too abstract. It had come to mean both everything and nothing.

During the discussion, the chair, Dr Ying Jin, asked the audience for a show of hands if they thought sustainability was the most important challenge in their lifetime. Only five or so hands were raised. This reinforced de Grey's point about the uselessness of the term; everyone had a different definition of sustainability, and many did not match with the narrow technical, resource based view of sustainability underpinning this session.

THE FUTURE CITY: REWRITING THE RULE BOOK

Drawing the day together, the last session focused on imaginative urban futures. The session was composed of Darryl Chen, Derek Walker and Karl Sharro, who each presented and defended their 'future cities' proposals to the audience and a panel of reviewers: Daniel Durrant, Penny Lewis and Biljana Savic. Vicky Richardson chaired the session.

Walker, the lead designer of Milton Keynes, reminisced about his work over the last 40 years. Chen explored the potential of new communication technologies for the future city; the Cellphone Bee. However, the animated and energetic architect and writer Karl Sharro 'stole the show' in this final session with his vision for Dubai in the United Arab Emirates. His proposal was radical – sky streets suspended between high-rise towers – but also plausible, and, he declared with conviction, it will be built.

Sharro was a fitting end to a day that had sought to open up debate on the future of cities. His work touched on many themes: culture, globalisation, transport and the sustainability of alternative lifestyle choices, all themes discussed in abstract terms during the day but finally placed in a specific context. In this sense the discussion reinforced the importance of context in debates about the future of cities and the origin of the underpinning theories used in analysis.

AN URBAN FUTURE

Minimum… or Maximum cities? was successful in terms of responding to the Department of Architecture's research tradition on urban issues. However, it broke new ground for the Department with its focus on big ideas, big thinking, and looking at the possibilities, rather than a concern for statistically validated claims of 'appropriate' urban growth.

The format, and indeed the spatial configuration of the lecture room, was extremely successful in terms of generating debate. No one thought the format would be easy – in fact we selected the format precisely because it was difficult, and challenging. But we believe that both speakers and audience rose admirably to the challenge. As Professor Koen Steemers, Head of the Department of Architecture reflected, 'one of the most interesting aspects of the day was to see how speakers responded when put under intellectual pressure to justify their arguments – something that doesn't happen often enough in conferences.' With such a format the role of the chair is very important: to order speakers' point of views, keep time, and guide feedback.

The debates demonstrated the future of cities is not prescribed, and that, contrary to dominant opinion, the future of cities has not already been written. There is still scope for thinking big and for big ideas that value and promote the urban condition as a force for good. In all sessions the popular paradigm of sustainability was questioned. By no means was sustainability dismissed, but rather participants and the audience involved themselves in fundamental issues of sustainability beyond seeing it as a purely technical problem to be solved.

One wonders what themes, speakers and debates would form a *Minimum… or Maximum Cities?* conference in the years 2019, 2029, and so on into the future. Maybe it will become a regular event in the Department's calendar thus providing a regular monitoring and recording period of thinking on cities. And on the success of 2009, it is a promising place to start.

SPEAKER LIST

The Anxious City: The Dilemmas of Growth
Alastair Donald, Min-Max-Cities group (Chair)
Anna Minton, Journalist, Author
Richard Williams, Dean of Postgraduate Studies, University of Edinburgh
Jon Coaffee, Professor, Centre for Urban and Regional Studies, University of Birmingham
Penny Lewis, Writer and Lecturer, Scott Sutherland School of Architecture

The Agile City: Local Ties versus Global Reach
Austin Williams, Director, Future Cities Project (Chair)
Joe Simpson, The Movement Design Bureau
John Adams, Emeritus Professor of Geography, University College London
Steve Melia, Senior Lecturer, University of West of England
Timandra Harkness, Journalist, Scriptwriter, Fellow of the RSA.

Powering the City: Innovations in Energy
Dr Ying Jin, Lecturer, Department of Architecture (Chair)
Rob Lyons, Deputy Editor, Spiked-online
Spencer de Grey, Head of Design, Foster and Partners
Peter Guthrie, Professor for Engineering for Sustainable Development, University of Cambridge

The Future City: Rewriting the Rule Book
Vicky Richardson, Editor, Blueprint (Chair)
Daryl Chen, Tomorrow's Thoughts Today
Derek Walker, Derek Walker Associates

Karl Sharro, Architect, Writer
Daniel Durrant, Regional Cities East
Penny Lewis, Writer and Lecturer, Scott Sutherland School of Architecture
Biljana Savic, CABE

ACKNOWLEDGEMENTS

Thank you to the other conference committee members: Alastair Donald, Ye Zhang, and Kam Shing Leung for their support in preparing this article.

(ENDNOTES)

1   Burdett, R. and D. Sudjic, (eds.), *The endless city, Phaidon*, London (2007).

2   Sudjic, D., *'Cities on the edge of chaos'*, The Observer (9th March, 2008).

3   Florida, R., *'How the crash will reshape America'*, The Atlantic (March 2009).

Proof

8734679R1

Made in the USA
Charleston, SC
09 July 2011